Advance Praise for The Berrigan Letters

As one whose own journey has been enriched and inspired by the
public witness of the Berrigans, it has been a moving experience,
through these letters, to enter into the intimate relationship they
shared and to understand the bonds of loyalty, love, and faith that
sustained their courageous work for peace and justice.

—**Martin Sheen,** actor and activist

Imagine my surprise as a young nun to see Phil and Dan on the
cover of *Time*, handcuffed and smiling, on their way to prison *on
purpose*. They claimed their act of civil disobedience as witness
to the gospel of Jesus, no less. Talk about rattling my religious
sensibility. These letters between the brothers trace their journey
from pious, obedient souls to revolutionaries for Jesus. May this
book live forever in testament to two brothers outrageously alive to
follow trouble-stirring Jesus, whom we so readily domesticate.

—**Sr. Helen Prejean,** author of *Dead Man Walking*

These letters reveal the intimate, loving relationship of brothers who
share their deepest selves with one another and, now, with all of us.
I read these letters with utmost respect for each of them and greater
awareness of the gifts they have been to me, to our church, and to
our human family.

—**Bishop Tom Gumbleton**

Watch Out. This book is going to make you pick up a pen, paper,
and envelope, and visit the venerable old Post Office. In prison
with pencil stubs, scribbled in haste on the way to the action or
the courthouse or the airport, labored over in the wee hours of the
morning—Phil and Dan wrote letters to one another (and countless
others) as they prayed and ministered, suffered and sacrificed,
resisted and rejoiced, loved and labored. This collection is a record
of two lives lived fully in the service of the human family and two
men who inspired and challenged and nurtured each other every
step of the way. After reading these epistles, you will be compelled
to write the people you care about and make indelible your
affection and appreciation. You have been warned.

—**Frida Berrigan,**
author of *It Runs in the Family: On Being Raised
by Radicals and Growing into Rebellious Motherhood*

As someone profoundly influenced by the Berrigans' mentoring and friendship, I am filled still with wonder at and gratitude for these pioneers of "liturgical direct action" and bearers of the prophetic tradition—surely our American Elijah and Elisha. This is a great gift to all of us shaped by the "movement" history these letters narrate so intimately.

—**Ched Myers,** author of *Binding the Strong Man*

The voices of these beloved brothers bring us pain, grief, love, and hope, enticing and admonishing us to remember, to pray, to act, to show the world, as they did, what is entailed in being followers of Christ. God's creation depends upon us to hear this call.

—**Martha Hennessy,** peace activist

I grew up under the emblem of Dan and Phil Berrigan's courage. When I was under attack for my anti-war and civil rights beliefs, I used to calm myself to sleep by thinking of their lack of fear. God bless them.

—**Jonathan Kozol,** author of
Savage Inequalities

Reading this book is like discovering the correspondence between the apostle brothers Peter and Andrew, or James and John. These letters radiate a steadfast discipleship to the nonviolent Jesus, a feisty love of life, and a passionate resistance to the culture of war. May they inspire us to give our lives as Dan and Phil did to the gospel work of peace and justice.

—**Rev. John Dear,** editor, *Daniel Berrigan: Essential Writings*

You cannot read these letters and not be deeply moved by the profound love the Berrigan brothers had for each other. I often wondered what sustained them in their work for disarmament and peace, and what gave them the courage to take care of the poor whilst challenging the military and war culture of their own American government. Now I know that for both it was knowing that God loved them, but knowing too that they had the love and solidarity of each other in their prophetic witness and struggle for justice and peace.

—**Mairead Maguire,** Nobel Peace Prize Laureate

The Berrigan Letters

THE BERRIGAN LETTERS

Personal Correspondence between Daniel and Philip Berrigan

Daniel Cosacchi and Eric Martin, editors

ORBIS ✦ BOOKS
Maryknoll, New York 10545

ORBIS BOOKS
Maryknoll, New York 10545

Fathers and Brothers
MARYKNOLL™
TOGETHER IN GOD'S MISSION OF MERCY

Founded in 1970, Orbis Books endeavors to publish works that enlighten the mind, nourish the spirit, and challenge the conscience. The publishing arm of the Maryknoll Fathers and Brothers, Orbis seeks to explore the global dimensions of the Christian faith and mission, to invite dialogue with diverse cultures and religious traditions, and to serve the cause of reconciliation and peace. The books published reflect the views of their authors and do not represent the official position of the Maryknoll Society. To learn more about Maryknoll and Orbis Books, please visit our website at www.maryknollsociety.org.

Published by Orbis Books, Maryknoll, New York 10545-0302.

Manufactured in the United States of America.

Manuscript editing and typesetting by Joan Weber Laflamme.

Library of Congress Cataloging-in-Publication Data

Names: Berrigan, Daniel, author. | Berrigan, Philip, author. | Cosacchi, Daniel, editor.
Title: The Berrigan letters : personal correspondence between Daniel and Philip Berrigan / edited by Daniel Cosacchi and Eric Martin.
Description: Maryknoll : Orbis Books, 2016. | Includes index.
Identifiers: LCCN 2015041704 | ISBN 9781626981645 (pbk.)
Subjects: LCSH: Berrigan, Daniel—Correspondence. | Berrigan, Philip—Correspondence.
Classification: LCC BX4705.B3845 A4 2016 | DDC 282.092/2—dc23 LC record available at http://lccn.loc.gov/2015041704

*To Dan Berrigan, Carol Berrigan, Jerry Berrigan,
Phil Berrigan, and Liz McAlister,
in gratitude for your faithful lives.*

Contents

Acknowledgments

We would like to thank first and foremost Phil and Dan Berrigan, who put in the real work for this book. They crafted their lives with diligence, deliberation, faith, and courage, and we hope to have reflected that justly in this collection. Thank you as well to the entire Berrigan family, particularly to Carol and Jerry for their inspiring lives and Jerry's organization of these letters, to Frida Berrigan for her help trying to track down missing letters, and to Liz McAlister, about whom we say more below.

We are extremely grateful to Ellen Grady and Saoirse for hosting us on three separate trips to the archives in Ithaca, New York, for a total of six days, each time on short notice. Our late night chats by the fireplace with a guitar were moments of grace to us. For opening your home, your table, and your family life to us, we cannot thank you enough. Thanks as well to Mary Anne Grady Flores for receiving us with a hearty dinner and regaling us with stories about the world in which we had immersed ourselves. We deeply appreciate their willingness to face jail for nonviolent resistance, along with all those at Upstate Drone Action.

Our conversations with Roger Haight, S.J., and the "Berriganistas" at Union Theological Seminary informed many of our editorial decisions. Richard Viladesau translated the Latin into English, which we could in no way have done ourselves. Thanks to Jim Keane at Orbis Books, whose searching eye caught many (sometimes embarrassing) mistakes. Our lively conversations together shaped this project with insightful details and an atmosphere of friendship, and we consider ourselves lucky to have had him as an editor. We also thank Robert Ellsberg for his oversight and for providing a framework for the book; we hope this book might approach in some way the quality of his own work as an editor. We have enjoyed the care of many friends, especially Beth and Kevin Glauber Ahern. And, of course, thank you to Julia Cosacchi and Anna Markowitz for their support in editing and every which way.

We would like to acknowledge our teachers and mentors at Boston College, including John Baldovin, S.J., Lisa Sowle Cahill, Dick Clifford, S.J., Francine Cardman, Steve Pope, and Randy Sachs, S.J. Dan Harrington, S.J. (d. 2014) was a model in all he did, whether biblical scholarship, preaching and teaching, or Boston sports analysis. Mark Massa, S.J., has consistently supported and encouraged us. We are warmly grateful for his enthusiasm for this book, our work on the Berrigans, and our futures.

Dan: I thank the many people who introduced me to the witness and thought of the Berrigans many years ago: Jim Marsh, Jim Fisher, and especially Brendan Coffey, nSJ, who made the pilgrimage twice to the former West Side Jesuit community to visit Dan with me many years ago and stayed up during many nights in college discussing their inspirational lives. It was Dan Berrigan whose life influenced me (in large part) to study theology. I remain grateful for that, and not least of all because of the theological community of graduate students with whom I have studied at Loyola University, Chicago: Christian Cintron, Michael McCarthy, Brent Little, Jason Renken, and Karen Ross (who always makes sure I have a place to stay when I visit). Joe Blankenship has heard me talk more about the Berrigans over these past years than any person should have to! And Mike Goode has asked constantly about the state of this book. Thanks to both of them for being such great friends. Finally, no one has supported me (in this project or any other) like my parents, Brian and Kathy Cosacchi.

Eric: Thanks to Kathy Boylan, Colleen McCarthy, Art Laffin, Michael Walli, and the entire community at the Dorothy Day Catholic Worker in DC for their friendship and example; Martha Hennessy, Carmen Trotta, Rebecca Sikora, and the Mary and St. Joseph Houses in New York; Geoff Gusoff and Rebecca and Paul Shoaf Kozak; Howard Gray; Ed Vacek, and John Shea; Kendrick Walker, a true teacher; all the folks at Casa Cushman for their unceasing hospitality (and keen eye for poetry); the LOMAH; the Pugsley Pilgrims; the Oratory of St. Maximus the Confessor; The 191st St. Jeremiah Group; Glenstal Abbey; Danielle Roberts, Jodi Dean, Sara Knutson, and Kristina Simes; my community at Fordham, especially Jeannine Hill Fletcher, Brenna Moore, Elizabeth Johnson, John Seitz, Jim Fisher, Christiana Peppard, Michael Lee, Christopher Dietrich, and Fordham Against Torture; Kevin Spicer and all at FASPE; Kate Mahon and Kate and Chris McCabe; Tyng and Arya Gulick for their spacious office; Elyse Raby; and Curtis Leighton and Jen Clem for our continuing adventures. All of you have contributed in some form to this project. A special thanks to my family, old and new, for everything.

Finally, thanks to Dan Berrigan, S.J., and Liz McAlister for supporting our efforts. They made this volume possible by granting their permission and opening their homes for memorable conversations (and sometimes delicious breakfasts). This project would have been impossible without their blessing and, more important, their inspiration, influence, and ongoing witness.

Thank you.

Preface

ELIZABETH MCALISTER

The brothers, Daniel and Philip Berrigan, whose faithful correspondence is the motivation for and the content of this manuscript, were the youngest sons of Freda and Thomas Berrigan. The brothers, in order of birth—at fairly consistent intervals of a year and a half—were Thomas, John, James, Jerome, Daniel, and Philip. A sister—stillborn—hyphenated the procession of males. As each left home, his mother made it clear that she expected him to write home, to keep in touch. And as long as she was able, she wrote to them. I know that Philip wrote to her every week; I believe Daniel did the same. Their brother Jerry lived most of his adult life in Syracuse where the parents lived; he and his family made it a priority not only to meet the needs of their parents but to treasure time with them. It should be no surprise that these brothers applied the discipline of correspondence to their relationship with one another as well as with their parents.

The letters between Daniel and Philip vary from a few lines dashed in haste (with a promise of more to come) to thoughtful sharing of plans, actions envisioned or accomplished, writings under way, travels, meetings, and friendships that influenced their lives, and so on. All will become clear as you read them. But whatever the content, the letters bespeak, above all, a profound love of each other; a deep trust in each other's advice, insight, support; and, as their awareness grew that America was not what the history books recorded, their need to walk together on the journey to become men of the gospel and to do all in their power to make oppression, poverty, war, and weapons rare if not obsolete.

Daniel's journey as a Jesuit priest often placed him in colleges and universities where he not only taught classes but worked with students building a sense of community and then sending the students to places where they would come face to face with human suffering—places where radical injustice was a day-to-day present tense, not something they'd encounter in a history book or film. These trips, these exposures were carefully planned by the two brothers because, by the time Dan was assigned to colleges and universities, Philip was a Josephite priest working in inner cities serving segregated and often impoverished African Americans. It was the time when segregation persisted as the practice and, in many places, the law of the land. One of Philip's early assignments was teaching in a black high school in New Orleans. Later, he was assigned to a black parish in one of Baltimore's ghettos. He would welcome Daniel's students as well as other student groups and expose them to aspects of life in the "Great Society" that were far from their own daily experience. The students—prepared for the experience by Daniel—would spend some weeks with Philip learning to organize, work, demonstrate, try to make a bit of difference in the lives of the folks they met, and, above all, learn a bit more about this country than the books recorded. (We at Jonah House in Baltimore continue to work with one of those students from the Jesuit College in Syracuse, New York, who with his wife began Viva House Catholic Worker—a ministry that continues to serve the poor of Baltimore to this day, nudging fifty years of dedication as I write this.)

While the struggle with endemic racism is far from over and while both brothers continued to confront it, the issues of war (Vietnam and, in time, the whole of South East Asia) and nuclear weapons became overwhelming—especially in the wake of the Cuban Missile Crisis. Philip was one of a number of people who prepared to travel the country addressing the issue of those weapons and did so with great fidelity. Dan, in consequence of his writings—both prose and poetry—was in constant demand as a retreat leader, speaker, guide.

The brothers—separately and together—agonized over the crimes of our nations. Their letters are replete with their concern and their search for ways to address their country's crimes and, hopefully, to redirect people into the ways of nonviolence, justice, and peace. Phil pressed for regular meetings with a circle of thoughtful, caring people; Dan pressed the Trappist priest Thomas Merton to host a retreat at Gethsemani with some outspoken men of faith who struggled for radical change in this nation. Could such a retreat help to inspire a movement that was spiritually based and serious?[1]

In the fall of 1964, Thomas Merton did host an unprecedented gathering of peace activists. Its aim—a search for spiritual roots to nurture sound motives for protest. This event, convened in an era

---

[1] The process and content of this retreat were captured in *Pursuing the Spiritual Roots of Protest* by Gordon Oyer. It is widely known that at the time of that retreat no woman could enter the cloister at Gethsemani.

of clear faith boundaries, brought together Catholics—both lay and clergy—mainline Protestants, historic Peace Church people, and Unitarians. Ages ranged from twenty-three to seventy-nine. Several among the fourteen participants are well known today among faith-based peace advocates: the Berrigan brothers, Jim Forest, Tom Cornell, John Howard Yoder, A. J. Muste, and Merton. Insights and wisdom from the varied traditions nourished one another. By the time they parted, they had set down solid roots and modeled interreligious collaboration for peace work that blossomed in subsequent decades.[2]

The work and the witness and the sacrifices that Philip and Daniel engaged were outstanding. Philip, with three accomplices, entered the draft board in Baltimore and poured blood on the 1-A (available for combat) files so that the records of men about to be drafted and sent to kill and to die in Vietnam, Laos, and Cambodia were compromised. Three of the four served long prison sentences in consequence. And between their conviction and their sentencing, two of the four—Philip and Tom Lewis—participated with Dan Berrigan and six others in the Catonsville 9 action—burning with homemade napalm the 1-A files in the Catonsville draft board. That trial was electric; hundreds of young men publicly burned their draft cards at demonstrations during the trial, and a group began meeting to plan for the next draft board action—the Milwaukee 14. So began a long history of nonviolent direct action—approximately three hundred such actions all across this country—that ultimately ended the draft as it was then practiced.

Philip, at that time, served thirty-nine months in federal prison; Dan, eighteen months. They emerged and began to study and understand our country's addiction to weapons. Their search was animated by the change in US nuclear policy and practice that made nuclear war more probable and more immanent. The Plowshares actions were one of the results of that period of study, prayer, reflection, and conversation. Dan and Phil were both participants in the first of the Plowshares actions, the Plowshares Eight. Phil participated in five or more Plowshares actions and spent years in prison. All the while Dan was organizing in New York City and bringing people together to pray, research, and organize resistance to the ubiquitous military presence and the work it was doing. Throughout their numerous arrests and the years and months and days each of them endured in

---

[2] Details of those discussions are reconstructed in a meticulously researched account of this event brought to life in Oyer's book. Their insights are still struggling to be heard against the inertia felt by so many in face of the ever more sophisticated war machine of our world.

jails and prisons, they worked with inmates and maintained intense correspondence with men and women who wrote to them searching for inspiration and for hope.

Phil's many years of prison radically compromised his health. He emerged from his last imprisonment very ill and died of cancer within the year. He died surrounded by his family and close friends and associates.

At this writing Jerry Berrigan's death at ninety-five is raw; he died at home on July 26, 2015. Dan is the only remaining brother of the six; I believe that he is in close communication with his own dying and the life that awaits him and all of us. Like Phil, like Jerry, it looks to me as if Dan is in touch with the life that lies beyond this one.

Introduction

When Daniel and Philip Berrigan joined seven other antiwar activists on May 17, 1968, in using homemade napalm to set fire to draft files in Catonsville, Maryland, they set themselves apart as national figures. The reality of their cases, however, is that the act of resistance was only the next step in an increasingly public struggle against injustice. The year before Phil had been arrested for his role in the Baltimore Four. Only days before this action, Dan had been arrested while protesting the Vietnam War outside of the Pentagon. They were the first Roman Catholic priests arrested for antiwar activity in the United States.

After Catonsville they would find themselves at the heart of the Catholic peace movement in the United States. Noteworthy about the Berrigans was their consistency on the issues: they embodied a "consistent ethic of life" long before Cardinal Joseph Bernardin coined the term; their important work against nuclear weapons, which was especially evident in the Plowshares movement; their ability to be a presence in the media; their insistence on the importance of community (whether Dan's membership in the Society of Jesus or Phil's co-founding Jonah House with Liz McAlister); their concern for the poor, sick, and dying; and their prolific writing.

While the large corpus of writings about the Berrigans continues to grow, we hope that publishing their correspondence will allow it to be read as they told it to each other, with the character and intimacy of their own voices.

In preparing a manuscript collecting the correspondence between two of the most historically significant American Catholics (and indeed, Americans!) of the twentieth century, editors are forced to make a number of difficult decisions. In our case the most difficult editorial decisions concerned which letters to set aside and which letters to preserve within these pages. In bringing together the letters here, we have tried to keep in mind seven criteria.

First, and most important, there emerges throughout each and every letter that the brothers write to one another a very genuine and quite touching statement of love. In some letters—most noteworthy on birthdays or anniversaries—the sentiment is expressed in a forth-right manner and with effusive praise. At other times the message is hidden between the lines. As a whole, this book is a story of mutual love more than anything else.

Second, we highlighted as much as possible the planning and re-flection upon their roles in activism. While they often made it clear that they believed the many actions in which they took part were egalitarian in nature, and a team effort, it is quite obvious that Dan and Phil were the ringleaders of almost every operation mentioned in these pages. By this, we mean that they often came up with the ideas for actions, funded the actions, invited the potential participants, planned the meetings, led the common prayer, and were the public faces in the media. Sometimes this role was thrust upon them due to lack of experience on the part of the others in their groups; at other times they seemed to yearn for this role. In all cases we found this material fascinating.

Third, it is obvious that these two men (especially Phil) spent a good deal of time in prison for their roles in the aforementioned ac-tions. We have attempted to make very vivid what these prison condi-tions were like by publishing as many of these letters as possible. Since prison has been a significant part of Christian discipleship ever since the time of Saint Paul, we felt that it was important to highlight the Berrigans' view on prison in these pages.

Fourth, there was a consistency throughout these letters in re-turning to the relationship of Dan and Phil with their family. Their relationships with their parents is a common thread. In particular, their common devotion to their mother, Freda, is a beautiful aspect of their fraternal bond. In this selection we were able to include only a fraction of their writings on family. We include these letters to il-lustrate their closeness. Their relationship to the three eldest brothers in the family—Thomas, John, and Jim—remains a bit of a mystery. For at least a time John and Tom were openly opposed to the actions of the youngest three brothers—Jerry, Dan, and Phil. As some letters indicate, Phil's marriage to Liz McAlister also proved to be a point of contention among the members of the Berrigan family.

Fifth, a constant theme in these pages is the relationship that the Berrigan brothers have with the church. Most often the rhetoric tends toward prophetically calling the church to embody more fully its faith and to live out its membership in the body of Christ. While the reader must decide exactly what this means, it is clear that both men retained a particular closeness with the church as the body of Christ throughout their lives. Under this theme we found quite interesting the relationship the brothers shared with a number of bishops (who were either closely or loosely affiliated with the peace movement) and their respective religious communities. This latter characteristic of the letters is most evident in Dan's writings. Finally, it is obvious that both men maintained a particular devotion to the celebration of the Eucharist. The reader will note this theme in their correspondence.

Sixth, as with almost all loving relationships there is conflict between these two men. While it only comes out in a few letters, it is clear that sometimes the actions of one brother made the other quite upset and critical. These blunt writings are fraught with pain and tension and inspire a hope that the recipient of the letter will carry out a deep and careful self-examination.

Seventh, and finally, there is a certain preoccupation with illness, death, and dying throughout these letters. One or the other brother is almost always sick in some way or close to someone who is gravely ill. Moreover, Dan ministers to those dying of AIDS and to others dying in a hospice in New York City. Furthermore, we read a number of touching letters that deal with Dan attending to his confrere Lew Cox, S.J., in the final days of his life. Phil is also surrounded by sickness, and ultimately we get a small glimpse into the pain and suffering of his final months in these letters.

There are some other items worth noting here. First, this volume presents a small sample of what is stored at Cornell University and DePaul University. There were just shy of twenty-two hundred letters, and fewer than a quarter of them appear in these pages. Almost none of them appear in full; they have been edited to avoid repetition and for the reader's interest. One regrettable result of this process is the underrepresentation of Jerry Berrigan, Phil and Dan's brother, and his wife Carol. Missing as well are the many additions of Phil's wife, Elizabeth McAlister, to the letters. Another full volume would be needed to capture these writings, and we consider their absence necessary to focus on the relationship between Phil and Dan. More of Phil's letters appear than Dan's, which reflects the whole of the archives. We have retained the unique spelling and grammar the brothers often used, providing editorial notes to clarify meaning when necessary.

Finally, we transcribed every letter between the brothers housed in the collections at Cornell and DePaul. To the best of our knowledge these hold all of the surviving letters between Phil and Dan. The reader will notice that some letters are either undated or mark only the year. We put these entries where their content suggests and are confident they have settled into, more or less, the correct spot. Some of Dan's letters to Phil are addressed "Dears," usually indicating that they were also meant for Liz and the other residents of Jonah House. Last, we elected to include editorial notes only when necessary, aiming to let the letters speak for themselves as much as possible.

On a "rainy, quiet day" in 1971, Dan confided to Phil that his letters gave him a sense of hope in the midst of prison. "Do you manage by the way," he asked, "to hang on to any of these immortal patchworks? They're about the closest thing I get to a diary of sorts these days. I keep yours—it is all part of an ongoing record; as well to read and read again."[1]

Much of this record has been placed back into original envelopes and interspersed among tens of thousands of other letters sent to the Berrigans. Whenever we finally found one between Dan and Phil, we were never certain what waited inside. Some held only letters, while others were filled with newspaper clippings tracking the latest news in Vietnam or the brothers' resistance activities. In some cases the clippings *were* the letter, with notes jotted in the margins, words circled, arrows cutting across the page, and a signature at the bottom. It was not rare to find envelopes stuffed to the brim with several articles folded at various angles, complemented with brochures, pictures, or book reviews. An occasional odd object—dried flowers, a toy ring, crayons—accompanied the paper contents. Upon unfolding one letter a mound of glitter spilled out from its creases and spread across the archive table. It was a fitting symbol of joyful irreverence in a silent, orderly space that fit the brothers' personalities.

The letters themselves matched their writers. Phil's daughter, Frida, remembers his letters from jail, "his handwriting neat and legible with a spidery slant" and usually written on lined yellow legal pad.[2] Dan's letters, however, are rarely neat and almost never legible. He often wrote in thick marker, in contrast to Phil's pen, and would decorate his letters with pictures, poems, or improvised designs. "I was interested in jiving up the awful prison paper," he told an interviewer, and so even on the atypical typewritten letter, he would sometimes sign his name with a crayon and draw colorful waves in the margins or behind the text to enliven the appearance. The writing itself occasionally changes direction or, in one case, appears entirely in spiral form (making the editor's task of reading it from a computer somewhat tedious). His

---

[1] September 11, 1971; p. 67 herein.

[2] Frida Berrigan, *It Runs in the Family: On Being Raised by Radicals and Growing into Rebellious Motherhood* (New York: OR Books, 2015), 26.

prison letters from Danbury almost uniformly contain unusual illustrations at the top, the product of creativity despite limited resources. "I carved out blocks of nickel erasers and got hold of a set of watercolors," he explained, "so that I was able to print designs on the letters I sent out. . . . They expressed my feeling that I was free even though in prison. I wanted, through some color and line and words and poetry, to say so to other people."[3]

Prison would leave its own mark on their letters. "They censor mail both ways here,"[4] Phil warned Dan from Baltimore City Jail, and the stamp of approval is a common sight in their correspondence. The inspection process sometimes took a week to complete, so it was not at all exceptional, for example, for Phil's letter of August 16, 1970, to bear a stamp from August 22. This delay in mailing caused some frustration, as writing to each other was their only link between visits, which were not always granted. "Yours of Nov. 20 last night," Phil wrote on the 27th. "The mail remains pitifully slow."[5] Dan summed up a recurring theme through the prison years when he said, "I always have a curious sense in writing, of being a sound track slightly out of whack with the image. The delayed mail, the late reports . . . make quite a game of time. And then when the letters are delayed—that must be something like Reel 8 played just before Reel 1 or something."[6]

The backup from censorship meant that letters often arrived in bunches, so letting the other brother know how many they received became a refrain in their greetings: "No less than 3 from youse today, all greeted with joy"; "three beeg ones from you tonight"; "A windfall of yours yesterday"; "3, yes 3 of yrs. arrived this PM"; "still digesting your 3 course banquet of last evening"; "I'm sittin pretty here, baskin in all the good letters that have flowed forth from yer parts."

The arrival of mail from each other, Liz, Jerry, and Carol was often the main event of the day. This only increased the brothers' irritation with the authorities when they interfered, which not only slowed down the pace of conversation but also dictated whether a note made it to its recipient intact. "Half of yours (Feb. 1) lost in transit, sadly enough," Phil complained to Dan. As would occur time and again,

---

[3] Lee Lockwood and Daniel Berrigan, *Absurd Convictions, Modest Hopes: Conversations after Prison with Lee Lockwood* (New York: Vintage Books, 1973), 61.

[4] November 1, 1967; pp. 37–38 herein.

[5] November 27, 1973; Cornell Archives, Box 105.

[6] September 1, 1971; pp. 60–61 herein.

however, he used the news as a chance to laud his brother: "But I sez—half a letter from Dan better than a whole from most."[7]

One valuable aspect of this collection is that it spans a key period of American history. The first letter appears in 1940, the year before Pearl Harbor was bombed and America entered World War II, and the last appears in 2002, in the immediate aftermath of 9/11. What this book provides, then, is a view of American history from the nation's rise as a superpower to its moment of national rupture and vulnerability, filtered through the writings of two brothers. These two events act as bookends, framing the evolution of the Berrigans from patriotic celebrants of the US victory (and of Phil's safe return from battle) to leaders in the American counterculture and its resistance against war and racism.

One of the more revealing contributions these letters provide is a view into Dan's early life while training for priesthood, including his view of God as "Him Who was a good Soldier." Trying to comfort Phil in the midst of his tour in Europe, he wrote, "To believe that our Lord wants you as surely in a field Artillery or Air Force . . . that's a grand faith and trust and high outlook that will solve a great deal, clear up a lot of moral issues."[8] Such passages highlight the extent of the conversion both brothers experienced, and the many that follow offer insight to the struggle, the reasoning, and the faith that guided their transformation.

The letters show that Phil and Dan always shared this slow work of change together, and so this book presents a love story between two Christians supporting each other in their attempts to live out a discipleship rooted in the gospels. ("I find it very hard to separate Phil's fate from mine, as a matter of affection and existence itself," Dan said. "I wouldn't know where his life began and mine ended."[9]) They unceasingly relied on each other for support in the midst of hardship, whether by prison, community building, exile from the country, a church they found lacking and lagging, a secret marriage, excommunication, persecution by the FBI, ailing health, or public scrutiny. Almost every letter contains an ode of love and admiration that conveys how much each leaned on the other. "Of all of us, your life shows the undivided self in Christ," Dan wrote. "You . . . are our (my) north star. That is your place in our firmament, fixed and bright. Thanks are redundant, but yet never so. Thank you brother."[10] Or, as

---

[7] February 3, 1972; pp. 83–84 herein.
[8] September 15, 1943; p. 7 herein.
[9] Lockwood, *Absurd Convictions, Modest Hopes*, 64.
[10] May 15, 1978; p. 146 herein.

Phil said, "God knows what a cabbage I am despite your care. But without it, I would be less than a vegetable—wandering, opaque and clinging to idols. In short, you have been grace and gift to thousands, but esp. to your kid brother."[11]

Perhaps no story better illustrates their intimate bond than when Dan lay on what he thought was his deathbed. In 1971, while he and Phil were serving time in Danbury prison together, Dan nearly died from a routine Novocaine injection gone wrong. As he slipped in and out of consciousness, it was Phil's name he called out. When things looked dire and another priest came in to give him the last rites, Dan waved him off, saying, "Well, I've just seen my brother, thank you." Asked if his brother gave him extreme unction, he replied, "I had Phil around—that was Extreme Unction."[12]

"Blessed are the peacemakers," Jesus taught in the Sermon on the Mount, "for they will be called children of God." Our ultimate aim in editing these letters is to pass on spiritual resources for those on this path, bringing them from seldom-handled archival storage boxes to a more accessible format. We hope those who work for the justice, peace, nonviolence, love, healing, and mercy of the gospels and prophets will find something in these pages to sustain them, and that all who read these letters can look beneath the historical events—the napalm-fueled pyres and the blood-stained warheads—to the hard-fought struggle for faith that founded such radical acts. Dan underscored the shared nature of this struggle when discussing his decision to join the Catonsville action that propelled them into the public eye. "There was only the force of a friendship, and an offer," he said. "I knew my brother. . . . I knew also his love for me. So there was no such element as pure darkness. How could there be? Instead of sight, or evidence, or logic, there was something better to go by—a hand in mine, someone to walk with. Enough, and more."[13]

This image of Phil and Dan holding hands in an act of faith fits well with how they signed off their letters for years, with a phrase that framed their relationship for the rest of their lives: "Devotedly in our Lord."

---

[11] May 2, 1992; p. 264 herein.

[12] Lockwood, *Absurd Convictions, Modest Hope*, 97, 101.

[13] Daniel Berrigan, *To Dwell in Peace* (New York: Harper & Row: 1987), 217–18.

1940–1955

[The first extant letter from Phil to Dan does not appear, unfortunately, until 1962; until then we only see Dan's correspondence to Phil. This allows a focus on Dan's early formation with the Jesuits, beginning at the age of eighteen on August 14, 1939, with a two-year novitiate at St. Andrew-on-Hudson in Poughkeepsie, New York. Dan recalls that upon entering the grounds, "the doors closed on us in a silence that seemed, at the time, both horrific and final. We arrived, we vanished into a new world." The oldest surviving letter reveals something of his daily life there and how dependent Dan had already become on letters from Phil, who was still attending high school in Syracuse.]

[1940]

Dear Phil,

I don't exactly know what prompts me to write two letters home in one week except perhaps the fact that I haven't heard from you in quite a while.—That I haven't the faintest inkling of how your basketball or studies, or how life in general is going with you. If I could only put into words how interested I am in everything about school, skating—everything, in fact, that was so common to us back a very short time ago! So I want it all in a good voluminous letter—your marks, all the basketball scores to date and how you figured in them, etc. etc.

There's never time heavy on your hands here at St. Andrew's. You really feel grateful when a half-hour is given in which to do a little extra letter writing, etc. I figure we have about 30 more or less cut and dried periods each day, excluding meals. But something is always coming up—recreation after dinner and supper by the now tightly frozen

1

Hudson, is something to thank God for. You can imagine for yourself what takes place when 68 up-to-then silent tongues are loosened for the first time after dinner. Then there's the deep element, two daily meditations, daily Mass and Communion, these three are your driving force and with your 7 or 8 visits to the Blessed Sacrament have melted even this black heart so that now his greatest fear is that he finds himself so terribly unworthy to be in such a Company as that bearing the Name of Jesus Itself. Father gives us our daily Confession in which we come to really know the Society and its spirit, encouragement, love.

Devotedly in our Lord,
Dan, S.J.

January 3, 1941

Dear Phil,

Your grand letter gave me a great lift—especially in the fact of your joyful Christmas together. I also want to thank you for writing so faithfully when I found it impossible because of our Christmas rush, to write you personally. Today was our second First Friday to Vows. It was more consoling than I can tell you to know that Ma and you were receiving in union with me. There seemed to be one idea predominant this morning at Mass and after Communion—Confidence in our Lord's promises that no matter what we are not, He will see us through.

Devotedly in our Lord,
Dan, S.J.

Saturday [1941?]

Dearest Philip,

The peace of Christ—I thought I would write you something in Latin, since you have now immersed yourself so fruitfully in this language. I really enjoy your letters, especially regarding your good success in studies. Every day, Philip, I thank our Lord for the divine goodness so well manifested in you.

It is fitting for me to say something about the Novitiate. Every day we read from the book by Father Fichter of our Society about Francisco Suarez, S.J. Father Suarez was a most renowned Spaniard, who is surpassed in church theological studies only by Saint Thomas

Aquinas; Suarez was not only erudite, but also holy, to our mind, and this holiness he put forth as the characteristic of glory.

I give thanks to all of you, Philip, for all your goodness to me on the Feast of the Resurrection. I am especially grateful for the Fanny Farmer candies, which I received this week. In my daily prayers I give my thanks that our glorified Lord may give you what I ask without merit. Please remember me in your prayers.

Devotedly yours in the Heart of Jesus,
Dan, nSJ

[In this letter, Dan laments the fact that Phil, who had been saving for college by living at home and scrubbing soot off railroad cars, had decided to enroll at St. Michael's College in Toronto rather than a Jesuit school. He would begin classes in the fall of 1942 and enter the military after having studied for only one semester.]

December 1941?

Dear Phil—

Your letter was like a burst of sunshine on our lady's beautiful feast last Monday. Not only did I enjoy the account of your work and interests, but it is a real and practical inspiration for me to read such an account of hard work and common sense. This life of studies might be more aptly termed a life of faith since one can go on for a very long time with honest, hard work and yet in a material sense at least, see little production. But the Society is very much like her mother the Church—in her timelessness; and in order to mould a perfect human instrument for souls' salvation, will wait and work—and wait again. And we Scholastics must wed ourselves faithfully to study and believe in spite of occasional difficulty that we, by doing God's will at this particular phase of our training, are doing more for men's souls than we could do in a parish or on the Missions—since this is what God wants.

I only wish that you could plan on enrolling under our Fathers in college, but since the matter is settled we can be grateful that you are going to an excellent college. Though by a year intervening you may lose a bit of your grasp on the studies, still you are gaining a hundredfold in experience and maturity. My boy—may I be brief—you're an inspiration to me. I pray every day that these years of college training may really materialize and you reap a hundredfold for the selflessness and grit of this year. I think of your railroad job and set the bit tighter into my own teeth.

Pray for me.

> Devotedly in our Lord,
> Dan, S.J.

October 12, 1942

Dear Phil—

I was delighted with your letter. You have a stiff setup in studies but with your characteristic energy there is no question of anything but success. I have found for myself that while study is a great sap on energies, it is irreplaceable for discipline and healthy thinking. You will know more of what I mean after a year of consistent work at the books.

The spiritual advantages you have at your disposal are magnificent; and make full use of them. You have so much power at your beck and call to pray for all—for great, far-reaching good. And pray for me. I need more of the aid and strength of supernatural oneness with our Lord. You see, my boy, a Jesuit is not in existence for himself—he is an instrument of our Lord sealed and set apart as the servant of men—to bear their burdens and forget his own.

My boy, I write to you as one who can be more than a brother; my great dream and never flagging prayer is that you will embrace the priesthood—the life of true joy and of satisfaction in loving and living Christ. You have all the gifts and talents required—that in itself, plus your good will, constitutes a vocation. St. Ignatius once said that it was much more sensible to look for an extraordinary sign from God telling one to remain out of Religion than to ask one to enter Religion since the first is so much more fraught with danger than the second. This determination to enter at the end of this year will give point and purpose to your study and assure you of God's help in your work.

Feast of All Saints, Nov. 1, 1942

Dear Phil—

Your fine letter was most welcome, as they always are. We cannot choose our own way of doing things these days; it seems that your plans for a year of College are to be entirely disrupted. One's only peace is a complete renunciation of will and opens into the living Hands of the Crucified.

You speak as though all plans for the Priesthood were completely abandoned. I can only hope and pray that such a step—almost frightening in its consequences to you and your future, was not taken before prayer and weighing of values. When you planned on a Technical Course at College—and especially from your last letter, where you announce your intention to join the Air Corps, I cannot but be forced to the conclusion that you were making altogether different plans. Well, God disposes, and it would be folly to try something you were convinced was not for you. But that is what will always cause me concern—whether or not you really plunked your heart to its bottom or whether the decision was taken lightly.

God bless and keep you. Pray for me.

Devotedly in our Lord,
Dan, S.J.

December 1942?

Dear Phil,

Be almost presumptual in asking for material and spiritual blessings for all, since you have so many Masses being offered for your intentions and favors. Ask the Almighty Father especially to pour out the Blood of our Lord—immolated every day, almost endlessly—upon the whole world, that these evil days be shortened and the incalculable harm being done to souls may be cut short. Perhaps oftener than not it is a simple lack of confidence and trust which makes our prayers so seemingly ineffectual—we tend to measure God's Infinite love and mercy by the yardstick of our petty fears and littleness. So walk the earth like a giant in your visits to the Blessed Sacrament—and touch every camp and warfront and hospital with Christ, who is God, at your side. You are a hundred times powerful because our Lord, who sees in secret, will also reward in secret your sacrifices on His behalf. Let's you and I be like lights on the mountain these days. Nothing can blow out a candle which God has lighted—we must be careful that the light is never hid under a bushel but shining out to lead the gropers to the True Light.

Pray for me, Phil—and again, a heartfelt thank you.

Devotedly in our Lord,
Dan, S.J.

*[Before leaving for basic training in January 1943, Phil made a four-
day retreat with Dan at St. Andrew's and briefly considered becoming a priest rather than joining the military. He ultimately headed
for training in Georgia, Florida, and North Carolina, where he was
confronted with the institutional racism that would drive his civil
rights work on his return from war. This letter represents several in
which Dan ties his support for Phil's service in the Air Force to the
Christian faith, underscoring the extremity of their later conversion
to nonviolence.]*

April 20, 1943

Dearest Phil,

Just a note before our grand silence of Holy Thursday settles down
over St. Andrew: a note to tell you of my prayer that your Easter
be holy and joyful—but above all, drenched in the peace our Lord
gives—peace in the cross and the doing of His Will.

Have received your letters regularly. Sinlessness is the hard-won,
fought-for reward of a clean heart which thinks too much of God
and itself to feed on swine-husks. You have our Lady, and the strong
consolations of faith, and above all, Holy Communion—fervent and
frequent as possible. My prayer for you is always double—your safety
of body and above all the clearness of soul which is your best proof
of the love of God, and which is freedom from smirch. So keep the
sword bright—bright in use, because the soldier-life you lead is in its
noblest view—inner and unseen—the fight for the approval of your
Captain Christian sinlessness.

All my love and prayer. Joyous Easter.

Devotedly in our Lord,
Dan, S.J.

*[In the fall of 1943, Dan moved near Baltimore, Maryland, to study
at Woodstock College. The poem mentioned here was published in
America on October 23, 1943, under the title "You Vested Us This
Morning (for four soldier brothers)" in honor of four of his brothers
(including Phil and Jerry) who were in the military at the time. Other
than Dan, only brother Jim had not joined the military. He had, however, joined the Civilian Conservation Corps.]*

September 15 1943—Our Lady of Sorrows

Dearest Phil—

America has promised to publish a poem of mine, which I have expressly dedicated—and they will state it so, to "four soldier brothers." Please say a prayer too that it does some good for the myriad of people who have their most precious possessions taken from them by war. You know our vocation is in plain words to help people, and all our learning and degrees are not worth a row of pins unless they help for that end. As if I have some tenuous writing ability pray I always keep it relative to the grand cause of souls and the glory of Christ Who has infallibly called me and wants not learning but the salvation of human souls: and this through all the sacrifice and devotion a soldier is called upon to give.

To realize that the soldiering of this war is a vocation too—that would solve some of your difficulties and loneliness and the vague worries too shadowy for definition, wouldn't it, Phil? To believe our Lord wants you as surely in a field Artillery or Air Force just as surely as he wants fifteen years of study and sweat from me—that's a grand faith and trust and high outlook that will solve a great deal, clear up a lot of moral issues, turn the whole situation (which is otherwise a pure mess) into part of the great plan to bring souls back to God their maker—the only thing that counts in life. And your part is to play the game (as you are doing superbly) looking on Him Who was a good Soldier—unto death. It is your faith which separates you from the mere animalism which can so preoccupy—I don't mean accepting it but its mere presence can blind one to the ideal and pure and beautiful—the sinlessness of our Lady—the sublime union of Holy Communion, the consolation of prayer, and the reliance on others' prayers—above all Ma's, to bring everything around. God bless you—my daily prayer.

> Devotedly in our Lord,
> Dan, S.J.

[No letters survive between 1943 and 1951, though much took place. Phil fought with the Air Force in England, France, the Netherlands, and Germany. On his return after the war he hitchhiked to Woodstock to celebrate with Dan. "We sang," he said, "toasting the war's end, patting ourselves on the back. . . . I carried the flag as we marched around the main building—a couple of platoons of soldiers, two

hundred Jesuits, friends, family, kids—all cheering our country's victory." He worked for a year in construction, drinking heavily, until his mother convinced him to enter the College of Holy Cross on the GI Bill; there he began to question the use of violence and the direction of his own life. He graduated in 1950 (fulfilling Dan's wish that he study with the Jesuits) and entered the Josephite order, whose focus on serving black Americans appealed to Phil's disgust with what he had seen in the American South and the military. Dan, having taught three years in prep school in New Jersey and now studying theology at Weston in Massachusetts, here attempts to prepare Phil for life as a seminarian.]

Monday in Holy Week [1951]

Dear Phil,

How full of meaning this Easter is for all of us in the family, and perhaps especially for yourself! In the events of this one week all of us can read our own biography—written, as [Thomas] Merton said, on His wounds. And those wounds, carried with Him into eternity and glory, still pour light into our souls as once they poured their saving blood.

When we choose Christ for our portion, we set in motion, like a stone dropped into a pool, forces that continue outward into eternity.—And at the little circle of light you are setting ablaze, how many who are lost, bewildered, discouraged, will come to be refreshed, to find their direction again in the night that surrounds them! 'God is Light, and no darkness finds any place in Him . . . God dwells in light; if we too live and move in light, there is fellowship between us, and the blood of His Son Jesus Christ washes us clean from all sin . . . the darkness is passed away now, and true Light shines instead . . . *ut filli lucis sitis*—that you may be sons of light.' All this involves a price, which you will begin to pay progressively this year, and whose cost will become clearer to you with the passing of time. But the 'son of light' does not ask a clear look into what is contained in the chalice—he says his 'I can!', trusting in Him who holds the chalice to his lips. And as you begin to pay in earnest the price of keeping your light untarnished, pure, bright, unwavering, you will see more clearly in its light, too—*in lumine Tuo videbimus Lumen*: in Thy light we shall see the Light.

These things I write mainly for the future; not that there should be the least wavering from trust but it is good to be wise as to what the years hold for those who will be the Christo-pheres, the luci-pheres, the Lightbearers for the world. It is seldom an easy life, but it is never a sad one, and Easter shows the true meaning of the wounds that are to come; shows their meaning even as Calvary never could—because the wounds are now glorious, they stream, as St. Bernard says, with light instead of with blood, to beckon us on to the consummation of love which '*Nunquam fatigatur — usque ad finem!*'

Devotedly in our Lord,
Dan, S.J.

[*In this letter Dan notifies Phil that his Jesuit superior has approved him for ordination. He would be ordained at Weston by Cardinal Cushing on June 21, 1952, a step that Dan said "struck a light that has never been extinguished."*]

Feb. 29 [1952]

Dear Phil—

This was in the nature of a great day and I wanted to share it with you before nightfall. Today received official '*promoveatur ad ordines*' from my Provincial; he acts as Bishop in our case, and his word is final approval of acceptance.

I doubt whether in 13 years a greater thing has happened to me. It was one of those occasions when all the jagged pieces slide into place finally and the picture fits. You will see what I mean; the ordinary days pummel me along in their wake + it's not often you hit a crest where the horizon is total.

God love you—

Devotedly in our Lord,
Dan, S.J.

[*Here, Dan alludes to the special Marian Year called for by Pope Pius XII in his encyclical* Fulgens Corona, *promulgated September 8, 1953, partially in order to celebrate the centenary of the proclamation of the Immaculate Conception of the Blessed Virgin Mary.*]

December 2 [1953]:

Dear Boys [Phil and Jerry],

I have both of you to thank for the good letters that bring the sunshine of Washington here.

The great Marian year gets underway on the Feast of the Immaculate Conception. I will offer the Holy Sacrifice for you both on that great day; and I thought it would be a good time for the three of us to make a special consecration of our lives and vocations, placing them totally in our Lady's hands for the year ahead, through December of '54. For the capital graces we all need, for perseverance, fervor, the spirit of sacrifice, it occurred to me it would be good to recite some special little prayer every day, if possible before the Blessed Sacrament, to keep the consecration alive. I ran across the following prayer in the life of Pere de Grandmaison, and it has been a favorite of mine for a long time. I thought it would keep us one in her, if we said it for one another this year . . . "Holy Mary, Mother of God, preserve in us the heart of a child, pure and clear as a fountainhead; Obtain for us a youthful heart, which is never obsessed with gloom; A heart great in the giving of itself, tender in its compassion; A heart generous and faithful; Which forgets no gift, and remembers no evil done it; Fashion for us a gentle, humble heart which loves without asking any return, and is joyous in losing itself in His Heart; A great unconquerable heart, which no ingratitude locks, no indifference withers; A heart tormented with the glory of Jesus Christ, wounded with His love, a heart whose wound will heal only in heaven. Amen.". . . . All goes superlatively here, with Christmas so near.

Yours for a great year with our Lady,
Dan, S.J.

[*In the fall of 1953, Dan went to France for Jesuit tertianship at Paray le Monial, near Lyons. Tertianship is the final stage of Jesuit formation; it occurs after a Jesuit has been ordained to the priesthood. During this year the Jesuit makes the thirty-day* Spiritual Exercises *retreat for a second time, having already completed the Ignatian retreat over a decade earlier during his novitiate. The trip was instrumental in awakening Dan to the issues that later drove his work. The squalor of postwar industry and its effects on laborers attuned him to material needs of ordinary people, while the collapsing war in Indochina alerted him to the evils of colonialism, which he began to see more clearly when his own country invaded Vietnam. His meeting with theologian Henri de Lubac, exiled from his community and prevented from teaching and censored in his writing for outpacing Vatican theology, presaged his own banishment for similar reasons twelve years later. This, along with witnessing Rome's dissolution of the French worker priests, who had labored in the factories with the workers to engage with "the world," led him to question his church in new ways. The Jesuit Pere Paul Magand, of whom Dan speaks here, was one such worker priest, and one hears the beginning of an impatience for theory, an admiration for immersion into society, and a need for experimentation with Christian living that Dan would later develop further.*]

Jan. 6 [1954]

Dear Jerry and Phil,

Phil's good letter came yesterday, with the good news that Christmas had been a time of perfect happiness for all; it was like a breath of home to get some of the details.

We have finished a triduum which proved a real inspiration. It was given by a priest worker from Lyons, Pere Magand, S.J. He has been in the factories there for some eight years, so can speak with authority. My admiration is unbounded for these men, who are carrying the world on their shoulders, often with such withering fire from the sidelines. He spoke with real passion, not so much on his own job, as on the need of charity, of justice, of poverty. It was unforgettable. He had come in on the evening train, in his old workers clothes, spoke to us in the same, even said Mass in them, without a cassock. He also brought to mind many things which have been simmering with me for some time; spoke for example of the 'irreality' of French Catholics, in the sense that so d- much theorizing, analyzing, orating, is done about conditions—and so little action. This is true of their churchmen as well; for whom elan, milieu, incarnation, esprit, and all the rest become after a period of genuine freshness, a series of wearying catchwords as old as the cliches they began by replacing. And that is why the priest workers represent such a marvelous and sacrificial and admirable departure; they are one of the few steps taken to put a tether on all the billowing theory and drag it to earth.

I must not close without some word of the interesting talk I was able to wrangle with P. Magand before his going. In view of the Rome decisions, and our own general's decree of removing Jebs from the priest workers as they stand now, he is uncertain of what his future will be. He thinks the priest workers are definitely not finished; they have only finished one phase, that of a daring experiment, I count our three days with him here one of the prime experiences of the year, and will not soon forget him. He is by the way a good friend of Pere de Lubac, who considers him as a good right hand, putting into practice all his own sublime theological development. I pray every day the priest workmen will flourish and reach maturity as an organ of Christ's Body—for the next fifty years, or a hundred, together with the Mission of France whose realignment we are still watching here, as their seminary opens again soon. There are few other signs as hopeful as these in the heavens. Keep them in your prayers.

> Prayers + all devotion—
> Dan, S.J.

[Dan reacts here to their brother Jerry's decision to leave studies for priesthood and marry.]

January 10 [1954]

Dear Phil,

Your letter came today, and I am trying to get this off in the afternoon mail in answer. I had a good long visit at the Blessed Sacrament, so feel much more steady than I could have thought possible. It is a great load from Jerry's heart, from yours and mine; for the family it will be harder.

All our effort and prayers now will go in Jerry's direction, praying for him the strength and courage to find himself with the new future. Certainly he will have taken a decision which was the most costly of his life.

For yourself now, be sure God's will, which is Love, has been accomplished, and go forward certain of His blessing, His light and peace. We have done, the three of us, everything humanly and Divinely possible; there is no point in dwelling on what is finished.

Believe me, my admiration and love have grown a hundredfold for you in these hard months past. It all goes into the making of a good priest, who can take sorrow as equably as joy because God is his first love.

You are never out of my Mass.

Dan, S.J.

[In June of 1955, Phil was ordained at the Shrine of the Immaculate Conception in Washington, D.C.]

The Innocent Throne
(for the Ordination of my brother; June, 1955)

> I
> Philip, since all is summed in you,
> I am a wastrel of fair words
> to send them loud and purposeless
> all frantic as a cage of birds.
> Possessing not my heart, my voice,
> they fret the lovely, listening day:
> then do not heed them. My word for you
> no word of mine will ever say.

II
My living memories arise
suddenly as those boughs our boyhood grew:
challenge and portent.
            Who dares climb
the stallion tree furiously striding heaven,
and ride, ride, beautifully to subdue,
to match to curb?
            Or diminished in Sunday twilight
what clean young figure, innocent of blood,
dares with his cape the avalanche, the horn?
My nightmare passes and the sweet day dawns.
But Christ, to what have You brought him? he rides
      now
the bleeding horn: he hangs from the furious bough.

III
Games were marvelous. To pretend king
set heart only on edge, gave the stick of sword
a superb damascan ring. And what more
could ten of the uncertain clock bring, awry,
authoritarian, than neighborhood children crying
hail, all hail, than passage to an innocent throne
and dragon years all slain?
            Folded the crown in dust
these twenty years: never an inquiry
the old air forms: wears he still at breast the heart
once at ten of clock, redressed our wrongs?
Now all the bells of heaven seize the sweet tale:
the young at heart, the pretend, were true: *all hail!*

IV
At play on summer's stream, they watched
paper boats, trees, themselves, flowering
in underwater light: and stretching a hand
to greet the stranger, found and lost
his shy image forever.
Then a cloud stole its wavering sun away
and downstream the logged boats limped into eve-
      ning.
But where had the game fled, the shouts
that scattered waters swifter than white flocks?

A first star knew, that could see for miles
the ins and outs of this most secret water—
where it wore proudly at the breast the childrens'
    faces
never to change, with no disfiguring tear
and all their songs carefully folded in echo.

V

Hide and seek, the dangerous twilight
stands with the lurking and lovely brother
who in a corner east of the new moon
is wound in such a spell, suddenly one stops
short of touch or shout. O is it time
that grows his shadow to an angry sky
or takes him suddenly by the hair of head
to the immeasurable treetop, or swings him
over a wall no love shall clamber?
Blind, count ten at the wall, and go
afraid and tiptoe under conniving trees:
he is here, he is there:—
      Heart, he is nowhere.
But age will show him, a sudden flare
lighting the sudden stranger.

VI

Now and again, apart in courageous
imagining, we wheeled upon the dark
and dealt with those tremendous cowards,
creating a charmed island for meek men
in a dangerous circle, with a sword chanting.
Again, we had merely to step on shore
and the first drum of a foot would send
tide and his dragon sliding back.
Knowledge was not in the mind: it was approach
slowly, watch from shelter, capture.
Knowledge raised its own device, gave the lie
to appearance, stood on the slain evil
or bending over a flower in the hand
heard secret heartbeat: or east of sun
standing, or west of moon, snapped the spells
that had wound men arrogantly in toils
and given bestial form to beauty.

It was good, turning quietly to slumber
to bid stars be wakeful, to bid one's dreams
create straightway a marvelous morning.

VII
A son's identity can startle
even the mother, upon whose limbs, upon whose life
this child has clung. He has stepped out of her
as image from its mirror, has danced before her
figures of her own grave and watchful will:
in the secret house of each, the other dwells:
she has walked easily into her child's eyes.

1962–1969

[Another gap in the letters appears between 1955 and 1962, a time of further political engagement for both brothers. After Phil's ordination he was assigned as assistant pastor at Our Lady of Perpetual Help parish in the Anacostia district of Washington, D.C.—"a huge plantation," in his words—helping black residents with inferior public housing. The next year he was transferred to teach English and religion at St. Augustine's high school in New Orleans, where his dedication to combating white supremacy intensified after one of his students was beaten by white Catholics with a tire iron in response to the integration of the city's Catholic schools. Dan gained recognition as a writer with the 1957 Lamont Prize for poetry and began teaching at Le Moyne College in Syracuse as associate professor in theology. As the civil rights movement gained momentum, both brothers' frustration with a largely absent Catholic Church increased when their attempt to join the Freedom Riders was thwarted by their superiors. Phil, en route to Jackson, Mississippi, was recalled at the Atlanta airport when Jackson's bishop pressured the head of the Josephites. The same bishop recalled Phil once again in 1963 after Phil met with CORE leader James Farmer in an effort to integrate facilities.

Letters remain sparse until 1968, but what few there are reveal a groping for what the Christian life demands in times of institutional racism and war, leading to feelings of estrangement from the institutional church, which tended to hinder Phil and Dan's efforts. This period sees them lean further toward the notion that, as Phil expresses, "fidelity to Christ means more and more the outside stance," a conclusion that would lead them to pay increasingly heavy prices for their faith. They began to glimpse a new vision of church in their relationships with Thomas Merton, Dorothy Day and the Catholic Worker, and those who were willing to commit radically to the downtrodden and resist their oppressors. The chapter closes with both brothers

17

sentenced to lengthy prison sentences and questioning their place in their religious orders. Here, Phil expresses some hope for the Second Vatican Council, which would begin in October.]

June 1962

Dan'l,

Your letter from Pa. today, and am immensely grateful, dear boy, the old horizon has receded a good bit with what you had to say. Have longed to talk over this large bit of Ecumenism with you for some time. Agree emphatically with what you say. As usual, it is your prerogative and gift to sense and act on what so many of us only dimly feel. And I suppose, it is your genius to beat the first paths to leave the far easier going to us. Have read [Hans] Küng's book [*Structures of the Church*] with complete approval—thank God—*Time* got hold of it and lent considerable authority to it. But as you say, we are a long way from the *mea culpa* that Küng suggested. I can't help but preserve some optimism about the Council. Cardinal Alfrink made an optimistic statement of his hopes recently—and I think we have real allies in scores of magnificent European churchmen, who can be counted on to do some powerful infighting. Time is the factor, as with everything today.

As for your letter on Ecumenism—will take it into my next session with the young Fathers. Incidentally, started at the 1st 2 hr. session with them today—the 1st of 5—a prospective of the historical development of the status, or lack of it, of the layman in the church. We'll go into a treatment of the lay roles of Priesthood, Kingship, Prophesy next with a few practical jolts. Four of the 10 taking the course are heavily involved with the laity now thank God. The others sort of ride with the shocks.

The work is going well and we're ahead of schedule. Have three of our Seminarians working steadily, and another who will go in September—the other three are needy cases, as they all are. But admirable kids! And great hopes wrapped up in them.

Looking forward to seeing youse more than I can say keep 'em coming, champ, and Christ's love.

And mine,
P.B.

[On June 25, Phil was relocated to Newburgh, New York, for inflammatory comments on race in New Orleans. His new home, which he

*called "a racial twilight zone," was in the archdiocese of the fiercely
patriotic Cardinal Spellman. Phil here expresses the hope, eventually
realized, that he and Dan would receive permission to join the March
on Washington for Jobs and Freedom on August 28. The letter suggests the brothers were in an ongoing conversation with close friend
and Trappist monk Thomas Merton about whether they should leave
the church and work from without. The three would continue to support one another's vocations up to Merton's death in 1968.]*

July 1963

Dear Dan,

Was very appreciative of the letter which arrived today, esp. in view
of the volume of work that faced you.

Merton's letter was marvelous—I guess he knows your dilemma
and mine because it's also his own. It did a great deal to quiet some
of the unanswered questions, and I think, without the slightest exaggeration, that we can proceed with confidence. I agree with him that
things on the racial scene are bound to get worse rather than better,
though perhaps there is reason for much more hope that he recently
expressed. But it is a very important point—in what context can you
and I do the most good? I am of the opinion now that it is within
the Church, because everything is working for what we believe, and
because men in authority are going to be forced into a position that
they hate and cringe from, and yet about which they have little or no
choice. And by this I mean Spellman or O'Dea or Shanahan.

Am finishing this up on Thurs. and I have most encouraging news
for you. [Archbishop of Washington Patrick] O'Boyle is blessing the
Aug. 28 march and will contribute to it in any way that he knows, full
participation of Priests and people. He is joined in this by Richmond
and Baltimore on the same terms. The only thing that he balks at is
this—he does not want to be known as a leader in this thing, and so
he is reluctant to send our letters to the other bishops inviting their
participation. But you can be sure that the good news will spread
and that places like Chicago, Boston and Atlanta will be involved by
way of the very minimum. The Bishops themselves will be meeting in
Chicago in the latter part of July and here the subject will be given
a full airing.

Can you get permission to become involved in the thing, or could
we be involved together? I foresee no difficulty in getting permission
myself, since I know that perhaps the full force of SSJ's in the local
area will be out. I think that this would be a vast source of personal

satisfaction for us both, having widespread effects within and without our communities that we can only guess at. What sayest thou?

Will get this off. Great to have been with you—I think such times clear away the fog as much or more than one factor. And there'll be more, thank God, in August.

Lovingly in Christ,
Phil, SSJ

[Phil here refers to Martin Luther King Jr.'s "Letter from a Birmingham Jail," written the previous April. Speaking on the Josephites, Phil said the letter "would draw some of us beyond sentiment, into the world of dogs and clubs, tear gas and jail cells."]

August 1963

Dear Dan,

One to answer your last and to bring you up to date on happenings here. Yes, I've seen King's letter and agree with you that it's magnificent. If anything will affect the thinking of Fr. Shanahan, this would be it.

Attended a meeting of labor leaders yesterday—A. Philip Randolph was the main speaker—the march is gaining all sorts of momentum—they make a conservative estimate that 25,000 will come from this area alone. They presently estimate that they will have no difficulty in getting a 100,000 minimum—I think that it may well go as high as 200,000—perhaps the largest social dem[onstration] that has ever taken place in the country.

Which comes back to my previous question, about which I badgered you in the last letter. Can you make it? What could be better than if we were to witness together, or appear with priests and ministers of like mind? A few more particulars on the March—they have already confirmed with the D.C. police, and are assured full help. In addition, no sit-ins will be allowed, and they are discouraging any sort of entrance to hotels or restaurants. Then I think, that provision for prayer and possibly some sort of an agape are suggestions that will be implemented.

The Archdiocese is still playing footsie with this deal, but they're sending rep to Chicago this weekend for the Conference on Religion and Race and maybe what will be told them will be crucial. We can keep hoping.

Best love ole sport. God's love and my thanks for everything.

In Jesu,
P.B.

[Dan's activism at Le Moyne led to his relocation, landing him in France yet again, where he received permission to tour Eastern Europe and discover life behind the Iron Curtain. He would never again have such a long tenure at a university, nor would he feel the same sense of home. "Henceforth," he wrote, "I would be a wanderer on the Earth."]

Budapest—Christmas Eve—[1963]

Dear Philly—

This will reach you after a rather long day here, but when one has been pumped so full of impressions and meetings as I have been, it is very hard to let go. I think the only urgency I feel is not that you should receive this at once but that I should write it at once—while the impact of my experiences is fresh on me. First I should say that with full approval from Rome I have come to be exposed to all degrees of Protestant and Catholic life; to meet ex-nuns and expelled religious, as well as those still allowed to function, and to touch in a way that is bound to be humbling, all degrees of effort and comprehension in the present social and political upheaval. I have no reason to believe that I am Alice admitted to Wonderland or victimized by the Soviet machine etc. etc. The machine is here, as everyone knows and lives with—but the real fact for Christians is that enlightened men and women are taking risks and making painful practical judgments on matters of import. Of import everywhere—the crucible is here, but the laboratory is worldwide, and international style of life and culture is emerging. Up to now the West, and Catholicism of the West, has pressed its face to the wall like Sunday visitors at a zoo—(the figure is used here and the reality deeply resented) as if to say—only the unwary get caught, but just wait; we are at hand and the holy war will yet free you. Meantime the thinking men are trying to fuse the *mystery—human life* experience into some reality that will be faithful to both elements, humbly conscious that the boiling point was reached here (and eastward) because here the Christian failure was confronting unkillable human ideological differences and energies. Could not Christians have been the first (and only) Marxists, if we had stopped, licking our wounds and wounding our neighbors, in good time? The Catholic story here, as the 20th century dawned, was so vulgar, naive, and brutal, so dead against social change, that only dead men could have remained immune to the threads it gave rise to, by claiming human attention and a place among men. The details are in the books.

Some eight Hungarian bishops have gone to the Council. It is to be hoped they may bring something alive home in their briefcase, like the Holy Ghost. Meantime a realistic Christian effort must meet 2 great obstacles, profoundly related, and (taken separately) absolutely reconcilable, 1) Christian division 2) Marxist society. No hope for impregnating the second except we are visionary enough and unselfish enough to get to work in the first. The workers, I must conclude, are few indeed. Both sides are kissing their relics and ignoring living men.

The living are largely Marxists. But the Catholics are mourning the loss of youth, not precisely to Marxism but more especially to—what? one hears here at the far end of the tunnel, of Paris, London, New York, where the international wave makes the Marxist problem indeed a local manifestation of some deep, mysterious universal undertow—a shift of consciousness away from Christianity everywhere,—as Christianity is almost everywhere practiced and preached. Thus I would venture there is no great Marxist 'threat' in our vulgar accepted sense, that does not point weapons at Christian institutions and ways of thought everywhere in the world. And in this sense there is much more justice in speaking of the Marxist contribution, as an echo of the prophetic tradition in the church, sternly determined to take in hand the forward rhythms of history, to infect mankind with the germ of hope and dignity. I am not being ideological here. I am reporting humbly the 15 year progress of working people who now have sufficient food, clothing, heat, a chance for their children—where these things did not exist before. Most of them no longer go to church—but it must be said too that until very recently, and even now, the Church never spoke of these things—and generally impeded their coming to pass.

Need I add that the heroes we know at home are also loved here? Pope John represented a voice unheard in all the ruinous centuries of Reform and counter reform. But they cannot meet with Catholics yet to any appreciable degree (in several cases the first meeting in their lifetime occurred when a minister accompanied me as interpreter of a Catholic priest). As a consequence, and this is my judgement, neither side is really meeting the Marxist wave, which in its present form, is indeed very open to a meeting. If the religious question were brought somewhere nearer a sensible human basis, both sides would gain, but this awaits (as I suggest to both priests and ministers) the changed attitudes which the Bishops *may* bring back from the Council—

All this suggests of course that Providence is acting as a mysterious limiting pressure forcing the faith back to its roots and concentrating the life force of Christ against some mysterious day of Ja[h]we[h]. I hope this is not a lazy man's judgment—one can easily use the bible as a surrogate for living risk and action. But when men as they are have been accepted as they are, and one has done all he can to offer whatever he can, there remains the situation—as it is. A certain measure of light and hope is always something. And we can learn from the East, from its dramatic shock of old and new forces, something extremely practical, and (almost) universally unadmitted—in the atomic stalemate, and the threat of universal destruction, no one who takes thought can place a realistic hope in anything but the basic human efforts of hope, communion, love, and their social structures. But then Christian bridgebuilding is as old a task as Christianity itself—"He has made the many to be one," . . . I pray that they may be one . . . "that the world may believe You have sent me."

We are not far off the track. It is in this simple hope I came to Eastern Europe.

> In the Lord,
> Dan

42, Rue de Grenelle, Paris, March 3, 1964

Dear Philly,

Merton writes things are tight, they have a new general, and some of his peace issues are due out in French this month, but the general lid stays on. He sounds quite tired, perhaps the mid lenten let down. . . . I am sorry and really distressed that yr. situation with regard to the superior remains tough. I'm praying like all get out that they will leave you in the NY area, where I've said from the start you belong and where the absolute sky is the limit for the talents you bring, and the contacts possible. But of course much of the picture remains out of the structure as they say and that's the rub. But the Holy Spirit is not sleeping, and I see more and more clearly that it does no good to get mad at men who are good men, but whose horizons are the end of the rolling press, keeping the wheels oiled and the factory going. But how could they be otherwise being products of such a formation???

Well anyway the S. African trip is shaping up through the endless formalities and shots and so on. I will stop on the way back, if possible, at Nairobi, Addis Abbaba and Cairo.

Thanx again, chumly, for everything. I was delighted to know Dorothy [Day] and youse were making a team. The great lady wrote me a nice note, and said she is going to publish a letter of mine in the Mar. issue. That shd. make some of the boys unhappy; also did youse see my short blast in the *Critic*; and the Queens work published the first installment of the letter to a college student. So it goes. Merton says you shoot a stone in the air and if someone calls out you know it was seen. Love, dear boy and keep em off guard.

> In the Lud,
> Daniel

42, Rue de Grenelle [1964?]

Dear Philly, Yrs. today a great comfort.

You're right, those socialists are a great bunch and for them to meet with you will be an eyeopener for them too. I think more and more that in God's irony the protestant and orthodox contributions to the world will increase rather than diminish and that this will do more than almost anything else to speed the day of reunion. Mainly because we will have to see ourselves increasingly left with s- on our hands from having done nothing while they stole the Lord's show and showed what love of the world really entails.

I am increasingly involved with students here, both in the house and the footloose Americans in town. We are planning a few hours recollection for the latter in the house here on Saturday. Then there is always counseling too. I probably wrote you that they are planning a tour for me in South Africa at Easter time, with Arch. [Denis] Hurley too. I take it as another of those once in a lifetime chances . . .

[Sent from Johannesburg, South Africa, where Dan met and worked with The Grail, a Christian group focused on developing communal leaders and living the gospel. In the 1960s they began to focus closely on resisting apartheid laws.]

1964 [March 31?]

Tuesday. Dear Phillie, I am in the midst of a most astonishing experience which I would not have missed for several worlds. I have had a major talk each day to groups brought together by the Grail, and in addition, they wanted me to get a taste of the segregated parish life, and transported me miles in all directions, while I helped at a different place each day with the H. Week services, preached, or acted as commentator. I preached in white and colored parishes, always on race. There was a member of the abominable Special Branch present in one place; these are strictly an SS Branch of police who report on all sermons and public gatherings; so undoubtedly there have been repercussions, tho word with the Grail whom I consulted with, was always go ahead and no holds barred. It was the first time many of the whites or Africans had heard a word on the subject in years; the clergy are silenced mostly by orders from the bishops,

Had 1½ hrs this PM with Arch. McCann of Capetown and the Bishop of Jo'burg. Very discouraging attitudes and most depressing. We left in a blue funk these two old very nearly useless men in purple sox and big rings who have nothing to say but profound abstraction-isms. I had a talk tonight to 50 of the J'burg laymen who assembled at the Grail. 3 talks tomorrow + a visit to the New Township where ¾ million Africans are isolated in the new modern animal farm. There are by the way 1 million black men isolated in "hostels" in white areas, ¾ of them unable to visit their families, except at very rare intervals. What more do we need to make hell local and visible. I was at one black community of 50,000 which is to be bulldozed out of existence to put up 'hostels' for 30,000 men + 30,000 women.

Love + please write,
Dan

[Phil writes in reaction to Father William DuBay's public request to Pope Paul VI to remove Cardinal James Francis McIntyre, archbishop of Los Angeles, for his failure to address American civil rights.]

Tues. Night, Fall 1964

Dear Dan,

Your letter deserves an answer, even though inadequate. But first of all—a world of thanks for the Mass, and a gem of a homily.

Your remarks deserve tremendous pondering. I often think that fidelity to Christ means more and more the outside stance, for the sake of whatever remnant is kicking around. I don't think that the frightened and fragmented people within can be much help unless this DuBay thing is respected and repeated often, in perhaps a more intelligent way. The crucial point—it seems to me is this—how to eliminate the last stubborn furniture of the old church, and in the process, get the new one to witness. I deeply feel that we should begin meeting—once a week—twice a month—perhaps no more than five of us—three clerics and two lay men. I have the deepest respect for Charles Kahle—the other lay man besides [John] Grady? Maybe one of the commonweal crowd. A paper could be given, booze available, and a lot of tough even vicious talk to consider what can be done—with an eye to taking a very exposed position of witness. I believe that we have history on our side, and more sentiment than we realize. I feel increasingly that if this is to be done—it will be done by a small community absolutely unanimous in dedication and purpose, and from a position so exposed that we cannot yet tell what it will be. I feel that I am less and less a part of what the church now is, and increasingly a part of what I discover in men like yourself, Grady and a few others.

Am beginning to be increasingly stifled here, though it is not yet painful. Am so tied up in pursuits having a little or nothing to do with the above, that complacency and inaction on the specific point could be a dangerous tendency. So preferably, we should begin this as soon as possible, and this is a selfish recommendation.

I feel not at all nonplussed at the possibility of being a cleric outside the structure, if it would come to that. Best love, dear boy—seeing you is to remember how hard the Spirit can urge.

In Jesu,
P.B.

[In March 1965, Phil and Dan met with Thomas Merton in Gethsemani to strategize nonviolent, gospel responses to the war and the civil rights struggle. They also joined Dr. King in the march from Selma to Montgomery as part of the voter registration drive. "We stepped out of rhetoric," Phil said, "into the realm of action, and the realm of consequence." One can see in this letter Phil, who had been assigned to St. Peter Claver Church in Baltimore, stepping further toward civil disobedience and understanding its possible consequences for his priesthood and freedom.]

May/June 1965

Dear Dan,

Some sort of haphazard reply to your great letter, which I appreciated so deeply. It was a further explanation of the enormous weight of your work and witness, and the usual spur to me. You at least are familiar with my heavy leaning on you over the years, and I am very sure that it will increase, including the heavy water that faces us both.

However, as they say. Without in the least challenging your thinking or Merton's, which I think are eminently right and Christian for you both, there are these perplexing considerations for me. I think the

V.N. [Vietnamese] cannot be disassociated from the overall context of the Cold War and the Arms Race—in terms of immediacy, in terms of ethos operating in both S.E. Asia and in the world situation, and most emphatically, in terms of the Church. Moreover, I am frightened by this thought, that the longer a moral voice is put off, in this case, from the Church, the more the gap grows between government policy and any sort of moral voice. To go a bit further, the more difficult it becomes for such as us to be heard, the less meaning is attached to our voice, the more time the power boys have to adapt to and smother what is said. Perhaps the two cases are only roughly parallel—but I will never forget your analysis of the situation in South Africa, and how it came to be. The fact of the matter is this—that apart from yourself, Merton and myself—the Church has no public voice on this issue from the clerical quarter—a quarter which has a worth and impact disproportionate to its real value, but nonetheless, there. The real danger to me is this—when will it be timely to confront the issue with what one has and is? The bombings intensified, the ground war is still being lost, the troop buildups will continue.

One can only conjecture what this means in the practical. I for one, and my situation is different than yours in this regard, will speak on the issue when the opportunity comes, though in disobedience to their version of obedience. Moreover, I feel at this time, that eventually I will have to expose myself to the public eye through the press, and perhaps go into civil disobedience and perhaps fastings, preferably in jail. Complications enter at this point and must be considered. Now I will be judged disobedient—before, I called the body to Baltimore and began work again—this time, I covertly go to D.C. or some other place, the structure all unknowing and lay it on the line. Hence, my position will be much more precarious in regard to the establishment. When the move is over, and while it is in progress, a frenzied debate will go on as to the whole quality of social witness and when it is allowable. And the Society will react in predictable terms, and will attempt to smother me even more effectively. Perhaps one's high point of efficacy has been reached at this point—one can only hope to grope in judgment again. But if the grand slide to war might have been slowed one iota, others may derive courage, the protest may grow, etc. I do not at this point envision leaving—it seems to me that the pillorying and suspicion and rejection must be accomplished within and without the institution.

To my mind, the historical guidelines do not exist—it's a matter of going by a conscience which is at best, hazy and fearful. And I don't know as though any sort of team up is possible, or possible only to a point. The mystery has among other things, an eerie quality about it.

Keep this feeble character at the altar, and somehow the Lord will make all things right.

> Lovingly in Him,
> Phil, SSJ

Jesuit Missions 45 East 78th Street: New York, 21, NY, Oct. 11 [1965]

Dear Bruv,

I have been bumbling about, in little mud puddles. Yesterday I was up to the Grail, Charlie someone, a young priest from Queens at whose parish you spoke on race last year, drove me up. He was exiled for saying something in English in the sanctuary. A great prophetic guy who split the day wide open by getting up after my talk, and saying simply that to do the Eucharist in anything but English after these thoughts and this response, would be a lie. He proceeded to launch into an impassioned and deeply moving half hour on the eucharist and life and change which obviously came out of his deep heart filled with scripture and suffering like a single wine. . . . Anyway we did the Thing in english and received under both forms and all the rest. It was a good day.

I am being led in the damnest directions; as usual, without any roadmap except that of good friends. I get a great kick out of it. It is uncomfortable at times, but I feel at the best times that I haven't even got the stopper out of the bottle yet, let alone know what the future smells or tastes like. Intriguing, no? and every time I try a new beginning and get some response, my bottom begins to itch again as though the Iceman had slipped an ice cube down my tail and said get moving or freeze here. . . . No doubt, every fresh start is only the most infantile sort of beginning.

Will you bear with me while I put down some (alcoholic no doubt) thoughts on where we (don't) stand?

1. Everyone who is at all thinking something through knows the old facade is down; what is valuable now is standing with the good victims within, our fellow priests and laymen, and much more difficult and unknown, the good people without, who are in a like bind due to the universal breakup.

2. What is outside is already in great part inside.

3. How to reach the outside is, for clerics, infinitely more crucial than retaining irrelevancies inside.

4. One way of reaching outside is to make all Sacred activity an immediate outside activity.

5. For the present, clerics have responsibility to listen + learn much more than to speak or teach.

6. 5 is modified for certain clerics who can help the inside clerics reach a greater measure of freedom in realizing the complications of what they are doing, as well as encouraging them to break the deadly law in the Spirit of love; thus opening a few windows on the (literally) benighted within.

7. I am not at all sure that in the long run, the preceding is not hogwash. The real job is in the world. In measure of this, some who have dedicated themselves either to sacred work within or to world activity within have eventually to step outside and exist and die outside as a matter of conscience. Leaving us in that desert as Someone's (sacred) imperative.

8. The corruption of the sacred is the suffocation of worldly instinct and sensibility.

9. Undoubtedly a time of recovery is necessary for those who have sickened within + are ready for life outside, like a fish with gills and legs—suddenly flung on the riverbank.

10. Practical contempt of Christ/as man is our sin. He, living a human life from brains to hands to scrotum. Busy about 1) making religion worldly—the man in the ditch, the cure of the man on the sabbath, 2) restoring the purity of worship, overturning the tables of old with who would "use" the sanctuary.

11. Who are the people who are forming the world by sacrificial action + what can we do with them? Forgetting all the hypocritical + self fulfilling activity that takes up most of our time + absorbs the time of so many laymen de-formed to our image?

12. What is the form of the cross for adults in the world? How does this give us leads on the nature of genuine (as opposed to masochistic or self-satisfying) suffering?

13. At what point is our job with laymen simply to urge them to give up on Church enterprises + get into the world—not as defeat but as victorious next step?

14. Why not public confessions before (public, presumably) Eucharist?

15. How much of what we know as Church will be dead in 100 years? How much we are ignorant of (as Church) will be in in 100 years? Why not begin now?

16. How much of the world can we afford to be ignorant of at the hour of our death? Presuming we are to meet a Christ who came,

died, rose in + for the world, not for, in, us? And if Judgement begins now, what of now?

17. Is our freedom a fidelity 1) to those struggling, who cannot meet our eyes, largely because of what we have done to them, and 2) those without who have forgotten we exist? I think both.

18. Is "to be forgotten as existing" not a good definition of who we are—can we start from there?

19. I think we are obliged only to what we see—as a maximum, not as a minimum—which is to say, our poverty + stupidity + alienation + sickness as the only riches we can claim.

Yours (at long last) in great love—
Daniel

[On November 9, 1965, twenty-two–year-old Roger LaPorte immolated himself in front of the United Nations in New York City in protest against the Vietnam War. Because Dan preached a homily for LaPorte at his memorial service on November 11, his Jesuit superiors "exiled" him to Latin America only days later, in the waning weeks of the Second Vatican Council. He would not return until March 8, 1966. The Centro de Investiaciones Culturales in Cuernavaca, Mexico, was a lay and religious commune run by Ivan Illich, a Catholic priest and critic of Western institutions. Unaware of student fasts at Notre Dame and demonstrations by Fordham students outside Spellman's Madison Avenue office to protest his exile, Dan fell into a depression that separated him from family and friends. Despite his state, he finds enthusiasm in this letter for Illich's community.]

Monday P.M. [1966], Cuernavaca, Mor., Mexico

Dear Philly,

Yer two arrived today. I am enormously grateful, yours and the others really keep me chugging. . . . Illich and a young Dominican have made me very quickly welcome, the liturgy is magnificent; some 120 nuns, priests and brothers, all out of the garb, all very free and hardworking and serious; a long day with two one hour talks on pastoral or something related, five hours of Spanish, and much good discussion. . . . It looks now as tho I will be leaving here in about ten days, with the next stop Caracas; but that is not settled by any means. Today while I was in class, Eric Fromm came out for two hours with the staff, he is studying problems of religious belief. Illich is trying to make sure I have every opportunity to sit in with the staff; he is starting in addition to the monthly reports from here, a series of otherwise unobtainable documentations on conditions in every country of L.A. [Latin America], with the help of a young Brazilian incendiary exile. Both the center and the Benedictines nearby are under heavy and constant fire from the Holy Office, so Illich is doing quite a balancing act, but he glories in it. You probably read that the Benedictines had a team of psychiatrists working on all the members of their community, to try and find out some of the roots of religious life. . . . They go about as far as they can in public with the liturgy; we usually start around tables in the dining room for the first part, then proceed to the chapel for the gospel, homily and the rest; on Saturday, no Mass, but an experimental prayer session and holy communion. We receive big chunks of wheaten bread broken up before communion, and all the priests, some 60, take the cup. The singing is glorious.

God bless dear boy and I know you won't waste any worries over me. Something is abuilding in which we are privileged to have part. Please, my very best love to yerself and all the amigos. Please have a little mercy in the flesh!!!

Daniel

Santiago [Chile], February 12, 1966

Dear Phil—

Yours of Jan. 30 was waiting for me on arrival here yesterday. We are staying with the Maryknollers and went over to the Center Bellarmine for an interview w- experts there and lo + behold a big packet, including letters from the Provincial. The Provincial sent a very peacemaking, hatchet burying letter, assuring me of his longing to have me back in May, etc.

Maryknoll's work is uninspired but solid, in American fashion. They have 1 Latin American in the order, who runs a program for slum leadership and seems way ahead of his American opposite members. Sunday we are flying 800 miles south to Osorno where the Maryland Jebs have a high school. Then back here and up to Peru, Ecuador, + Colombia. And go home!

The damn war news hits like a knife. But at least as you say, there seems to be some degree of Senate awakening.

Dan

Wed. Apr. 6, 1966

Dear Dan,

A short one for your birthday. Another milestone for you, and more encouragement for the rest of us. You came from the Southern jaunt with limitless courage and grace, to show the rest of us what it means to be misused, and yet always on top of a situation.

And so my love and respect for you grows with the years. I recall you remembering a few great priests in your life, and how they influenced you. For me there has been but one, and it is graphically and emphatically you. If this were all the Lord chose to give me, it would be enough, but the hundredfold is also there with you, but mostly because of you.

And with this comes the explicit confidence that as the plot thickens in these mysterious times, there will be one clear voice to listen to, and a great heart to join.

Christ love you, will offer the Holy Sacrifice for you next Monday.

Love from
Ole Phil

[Phil describes what would become his first act of civil disobedience in March or April of 1967, which he called "my first step across the line separating polite discourse from direct action."]

Oct/Nov. 1966

Dear Dan,

Am about on my way to Fred Weisgal's house—our Civil Rights lawyer. The plan is generally this, and we hope to pull it off soon after the first of March, if not before. We intended to get into Ft. Myers (no problem)—head directly to Gen. Wheeler's mansion, and begin a vigil. The rationale is some sort of moral challenge to the military, and the growing power they have in foreign policy. Of course, we know that behind them is American business interests, but one has to start somewhere. Wheeler is Chairman of the Joint Chiefs of Staff. Now the law makes no provision for our type of action, for or against,—it deals with trespassing in the sense of forced entry, damage to real estate, equipment or personnel. It says nothing against those on a military post for reasons of dissent, and the beauty of this is that if one could get arrested, one would at the same time, take on the inadequacy of the law, as well as the

consequent immunity of the military from any sort of civilian protest. In a word, it's Weisgal's view that the MP's will try very hard
not to arrest us—they will try to bluster at us, threaten us, and when
this is unavailing, try to eject us from the base. At this point, the fun
begins, or it may begin. It might be that they will eject us forcibly
(us non-cooperating), and no more would come of it. Or it might
be that we would sufficiently provoke them to have them haul us
in. At this point, maybe the central problem is how to get arrested.
Personally, I see only limited effect coming from a trip to Myers,
getting on the base, getting thrown off, getting a fairly good notice
in the *Washington Post*, etc. We will be profoundly admired by the
peaceniks, will shakeup DC a very little bit, and that's all. If arrest
comes, however, and it goes before a Federal Court in Virginia or
elsewhere, the complexion changes, it will be a test case of the first
kind, and the real service will be done in the courtroom.

If arrest comes, we have agreed to remain in jail—all of us—a minimum of 24 hrs. Then we have decided to resist the idea of bail, since
we're benefactors and not criminals. The thing to be opted for here is
release on recognizance, and later on, trial. Weisgal almost guarantees
a hung jury, but if this does not happen and we're convicted, he says
he can fight it for 3 yrs. up to the Supreme Court. I for one thought it
a good thing if some or all are sentenced and got a couple of yrs. But
whatever the case, the spectacle itself would rock the law, the country
and the Church. The position of the seminarians would be esp. interesting—it might break this freedom of conscience thing once and for all.

Give us your particular insights. We'll do what we can, and if we
fail here, there's always another round. Keep the lamp burning, ole
top. And the Lord's vigah. Luv ya,

> In the Lord,
> Phil, SSJ

Early November 1966

Dear Dan,

Am writing [Josephite Superior General George] O'Dea this weekend and asking him for a year away for decision-making as to whether
to remain with the Society. Beginning next Sept. want time to do this
book, and to move for peace and for the poor. And in NYC. Of course,
the SSJ's have been good to me, and I will never forget this. But it is
going nowhere, the new farms are needed, and perhaps I can help to
build them.

Hope you can come to DC at the end of the month. Know you slew'em in Mexico. Content to have you in the rearguard, and grateful to bring up the rear. Best love and the Lord's peace.

In Jesu,
P.B.

Mar/Apr 1967

Dear Dan,
    Too short a talk with you, ole man. The stint at Ft. Myers was profitable in a sense, and a little disappointing, too. Wheeler was in Saigon and this hurt us. We had a grand crew—almost 30 stalwarts. At least, the MP's blocked off the street in order to cut down visibility. We picketed for a solid hr. and were just on the point of leaving when up comes the base Commandant, very nervous, very angry, very unsure of himself. Told us he had no intention of arresting us, or forcibly ejecting us, he merely was asking us to leave. Told him we had no intention of leaving, that we were there under legal right to protest this war. He said he would have to use other means to get us off, but after pumping him repeatedly as to the other means—he had no answer. I think we could have provoked him to arrest us, but whether this would be possible while preserving a strong case for court, is unlikely. So we left.
    But now the bubble of military invulnerability has burst, and a whole new horizon of protest has geared up. If we don't get suff[icient] publicity to encourage people to go there to protest, there will be other times. I told our poor military friend that we'd be back, and of course, we will.
    A blessed & peaceful Easter. The light will come up in rather rare darkness, but that's perhaps as it should be.

Lovingly,
Phil

[Phil alludes to Rev. Charles Curran, one of the most prolific Catholic moral theologians of the twentieth century. Only one year after this letter was written, Curran would publicly dissent from Pope Paul VI's encyclical Humanae vitae, *which upheld the Catholic prohibition of artificial birth control. Also referenced in the letter is Robert Mitchell, S.J., the provincial superior of the New York Province from 1966 to 1972.]*

April 1967

Dear Dan,

Some sort of answer to your special delivery. It strikes one that you're taking the whole bitter fiasco with your usual clarity of vision. Your conscience can be entirely clear, as it always has been, that you paid your dues to the Order, and attempted to make it something more Christian.

I feel that if the visa goes through and you do go to Hanoi, they will either not dare to touch you (and the brush with the law will be minor), or they will try to discipline you and will be whipped back into their holes. If Charlie Curran could spark such protest at C.U. what can you well expect, an infinitely more important man, who first took every effort to get Mitchell and others to recognize both issues of conscience and war? It seems to me that national response will surprise even you, who experienced something similar at your exile.

To me this response would be almost a certainty, yet it does not save you from painful groping, and a lack of support from those best in the position to give it. Yet I've long felt that the Lord burdens only men of grace, or the burden fits the man. One way of saying why I have no burdens.

At any rate, we are with you 110%, which on reflection says not a great deal save that we love and revere you, and pray that Christ's saving Will be accomplished. And where you're concerned, that's a certainty.

> Love ya, pal—good cheer,
> Phil

Sunday (late April) 1967

Dear Dan,

Didn't think the sum total of yesterday imp. enough to call, but here it is. 17 of us went—the press had tipped off the base, and I was stopped by MP's at the entrance. They were looking for collars and signs, both of which they found in our car. But nonetheless, three cars got through. Our load and one other fumbled through Arlington Cemetery and finally got on the base. By this time, the others had been picked up—they had gotten to the parade ground with signs, when MP's descended on them like avenging angels, ripped away the signs and took them into custody. I came on the scene just as a colonel was writing out notices for them that reentry would mean $500 fine and 6 mos. jail. He promptly issued me one also.

But it was hopeful—they can't keep the base closed to us—next time we'll take the press with us. And I don't see how they can avoid arresting us. We were all heartened by the spectacle of frightened, bewildered, young MP's—a Major General screaming orders, and the ridiculous procedure of the "cease and desist" orders. It was as though a band of V.C. had appeared in their midst.

This for your birthday also, dear boy. This makes 46, huh? God, what a life? I remember remarking after 10 yrs. of the priesthood that you saw little or nothing accomplished. Such might be a safe view for you—it will never be an accurate one for me. You've been a vessel of grace to all who know you, met you, heard you or read you. So your birthdays as they come are in a sense, milestones for us all—better still, sources of hope. For thousands would not have such a view of the faithful servant without you. Christ's blessing and increase—ole pard—His love and peace. And my own, which grows with every sight of you, and every word from you.

Phil

Late April 1967

Dear Dan,

A word to tell you how much it meant to see yourself, Carol & Jerry. And to say that I was once more thrown into wonder by your courage and dedication. The rest of us can do little more than recognize this, and then attempt to imitate it.

I know that trying to pin down the diversities of this Hanoi junket must be harrowing, mostly because you cannot count on one man in position who understands what you're talking about. And yet, I wonder if it has ever been otherwise? And is the fate of you and I to be one who talks to the establishment from the fringe, or rather, one step beyond it? I put myself haltingly in your company because I have sensed that sooner or later it would come to this for me. And because I feel increasingly that my composition is untenable outside of jail. The only problem really is to do the utmost to have a stand that can be clearly expressed and adhered to. In other words, not just arrest for its own sake, though ultimately, it may come to that.

This is of no help to you, though it may be of some consolation. I believe so profoundly in your conscience that I hesitate to even suggest one thing or another in regard to Hanoi. In the last analysis, you will have to rely on the Spirit and on yourself.

Your last book is perhaps your finest—does a great ministry to me in that it faces me with myself, a picture that is neither consoling nor cheering. I thank you for it, and for yourself. Having you is a blessing from God, reason enough for a daily Te Deum.

Lovingly,
Phil

[On October 27, 1967, while Dan (now teaching at Cornell) was in jail for a Pentagon protest, Phil, Tom Lewis, David Eberhardt, and Rev. James Mengel entered the Selective Service Board in the Customs House, Baltimore, and poured blood on draft files. They became known as the Baltimore Four. Here, Phil reassures Dan about the plans before the event.]

Mon. Morning (Oct. 1967)

Dan—A quick one—

Sorry I didn't make the action clearer—it must have caused you great concern. No, I would never do anything that would harm people physically—but the property that is part of these bloody gearboxes, thass another thing. We set a tentative date for Oct. 27—now it's a mere question of working on details.

Sez I to the young guys on return—"I've got a great brother, wat?" And they agreed emphatically, and said you're slowly setting Cornell on its ear. Sez I "what else?"

Thanks mucho and best love,
Phil

[Phil and Tom Lewis refused to sign a promissory note to appear in court after the action and were sent to the Baltimore City Jail, where Phil "was shocked by the misery and the ugliness of life" but "felt a great satisfaction being there."]

Balt. City Jail—Nov. 1st—Wed (1967)

Dear Dan—

They censor mail both ways here—your air-mail spec. delivery got here Wed. noon—profoundly grateful for it. Have been getting about 1,000 words of speculation out every day to *Commonweal, NCR, Christianity + Crisis, Ave Maria,* etc. One set was lost, or complicated by the Federal Marshals.

Will try to get a few ideas out to you as long as we're here, and either send them later or presently through someone to spirit them out. We're finishing our 6th day of fast, but feeling great. I have no doubt that we could continue indefinitely if conditions warranted this. Tom right in there—an angel, and a very powerful one. He sends his love—you mean a great deal to him.

We are trying to keep initiative from the government, and to keep it ourselves. The Federal Commissioner here is a brilliant young Jew named Steve Sachs, whom we suspect is against Vietnam. Monday at the hearing, Sachs botched it by not proving that Dave Eberhardt poured blood (he did), or that Mengel did anything but come in and pass out N.T.'s. Then one of Sachs' men read parts of our statement which supposedly proved that all were involved (we were, to 1 degree or another). But in a human sense, the excerpts he read were damning to the government's cause—it merely showed the inadequacy of this law, and made them look quite ridiculous. Then Tom and I stood up at the end of the charade and refused to sign bond for release—another tactical defeat for them. Tom told the judge, "I'm not a criminal, I'm a Christian. We'll continue our fast in jail."

Tomorrow a large demonstration planned outside this jail. We think it will force Sachs to force us out—another tactical defeat. We intended to continue pasting the govn't at every turn—to plan the trial well—it probably won't be called until January, and then return to jail with pennants flying.

I see we made *Time* this week, those ambiguous bastards. It is the last of my ambitions to gain mention from them. Glad the folks are taking it well—with Jerry and Carol there, we can count on the home scene being pinned down. Our bouts with jail ought to provide an atmosphere of sorts for Rosalie and Jim's homecoming.

Thurs. Nov. 2nd—We had counted, as had the warden, on a big demonstration here today, but the weather was abominable, and it was undoubtedly called off for good reason. Perhaps something tomorrow.

Communication is very difficult. Only clerics and specially selected lay folks can visit us—so we are largely cut off. This is not necessarily discouraging, since in spite of it, we know people are keeping the pot brewing or preparing to light a fire.

We are playing our exit from here loose, but reasons for remaining on here seem to be slowly evaporating. It may be a question of signing out tomorrow, calling a press conference and then going on from there. It is a question too, I suppose, of facing my gallant leaders at headquarters, in order to get their mind on my future. They have little choice with one it seems—the political repercussions of putting me on ice in one way or another would be too great. Then too, I'll undoubtedly be sentenced to jail within 2 mos., and must remain based in Baltimore for that reason. Whatever the case, I'll probably be illumined on the cast of unilateralism to them.

We have a great time here with our black brothers—some of them are real leaders who unconsciously screw the system for all it's worth. The word of course, is around as to who we are, and when it is understood why we're here, the acceptance is total and very graceful. More later.

[The trial for the Baltimore Four began in April 1968.]

Wed. Apr. 10, 1968

Dan Baby—

Courage coming from yer very appearance, ole chum—everbuddy says so. So grateful you could reinvigorate us. We'll try to go on in the tradition.

Just a word about today—His Honor made it clear that the law could not consider subjectivity, which in effect meant, it could not consider the reality prompting us to move. In a word, the court will allow no indictment of the government or itself. Which is not surprising.

Which strengthens our hand rather than weakening it. For if we thought to get justice, it would have been a serious lapse in judgment.

Jerry + Carol coming down on Monday. The reaction from the Maryknollers in DC looks hopeful. Will probably act some time after conviction.

> Luv ya, pard. Peace of Christ,
> Phil

[Phil refers here to the Melvilles—Thomas Melville (a former Maryknoll priest) and his wife, Marjorie Melville. One month later they would achieve prominence for their role alongside Dan and Phil as members of the Catonsville Nine.]

April 1968

Dear Dan—

We are planning a summit meeting in D.C. on Monday, May 6th. People coming in from St. Louis and Boston, and of course, the full contingent of Maryknollers, including the Melvilles. In effect, the outside people must decide what needs to be done, or if the time is right in light of Paris.

I feel very badly about the concern I'm causing with you and other members of the Community. I guess in such peculiar circumstances, suffering is greater in the people one loves than in oneself. But as you know, I have little hope for man as long as this country pursues its insanity. And I have great hope for revolution, and the kind of witness the Gospel seems to suggest.

Will take off here Wed. May 8th, and if you're home at Cornell, will drop by. Seeing you is always enough to get the biceps flexed again. Will call before leaving.

The Lord has us all in His hip pocket. Luv ya pard—great gratitude again.

> Peace of Christ,
> Phil

[On May 17, Phil, Dan, and seven others entered the draft board in Catonsville, Maryland, and burned draft files in front of media cameras. The group became known as the Catonsville Nine. Phil was refused bail due to his actions with the Baltimore Four and therefore writes from jail. On May 24, Phil received six years for the Baltimore Four action. Despite the heavy sentence, he was "neither depressed nor frightened" but "exalted."]

Baltimore County Jail
Sat. morning May 25th (1968)

Dear Bruv—

Know you won't have the slightest tinge of anxiety about us. We're in great health and spirits, and could want for literally nothing. Lewis and I must sit down and talk over this jail thing in prospect of bail. Of course, we'd have a double bail situation—the first would involve an explicit premise to stay away from fire and blood; the other, travel restrictions of the like you're under. Then, there's the possible gain of getting into a new dimension (jail for both of us). Though I have trouble with that, since it would be less costly than staying outside and working with this society.

But we'll see. Lewis and I can't say enough about what it meant to have you with us. Certainly, the fiery seven, if not nine, looked to you for your marvelous insights, good grace and humor. And strength most importantly. It is not so much that I miss you—which I assuredly do—but that I figger you left so much of yourself with me, and with Tom, that we are overarmed to continue. How good can one have it?

Luv then bruv from us both. Pop warns against stressing the obvious, but it has its uses—you are the greatest. You've meant the Church to me at its best and noblest. And no one else has had that asset and privilege, to the extent that I have. Luv ya.

In Jesu,
P.B.

[The Mrs. Murphy referred to is Mary Murphy, receptionist at the draft board house, who cut her finger while trying to wrest away from Phil the trash bin used for burning the files. Phil notes the unease at the action showed by the archbishop of Baltimore, Cardinal Lawrence Shehan. In the following letter Shehan revokes Phil's priestly faculties to celebrate the sacraments.]

Tues morning May 28th

Dear Dan—

Thought I'd give you an idea of recent developments. We've been charged in the county for acts of sabotage, and for assault on Mrs. Murphy. Apparently, a good deal was done by the Federal authorities to forestall this, but it seems the county people want a piece of the action, and especially, an opportunity to show the Feds how God fearing people tend their own bailiwick. Weisgal was pretty discouraged about it. But Tom and I take a different view of it—after all, the local people are only doing what the government has done and will do again. Another way of instructing us "where it's at."

Meanwhile, the bail thing continues to hang. We should however, know within ten days—otherwise, it's ship out of here, probably to Lewisburg. The Cardinal finally burst out of silence on Sunday—said that he could not condone acts of violence against persons, or destruction of property, or blanket condemnation of the Church as racist or war supportive. While in another breath, he guaranteed the rights of conscience, and obligated priests and laymen to exercise their moral judgment upon the war and injustice. It's the familiar pattern of being all things to all men by being on both sides of a question at once.

But lots to do here, and much blessed time to do it. We've got a new cellmate. So the community builds up again. Hello to all our friends at Cornell—love and gratitude to you all. Great times we will agree. Lewis sends love.

                              In Jesu,
                              P.B.

Wed. June 4, '68

Dear Dan—

Just back from appeals court—We will know their verdict on Monday. I am decidedly neutral on the thing, seeing advantages on both sides. My stand at this point is to leave it up to the community, and to let the course of events decide what is to happen to us. There are great advantages, it seems to me, to let power decide, and thereby allow Providence to be more free in our regard.

Bobby Kennedy's shooting the latest episode in dissolution. Events seem to indicate that we will come to the domestic brink before people counted on seeing it. And now, hot summer looms ahead.

Nonetheless, bruv, we're trying to stay with it. Be sure that there is nothing wrong with our spirits—and I hope, our perspective. Lewis continues to be a great source of balance and encouragement.

                    Luv from all of us to the whole com-
                    munity—esp. youse,
                    Phil

Mon, June 10 (68)

Dear Dan—

A bunch of Quakers came out yesterday and prayed in front of the jail. Really kind of touching. We hope to get some breakthrough from the Warden by way of provision for me to work on the book, and for Tom to do some painting.

Did I tell you the Cardinal quietly took away my faculties, sort of an informal, archdiocesan suspension, meaning in effect, that even were I free, I could not operate as a priest. In fact, I'm not supposed to operate here. It's all so amusing—they're intent upon doing their best to disown me.

Hope to hear from youse today. Great shape, bruv—no sweat, no pain.

                              Luv ya,
                              Phil

Sun. morning June 23 (68)

Dear Dan—

Am going down to the Eucharist in a few moments—they restored my faculties. For which I give them no credit at all—they were merely smart enough to see the makings of a fight. And they figured that more would be lost than gained—by fighting.

Stay well, dear brother,
Phil

[Phil was moved to maximum-security Lewisburg Prison in Pennsylvania in late June, after becoming the first Catholic priest in US history to be tried and imprisoned for a political crime. He remained there until December.]

July 6th, '68

Dear Dan,

Last stop before Allenwood, or so they tell us. The marshals brought us up yesterday. Quite a surprise, since we had been pretty well convinced that Warden Foster wanted us to remain at the County Jail, and would manage it. At any rate, he left with his family for a short vacation, and perhaps didn't have time to conclude anything before leaving. As Tom reminds me, "it's out of our hands, and therefore, for the best."

Kind of a magnificent place—this one—set in the middle of the countryside like a little medieval city. It is beautifully tended and clean, most of the prisoners I've talked with far prefer it to any other prison. The food is superb—a great deal of freedom is allowed—and the prison yard is spacious and jammed with nearly every sports activity one can think of. Tom and I went up to the library last night—amazingly good for a prison library. Hoffa is here. About 1,600 men.

At the first opportunity, I'll let you know about writing and visiting privileges, which differ here slightly from Allenwood. Will get word out to you at the first development. Love to yourself and everyone. Have no anxiety—we're at least with it, if not ahead of it.

Peace, ole bruv,
Phil, SSJ

Tues. Aug. 6th, 1968

Dear Dan—

A quick one, ole bruv, to let you know how I rejoiced seeing you, Rosalie, Jim and the girls. It was an event, let me tell you—and I was profoundly grateful for it. Moreover, your appraisal of recent domestic and world phenomena substantiated so much of what we both feel and decided. I think it is relatively rare that people enjoy such a sanction upon judgment.

The Transfiguration today, and the anniversary of another Transfiguration in Japan twenty-three years ago. Significant, I think, was a concelebrated Mass I offered this morning—the first Mass I've offered in some six weeks. And then, some of us will do what we can do today and on Friday, to atone for what has been done, and what is being done.

Might I say in closing what it meant to see you, and to see you as well as you are. The Lord's hundredfold is personified in you, or at least, about 98% of it. Thank you again—best of love and grace. We will continue on with élan and a flourish.

In Jesu,
Phil

Wed. Aug. 7 (1968)

Dear Dan—

Can't close down the evening without a note to you. Yours came in with a big packet of letters. The high point was yer own. Must say that I had not the slightest idea the back was kicking up. But then, I remember several other occasions when you were in even greater pain—yet for the sake of others, were in your finest form. So it was Sunday—everything very calm and serene, and yet all of us looking to you for those enormous reservoirs that you're always so prompt to empty. I hope the pain clears up, and that troublesome little disc keeps where it belongs.

As for myself, it is a simple fact that I've been led to this by others—particularly you—and that it's a simple question of living with the implications. And being grateful for a chance at them. I feel that the struggle to maintain some sort of integrity within and without the church has now reached a current high point with both of us. There will be others—this period is no more than basic training for what is to come. The Lord insists on staying with both of us because we don't refuse him, and we won't be finessed out of His plans.

Without going for the sticky, I must say—as I haven't said before or often enough: You're the greatest priest I know, and the greatest human being I know. The connection is essential. And you're my brother. As the Lord has given to you, He will also take, and take heavily. But you will always be equal to His taking, and those of us less sensitive to his wishes will then be empowered to follow.

The separation between us will go on in the months ahead, perhaps for years. But that will only tend to confirm the reality of events. I reflected after you left that our freedom from one another in the family grows apace, while proportionately we love one another more. So the great mystery unfolds—but it began with you, and it will have clarification only from you. The rest of us wait and try to listen.

I no longer have the slightest apprehension about the future—not even while I watch the Republican Convention. The Lord has quietly formed His remnant, and quietly builds it up. And we would not have membership if it weren't for the general failure to join. In any event, as long as the club is around, the divine mercy will be felt. Which is more theologizing then I've done in years.

I know you'll tell near and far that we couldn't be better, and that gratitude + peace goes out to all. And to you, thanks for things I don't even know about, or can't imagine. And best love, Dan.

In Jesu,
P.B.

[In January 1968, Dan had flown to Hanoi with historian and activist Howard Zinn to pick up three American prisoners of war. He spent two weeks meeting with delegates of North Vietnam; during that time he had to hide in a bomb shelter during an American attack. He published Night Flight to Hanoi *as a result, to which he refers here.]*

September 14 [1968]

Dear Philly,

I arrived here about 2:00 AM to discover a sizzler of a letter from [James] Somerville. Its purport was that two recent events 1) my refusal to submit to book censorship in the case of the Hanoi diary, and 2) my unprecedented attack on the Society in St. Louis raised grave doubts, etc., etc. Now I took it 2:30 (by then) AM was a great time to allow the dawn humors to enter the head, and to compose an answer to Fr. James. Which I did. Pointing out that as 'unworthy servants' we were called to corporate examination of conscience now and then, and that what I was attacking was by no means the 'corruption' of the Society (his term, not mine; too corrupted by others) but the institutional immobilization based on indebtedness to big government and big benefactors—this preventing us from saying the simple evangelical word to the Powers. That the same questions would haunt the Society, whether or not they accepted my continuing presence. That we were obviously hearing from very different Jesuits, since I was receiving letters thanking me, and asking me to hold on for the sake of the young Jebs., etc.

A few conclusions may be in order.

1) Since I love the Society, and one tries to save what he loves, one applies force counter to forces he no longer believes in, no longer believes are Jesuit, no longer have power over his. Mainly to get conversation going, about Christ, about community and conscience. There is no point in trying to write off the Thing as not one own's thing; I'm too far gone in my marriage to be capable of divorce. I begat too many children and absorbed the real thing too long.

2) On the other hand, anything like a revolutionary stance requires that one's love stay stern as well as tender—esp. in regard to those who claim the real marriage, but have reduced it to a rotarian gentlemen's agreement, with all sorts of weekend episodes with Uncle Sam and Uncle Spellman. Let them break up the marriage, but I won't. And if they do, the consequences are their own, including public horror, disaffection, the continuing loss of the best of the family.

3) Given everything, jail and the equivalent of jail are coming to be the only scene from which to declare the integrity of the marriage bond. One is freed of the accusation of special interest (there is literally nothing one can bridle at losing), and there is a growing wave of support from those who by reason of youth, integrity, or simple decency, will not see good men ground into material for cook outs.

4) When the chips are down, and the rhetoric is peeled away, the Church is only slightly more capable of conversion than is the state. I say this tentatively. But the 'slightly' is all the point. It has to do with that slight edge of wisdom, courage, continuity, and vision which Christ offers us, and through (even) us, others. But the lever or scalpel or whatever have to be operated with precision, delicacy and purpose. I cannot waver, even while I listen. I will not submit, even while I submit. I will be a man, even though I must be the last man.

5) The slow inching forward of hope. Real change is so imperceptible. And in this sense of things, it has no master plan, no blue print. Those Platonists who still think so, are going against humanity to do the thing we are going to prison to say no to.

6) Not to make their scene is unimportant. To create a scene is of the essence. The creation of a scene is done not by coaching actors and painting scenery. It is by getting on stage, tragicomedian, improvising the script, and allowing the outcome to grow as naturally as yeast or a baby. Grace under pressure. Prison with freedom. Christianity is not winning in history, it means merely being in the right place through history, in view of the end.

7) Mitchell's assumption is that he has a master plan for the Society. Maybe. But I have seen this mentality operating in destructive ways, to the point where I distrust it completely. It allows of omnipotence, which God does not—even in himself. "Took the form of servant." The advocates of the master plan, or of the master race, presume, as a working hypothesis, that the Lord 'became servant' only as a temporary role; after that edifying spectacle, He mounted Olympus once more. And speaks through Us.

Well, I'll close this, hoping it contributes to the incoming tides.

Love to all yrs. in Man

[Elizabeth Bartelme, Dan's editor at Macmillan, suggested making changes to what would become his play, The Catonsville Nine, *to which Phil responds here.]*

Fri. night. (9/20/68?)

Dear Dan:

You'll pardon me if I expressed the opinion that the last thing we need in this fair world is editor problems. I don't think our friend has caught our action at all. Perhaps she considers the action as taking one of the best writers in the business out of circulation, and a dear friend to boot. A degree of truth there. However, her letters to me since the action have been kind of infantile, rather in the tone of Dorothy Day's letter.

Another opinion—our words are no longer those of Church liberals—we are practically the only ones in the Church talking sense about corruption and cowardice, and doing it as well—or better—than anyone in America. Esp. you. I no longer feel that we have to go hat in hand to anyone in the publishing business, and that's what I'm doing at the present time. I don't know, it may be a very good thing not to have one person sitting like a grande dame over our literary efforts—bureaucrats, certainly those in publishing as well, have a way of getting smug over a sure thing.

If any change is impossible in the present decision, you know that you can use anything I write with punity or inpunity. I realize my own limitations, and they are not a few. And you know them better—but if anything can be of use, you know that what we have is ours. So we have always acted.

Luv ya man—youse are the mostest. Let me know your mind on this when I see you—there's no hurry. And thank you for being Dan, my brother. The Lord's peace.

Phil

[On September 24, The Milwaukee 14, inspired by the Catonsville Nine, burned ten thousand draft files with napalm.]

Wed. Sept. 25th (1968)

Dear Dan—

Lewis and I have been doing a little fasting for the soul, and as some sort of deeper tie with events. Reports have it that support is beginning to blossom in all quarters. I think we're in for a relatively big thing. Will send you another letter in a day or two—have been waiting for a typewriter. But even that may become impossible.

Know you're pushin' hard, kid—but drop us a line. Knowing of your whereabouts and doing is drink to this parched soul. Lewis says he'd die of beatitude if he was any better. So would I. Peace + love.

In Jesu,
P.B.

[On October 7, the trial for the Catonsville Nine began, and on October 9, the jury found them guilty of destruction of US government property, destruction of Selective Service records, and interference with the Selective Service Act of 1967, with sentencing to take place in November.]

Sun. (Oct. 20? 1968)

Dear Dan—

Have been busily getting down a few things on the trial, so now a few ideas for youse. Maybe this will be awaiting you when you get back from the West Coast.

The pressure stays on. Gov. Agnew spoke Fri. night at Towson State—where you were arrested, and was very nearly shut down by students, who promptly came here to stage a lovely demonstration at the rear of the jail.

As a young seminarian said to me this morning, "Jail is the only place for a priest to be." I suppose so—the idea seems to be catching. Incidentally, the seminarians were out in force behind us—several hundred of them. They have been turned on in a way I didn't think possible.

I am overwhelmed with the dedication. And with your presence + words at the trial. It would have been quite a different scene without you. Lemme know what you think. Thank youse.

> Lovingly,
> Phil

[Dan received a three-year sentence and was immediately granted bail, while Phil and Tom Lewis received three and a half years to run concurrently with the Baltimore Four sentence and were remanded to prison, from where Phil here writes.]

Tues. night, Nov. 26 (1968)

Dear Dan:

Beaucoup thanks for the great letter, which Tom and I devoured with relish. What I'm going to offer here are just reflections on what you sent on. And they in no way compromised the great, great satisfaction that we feel at the great efforts being made, and especially with your confidence.

I would personally hesitate to conclude that the Viets are in such a precarious political position that it would be best for them to be uninvolved. To me, they are in the strongest political position, and give indication of understanding this all the time. Therefore, for them to agree that they are releasing airmen to American peace representatives, and only to them, is not asking too much. After all, we share with them a common adversary. Then when we approach the powers, we have confidence that the Viets will go along with the conditions we suggest. I don't see how it is possible to have any leverage with the powers unless this is a minimal agreement by the Viets. Sure, we might be open to charges of conniving with the enemy, but there are countercharges as well—how about the quality of this war? How about the fact that the airmen are imprisoned justly and antiwar people unjustly, and that the powers hesitate to free peace people—even for a time—to pick up its terrorists? What about the powers' concern for its red-blooded bandits then?

I feel that it is high time that both us and the Viets realize that we are allies, and that this coalition—unequal as it is, sez I shamedfacedly—is a fundamental fact from which to plan resistance. They have, with incredible valor, taken more and more control of the military and political situation in their country. They should do the same in Paris, and in this current deal. "We'll release the airmen on conditions set by our friends in America. If you reject the conditions, no airmen! Savvy?" There are elements of the press in this country, and abroad, who will carry this golden ball journalistically, and do it with relish. The power's embarrassment would be profound, it seems to me. Another case of impotent power—the Viets are good at proving power impotent. Let them do it diplomatically as well—with us.

It is utterly up to your discretion how to use this. I think there might be slight differences with [Dave] Dellinger et al. because we view this society differently. We're looking at it from within—he's not. And the Viets are looking at it from within also. I think we'd find a surprisingly common bond and language. But as you say, I don't want to seem clairvoyant on this. It's only an opinion, and perhaps a not very helpful one.

Happy Thanksgiving—our debts to the Lord increase year by year.

Luv and grace from us both,
Tom + Phil

[On December 10, 1968, Thomas Merton died of accidental electrocution in Bangkok, Thailand. Phil, now released from prison on appeal, also makes reference to Richard Nixon being sworn in as president earlier on the day he was writing.]

Jan 20th (1969)

Dan—

In my dim way, I am catching up to what the loss of Merton means.

Things booming along here in the most hopeful fashion. We'll give you reports on these realities soon. I think some of yer brethren in the Society are coming to terms with what you mean. And you may take pride in them yet.

Today is a happy day for the nation. I would be in D.C. celebrating Pres. Nixon and his Administration, except that I feel there are better ways of doing it. We must all work for the unity he seeks according to our lights.

> Christ's joy + peace,
> Phil

Aug. 6th (1969)

Dear Dan—

Hiroshima Day! Maybe we're beginning to live it down. I dunno. Remember 24 yrs. ago at Woodstock? We've been reborn since.

Luv ya, ole pal. And the big thanks.

> In Jesu,
> P.B.

Balto. 21202
Sept. 13th (1969)

Dear Dan—

I'll see some of the D.C. Nine tonight and try to get them moving— we need to organize a NYC retreat and possibly, a Balt. one. There are enough resources in Boston to stage an extravaganza there—whereas Detroit should be an important discussion-topic in the Midwest. I hope to have enough notice on these to give you notice—you can sense the difficulty.

So much to do, bruv.

Miss youse—send this with all love. And Jesus' peace.

> Lemme know,
> Phil

[The passing of Phil and Dan's father, Thomas Berrigan, opened complex emotions, as seen in the letters below. Though his union work and hospitality to wanderers during the Depression influenced the brothers' social outlook, his domineering and sometimes violent tendencies colored their relationship even after his death.]

1130 No. Calvert
Balto 21202
Oct. 15th (1969)

Dan Bruv—

Grateful to you for so much—you're constantly saving the chestnuts for this yokel. More particularly, for being with Pop at his death, for working out the rich experience his death became, for keeping all of us sensible and restrained. Forgive me for not saying anything at the little evening service—I was blank and bushed (common occurrences these days).

But not depressed, you took care of that. So thanks bruv, for the hope and understanding and love, you're always there where you're needed—the Lord has managed you as gift to us. Luv youse.

                                        In Jesu,
                                        P.B.

[Phil refers here to three actions. On November 1, in what would become known as the Beaver 55, eight people shredded induction files at the Indianapolis Selective Service complex. On November 7, the same group destroyed biological and chemical research in Dow Chemical's data center in Midland, Michigan. Also, on November 7, the Boston Eight entered four Boston Selective Service offices and destroyed 100,000 draft files with paint and ink. The only named participant in these actions—Mary Cain—went on to participate in the Harrisburg Seven and would take the surname Scoblick after her marriage to Anthony Scoblick.]

Balto 21202
Nov. 8th (1969)

Dear Dan—

Well baby, they did it—and in the process, took out 70% of the S.S. capacity of Boston. In view of an irresponsible and stupid raid—quite ineffectual—on 1 draft complex a week earlier. A rare example of courage and discipline.

Left them at 8 PM last night to fly back here. At 5 AM got a call and the party was on. Grady was magnificent—he has a sense of both theoretical and tactical that is unerring. 4 centers were knocked out, and if I know our people, they did it thoroughly.

Now we must go through the painful process of seeing that they can surface in D.C. No easy task, with the hyper politicizing and maneuvering of the Mob Committee.

The group includes two priests—one S.J. (a grad student at Harvard), an SSJ (one yr. ordained), a great young nun from Baltimore (Mary Cain), and a superb young seminarian from here. And then sordid Resistance types (all Cath. but two).

Voila! I can only thank God. Meanwhile, another group—with whom we've worked closely—has done S.S. in Indianapolis, the data processing center at Dow (Midlands, Mich.) and hope to do two other sites before surface in D.C. A lot of them ex-YCS. Luvya pard.

In Jesu,
Phil

Dec. 15th (1969)

Dear Dan—

Just wanna say what I think of *Father* which you sent on. It is a devastating piece of work—I've been through it about 4 times, the last time before getting some shuteye last night. It caused the early years to flood back with amazing clarity—I became a 10 yr. old with him—breaking the immense "lumps" with a long handled shovel.

I've been trying to reflect upon my conscious indifference to his death—unconsciously, it shook me—in contrast to the obvious anguish that you + Jerry felt. And have concluded that I've been protecting myself against him for years. For better or worse, I would not expose myself to him—his quality of madness was too patent and destructive to deal with. One could only oppose it when it became too manifest, and do the high wire act of compromise when it was somewhat more livable. But I am deeply grateful to him in my own way—I don't think you and I would be the men we are—let's face it, unique—if we had not been toughened by him. So I pray for him every day, that he may have the rest and peace which he denied himself. And the love which he almost never gave.

Luv youse, bruv—hope to see you puhlenty during holidays.

Phil

1970–1972

[No letters between the brothers exist from 1970 before August 16, for understandable reasons. According to their biography, rather than appear for his prison sentence after being denied appeal, Phil instead secretly reported to a retreat house owned by the Religious of the Sacred Heart of Mary (R.S.H.M.) community of women religious in Sea Girt, New Jersey, on April 8. The next day Dan also decided to go underground rather than submit himself to prison. The FBI arrested Phil at St. Gregory the Great Church in New York shortly before he was to make a speech on April 21. Dan, on the other hand, appeared and spoke only days earlier at a Cornell event held in his honor and dramatically escaped from the agents in the crowd, hidden in a mascot's outfit of a disciple. Enraged and embarrassed, J. Edgar Hoover placed him on the FBI's Ten Most Wanted List as Dan continued to give recorded sermons to congregations on the East Coast. At Lewisburg once again, Phil protested prison conditions on July 6 and was sent to solitary confinement in the "hole," where he fasted for over two weeks to continue his protest. Finally, on August 11, the FBI arrested Dan on Block Island at the home of friend and writer William Stringfellow. He was sent to Danbury prison in Connecticut, where Phil would join him on August 26.

The two remained together for a year. During that time they heard each other's confessions, celebrated the Eucharist together in private, and co-taught a Great Books session that quickly turned into a resistance community. Dan nearly died while receiving a novocaine injection in June and was denied parole while still recovering. Phil responded by sparking a "prison-wide work strike to protest the parole board's arbitrariness and secrecy," hunger striking for thirty-three days and getting shipped to the Bureau of Prisons' Medical Center in Springfield, Missouri.

This compact period is characterized by the struggles of prison and the FBI's accusations that Phil conspired to kidnap Henry Kissinger and destroy heating pipes in government buildings, for which he faced life in prison. The brothers increasingly relied on each other and expressed this in their letters. Phil wrote, "Our greatest achievement in jail was learning our meaning to one another and trusting it implicitly," and he signed off the last letter of 1972 with hopes that the ghost of John XXIII would guide them forward now that they were both released.

The most significant development, however, was Phil's marriage to Elizabeth—Liz—McAlister, a sister of the R.S.H.M. since 1959 who taught art criticism at Marymount, a college for Catholic women. Coming from a patriotic family, she had become an antiwar activist as the Vietnam War escalated and began crossing paths with Phil at rallies and demonstrations. Originally married in 1969, they kept their nuptials a secret in order to continue their work in their orders. Even Dan did not know until shortly before their renewal of their vows in Danbury prison in January 1972; they did not announce their marriage publicly until June of 1973. They were excommunicated the very next day. While the excommunication was later lifted, there is little indication of how that transpired. Liz opened new avenues in their experiments with community building and resistance. A reflection of her importance to both of their lives is found in Phil's message to Dan in 2000, reading, "It's all one, you + ourselves!" to which Dan replied, "How right, how deep, what precious truth."]

Sun Aug. 16, '70

Dear Dan—

I would have attempted to get a note out sooner, but there has been nothing official on my status until last Friday, when I talked out the matter thoroughly with the new warden. We agreed that it might be best to join you at Danbury. And so, we ought to have a reunion of sorts there. Who knows?—perhaps the best yet.

I deeply hope that Carol and Jerry have been to see you. Prior to your capture, they planned to come here on Aug. 23rd, but wrote them suggesting a reroute, and a plan of seeing you first in August. If they arrived, you will have heard that Freda is gamely struggling with the walker—determined to be self-sufficient. All balance and heart—that's our girl.

Read in account that Barney Skolnik—the Ass't U.S. Prosecutor from Baltimore—remarked that you had been quite an egg in FBI faces. You have developed a huge following here—the guys take a personal interest in you, passing on newspaper accounts from their home cities all over the East + Midwest. Which is to say something positive about wider following, and a sterling work of education.

I'll tell you when I see you how proud we are of you. Part of the living annals, if this age ever produces any. Until we meet, dear brother—best of the Lord's love, peace, hope.

Phil

May 9, 1971

> i thank you God for this most amazing day. . . .
> (i who have died am alive again today,
> and this is the sun's birthday; this is the
> birthday of life and of love and
> wings: and of the gay great
> happening illimitably earth)
> —ee cummings

More importantly, this is your birthday, and it is one of life and love and wings. You give us these things. So we thank God for this most amazing day, and for you.

With mucho love from,
Phil

[Phil writes here from the Missouri Medical Center and describes his new surroundings.]

Thurs. Aug. 12, 1971

Dear Dan—

Well, ah tell you bruv, quite a scenario! And quite surprising! I had not fully grasped the hypertension in the atmosphere, or overeffect following under cause. But it was a panic! The security forces are becoming a kind of overpopulation factor, so it was on the way to the plane, and at every point after. Nonetheless, we flew here in grand style in two small planes, with kindness the rule, and fine quarters awaiting us at the end of the trail.

This is a sprawling place—900 inmates—seems relaxed enough, though I've seen only our share of it. We have correspondence and visiting permissions, and expect in time to get to commissary. I imagine that the lawyers will hop to it and get here muy pronto, but if they need reminding, I know you'll remind them. Sorry as hell about the distance people will have to come, but that's how things line up these days.

Anyway, affairs couldn't be better with the community, everyone practicing true grit, and doing their push-ups. Incidentally, please get puhlenty of exercise yourself—I've found it somewhat like prayer—it keeps one going. Love to you and to our friends—peace of the Lord, courage—from everyone here.

In Christ,
Phil

Tues. Aug. 17th, 1971

Dear Dan—

The local bishop (Springfield-Cape Girardean) Bill Baum, came to see me yesterday. He's a Roman PhD (Angelicum) but more importantly, knows something about the Bible, has a background with the Liturgical Commission, pretty much sharing that kind of thinking. But he was kind and responsive, if quite non-political. He asked very feelingly for you, and I gave him some genesis on our latest escapade (this one). He has the whole southern part of the state, and spends fully half his time on the road—his people are, for the most part, fundamentalist and rural. As we parted, he promised to come again.

We continue [the fast] excellently. The first bunch have been at it for 12 days, ourselves 9, and everyone is very much together, despite the loss of weight—close to 20 lbs. in most cases. We have a very fine young doc, and as good a set of guards, with whom we've become quite chummy.

Will look for a note from youse one of these days. I know that despite the pain of separation, you'll waste no worries on us. I know also that your great heart will direct you to husband your strength and to rebuild it slowly. For the future, and for us. Love from us all. Peace of Christ—light and life. We miss youse.

In Him,
Phil

[On August 21, a riot broke out at San Quentin State Prison in California in the midst of an escape attempt. Three guards and three prisoners were killed, including George Jackson, founder of the Black Guerrilla Family and symbol against racial injustice in US prison systems.]

Sunday—August 21 [1971]

I said to my soul be still and wait without hope for hope would be hope for the wrong thing—wait without love for love would be love of the wrong thing yet there is faith but the faith and the love and the hope are ALL IN THE WAITING.

Bruv Dear—

We are all down 10 notches after the bloody news from San Quentin. Jackson's life went with the marked mobility of a Greek drama: he was his own prophet, as it sorrowfully turns out—to the loss of all. I am wondering if the truth will ever be known about his death?

I am reading another completely charming fairy tale by CS Lewis in the series I started in hospital. Never quite got to him before. But these tales are irresistible. I think they bring joy + primary colors back to the Christian thing—in a way I disremember happening for years. Also a great anthology of Amer. poetry. Makes me yell out a hope you are getting some books there. . . . A group of us talk about Matthew's gospel as well.

Nothing but hopes, waitin' on you + the community from there. Everyone to everyone, we enfold you in thankful prayer. Nothing better + nothing else, in fact.

Daniel

[Dan's invocation of the Confessing Church refers to a German church that broke from state-sanctioned Christianity and declared its opposition to Nazi doctrine. His use of the term underscores the severity of their critique of the American government.]

Saturday 8/28/71

Dear Bruv,

The San Quentin horror continues now, a kind of the Texas horrors of '63 with everyone in sight 'indicted' in a sense, or clubbed, or killed, to supply new grist for an original sin. Are we ever to get at the truth of such events? It seems to me that the truth would be strictly beyond bearing—in the sense that it would demand such change in the guarded zoos of the 50 states as would indicate a sudden universal onslaught of sanity. No more peasant deaths, no more black deaths, no more body scores to justify the day and placate the night. . . . But I suspect we are short of all this, and Jackson's blood must flow for some time underground "beneath the theme of the Lamb"—underground in conjunction with the other innocents—in a limbo where death seems a total power, but the number of the just is not yet "complete," in the sense of energizing a rebirth.

Forgotten and scattered as the limbs of the children at My Lai, or indeed the freely accepted sufferings of 11 prisoners of note; and yet apprehended and taken into account indeed. Elsewhere.

Fasting. I think this refusal of ever good and necessary things in creation has slowed the show, and given pause to a few intemperate hearts. A sign of life to us, a sign of death to them. Even if nothing more were to happen, this has happened, Alleluia!

Your reference to the confessing church sets me wondering. Whether or not the time has not come to think of comparing a "confession" similarly to the one which Bonhoeffer's seminarians agreed to. Relative to church + Caesar + to the times! More + more seem 2 be involved in what the vulgar *NY Times* in its fickle majesty is pleased to call the Catholic left: more will be in law courts + prison, more involved in liturgies of note. This wd. by no means be a ticket of admission 2 some elite, but a way of declaring where one stood, mainly for the sake of his own soul + the brethren. Let me know if this has vibes corresponding.

And much Love from ALL to ALL,
Daniel

Wednesday, Sept. 1.

Dear Bruv,

Yrs. marvelously of Friday 27 here this PM. I always have a curious sense in writing, of being a sound track slightly out of whack with the image. The delayed mail, the late reports, the newspaper and TV, all make quite a game of time. And then when the letters are delayed—that must be something like Reel 8 played just before Reel 1 or something. At least one can always manage to laugh.

The health thing has been up + down but a great help has been settling my job situation. These days you know my lazy zen eggs only scramble into less useless configuration in appearance of malaria or marmalade. There is something of both about these days. If I were not so determined not to be lonely I wd. jump into my own yawn and make zero a positive thing. Trouble is there is always interest in working hard at meeting the next hour—simply sometimes because it is there with people aboard. That ought to be and usually is enough. I have only to think of you all and my mind starts sweat-juicin' like a tapped maple in April. Smells good, tastes better. All the bureaucratic hemlock in creation not enuf to undo that sweetness + strength.

Well if you get this alone or with 4 other missives! No matter! So it goes. All ask + ask + ask about yez. We rejoice and love yez, and love to an end and a new beginning.

Daniel

[Dan here refers to a visit from the New York provincial, Robert Mitchell. Dan also refers to the "new Mass." The Mass was celebrated in Latin until 1964, at which point it transitioned into a temporary translation, which was in effect until 1970. In that year the second translation of the Roman Missal was implemented, which changed some of the language even further.]

Friday Night Sept 3, 1971

Dear Bruv,

Fr. Mitchell was here today; spite all. He showed an appropriate concern on the health thing. He was at pains to open his soul on the recent sacred liturgies, and to get my views on the matter. Much disturbed, it seems as though he subscribes to a view of more measured change, esp. as regards the younger priests.

M is appalled that the "new Mass" so polarizes the province, that there is no prior consultation, etc. We at least reviewed a few ideas on community, etc. + I suggested he search his heart to discover whether the principle of community openness did not depend on the measure of trust he was able to awaken. He listened. He is going to talk to the young priests, I suspect at least a doubt has been sown in his mind, an area as free of these as good ground of tares, stones, etc. Purportedly. We shall see.

People think I must be in the dumps at your going, or you in likewise at my staying. 'Weep for yourselves + for your children.' Your being here was a gift. Your being elsewhere is justly a gift to that place + people. I do not mean to say one does not have a stone in his guts, a weight of loneliness. That taste like every other one connected with the crannies of a place like this, is straight out of nature; and so good, and so a healing. Whatever comes, I quake when I say it; and will say it anyway. There will be much more to bear before we are done. The very stars are wrong; the coloration of blood.

And who will begin even to deal with the moral aberration, madness, blindness, persnickety, puritanism, gunsmanship, law'n'order lawless disorder—the changes that keep people off base morally and on the scent of the victim—'The day will come when the one who puts you to death will do so as an act of worship of God [Jn 16:2].' We are quite near that day. I think.

I judge fasting as long as you have must carry the most profound soul effects with it. If anyone had the least sense of the interplay of spirit on spirit he would long to be in yr. midst, mostly as silent observer. Anyway short of that, one tries to be calm enough of spirit to catch a few of the notes you send us. Concern is everywhere, the length of your shadow was never so encompassing—a shadow that grants light.

Love,
Daniel

Sun. evening, Sept. 5th, '71

Dear Dan—

Re the Bonhoeffer idea and a transplant of his Confessional Church. It's a damn good idea, and ought to be pushed. It strikes me that we have no need for the name, nor a need to equate comparable situations—here and Germany. I would prefer profession to confession. The preliminary need however, is for a manifesto, direct enough and pointed enough to remain true to the gospel, and get invitational, esp. to the young. How about work on the manifesto—gospel, non-violence, human rights, community, refusal to burn incense? You're the obvious composer of such an opus. Then lay it on the churches—but hard. Perhaps it's one of the links we've searched for in the dark, and still haven't found. I will scrounge further for ideas.

You are in our hearts and prayers—we send best love + thanks.

In Christ,
Phil

Labor Day about Noon [Sept. 6]

Dear Brother,

Happy Labor Day. Some say God labored over the world. Some say he danced and sang like a clown. Anyway the Jews have a big thing in a Sabbath rest—the work is a tendency, a leaning toward; not toward more work (slavery under the corporate whip) but rest, fruition, enjoyment, non profit organisms of prophets at play. R+R not as the rancid fruit of war but the flowering of peace.

I think the technocrats destroy both—the way + the end.

The means are so important because we have to live with them—so do others. Also because most of us are not going to live to see anything else. Also because out of them, if a man can see, the end is lurking + taking shape.

I think we know enough by now to know that the non-violent resistance is the only sector of the peace movement which has been able to keep the above in mind. I don't mean anything mild by this. I mean sanity: right ordering of means so the end is always as concrete + compelling as my treatment of a single other person.

Maybe only in the case of a few like Gandhi or Jesus, does one lifetime show both means and end in conjunction. Gandhi by living long + so finishing a stage of the work; Jesus by foreknowledge and vision. The rest of us I guess have to muck about among the means which stay themselves (and get transformed) by being respected; like good plans mutually arrived at, or dropped like the wrong end of a hot porker (w. the right end of a gun.)

We love you and think of you + hope with you. Here's to more day + less labor.

♥ Daniel

When my brothers fasted for me
they fleshed out the shin of survival
they fleshed out the soul, thinning themselves
in that desert carnival
where the devil rides Quixote
like an ass the spine of a man
and 3 temptations stalk 1) all is bread
to the capital gain of the brain and
2) throwing your weight around gives
employment to idling angels and
3) when the devil pisses ambrosia let
God bend his knee SAY NO AND NO AND NO

Tuesday Sept. 7

Tried a bit of quiet and fasting yesterday in union with youse. Not too good. Sometime we'll have to have a long heart-to-brother on the Perils of Almost Going And Hardly Returning. About all I can offer these days is the ordinary plowman's plod and then some cheering from the sidelines. Would it were a thousand percent more!

Much much thought of you and many hopes riding on tomorrow, for so many, beyond ourselves.

They tell me there was quite a story in mag. *Times* Sunday, on an officer who ran into concrete walls trying to tell of V.N. atrocities. I guess I've reflected with you previously on the mystery of how people seem to attain a slavish adjustment to new criminality—the Bible I suppose speaks of 'hardening of heart', but have we ever seen it on such a scale? I mean where almost every institutional exposure or involvement means that one becomes inured to suffering and immunized against compassion? And the social scene becomes one great crustacean, resistant to change like a snap of the jaws?

What does the religious man do? ought to be the equivalent of the question—what does a man do? at least as far as meeting of minds go. Otherwise I think we trip over our own phylacteries.

Well enough tirade. I pray you brother + all brothers can reach in empty air and touch our hands which stretch out to you also. May a happy issue crown the good thoughts of those who scatter head 4 the birds of heaven + the children of men!

♥ Daniel

If I were the last
felon in lockup, my brothers
would fast for me. The proposition
strives
to make a point, it ignores
the bloodshot fact—man is
a cage-constructing animal.
Fasting thus becomes in a curious
Marxist phrase a "class action."
Self-denial releases like a
                    pierced heart
enormous consequence
 as though man the iron-monger
[whose hand like a bloody stump
must be fitted to a lethal claw,
            key gun
to "feel right" with the anthro-
pology of manifest destiny]
WERE GRABBED BY AN EPI-
PHANY FROM THE CLOUDS
            OF HEAVEN AND

DROPPED THOSE DEADLY PROSTHESES
flexed his ten fingers with a view toward
flexing his forked transfigured being
        into a peace sign
  or stranger still
    wept from his bullseye eyes—
        a use that died
      with the last murdered saint

Wednesday—Sept. 8—Mary's Day

    I wish you a thousand buds of taste blossoming beside still waters.
I wish you the joy of accomplishment which is unknown to the world
(more: unknowable) and in that degree, for real.

    I hope you may find in the making of bread that Lord who is a
stranger until the bread is broken.

    I hope you may find in the bread that God who (Gandhi said) must
come as bread, since there are so many hungry people.

                    We thinks of yez. Love all around.
                    ♥ Daniel

Sept. 11 (1971)

    Denying ones
    self the good
    things of the
    world thus be-
    comes
    good news for
    the world
    bread refused
    goes further.
    Men eat
    as though the
    bread tree
    of the universe
    savored in its
    sap the blood
    and sweat
    that fell to
    its soil—

a laborer's
bloody sweat.
Those speaking
leaves bestir—
FREEDOM NOW!

Fri. night Sept. 10th (1971)

Dear Dan—

No less than three from you today—one preceding your Labor Day letter (Fri. Sat. Sun.). I heard from Jerry today, fresh from his visit to you. He gave a sobering account, filling in all the gaps that inevitably one gets from others. I love him for telling me, because I know he was relating things you wouldn't tell me about yourself, fearing I'd worry. I have a gnawing realization that this simple path has been firmly paved with the stones of anguish and physical suffering you have laid, plus your prayers, insomnia, battling with the local demons. Am also realizing that while I may take on and deal with a few physical burdens from time to time—you are much more profoundly engaged in the spiritual lists, where the demons roar a hellova lot louder, and show far more muscle. It reminds me of some of the struggles the Cure' d'Ars once had—or for that matter, your John of the Cross. It's a dimension probably closed to me personally, closed permanently perhaps—it's basically the difference between a meat and potatoes man and a mystic-activist.

But enuf. Bishop Baum came in again today—he's going to Rome and the Bishops Synod. Paul appointed him—out of the blue (I wonder why?) to complement Cooke, Krol, Carberry and Lee Byrne from St. Paul. Dearden is also in there somewhere. Theme? Priesthood + world peace + justice. I am going to write him a few ideas which he will take with him. I'll make sure to send regards to Paul VI in the name of us both, perhaps remarking that while we consider ourselves duty-bound to visit the Powers, we are rather tired of resisting him.

Hang on, eat heartily when you can, sleep soundly when that's possible, and let your great spirit wax stronger on our mutual love and hope. The guys here revere you in a totally selfless way—and have their heads together on alternatives. Love you—thanks for yourself, which is a servant to the point of blood.

In Jesu,
Phil

Let us Pray

> Find it hard; forgive the big ones, Father
> who pull down, capricious children
> your mild & serviceable earth.
> Be it the pride of your metaphysic
> to see deep. Perplex long long above
> the plumbless pits of their wrongdoing.
> They devise triumphant & cast in face
> of you and yours their tricky tinny wares
> dare fashion yes to your thunderstruck gaze
> idols, foul proximates
> through clacking jaws to mime, mock you
> & for passing of base coin, pretend forgive.
> Forgive them Father straitway hard & fast.
> Bind up voracious wounds. For surgeon
> induct the meek of earth. Their hands
> acquainted as yours with wounds, empty
> of base won gain. Groans of the sinner,
> groans of the healer. Resound in you
> concomitant distemper, second birth.
> Bring men a new heart majesty save
> all things your tears & mirth called forth.

Saturday, Sept. 11

Dear Philly,
   Just mulling of your last three brings me such hope.
   Do you manage by the way to hang on to any of these immortal patchworks? They're about the closest I get to a diary of sorts these days. I keep yours—it is all part of an ongoing record; as well to read and read again.
   A rainy quiet day here, no visitor. You remember the peculiar taste + smell of rain + Saturday—something like drawing sawdust up the nasal tract. All hail all there. In your hearts you incubate the future.
                    Pray with us.
                    Daniel

Sun. Sept. 12 (1971)

Dear Dan—

Just out of the evening's discussion—some good stuff on Gandhi's sense of experimentation—basing his whole life on it, and from it gaining vision and clarity of purpose. Went down to the Eucharist alone this morning—the young guys have seen enough of the chilling experience. Sort of ritualized incoherence—both spiritually and politically. I find it profitable however, in the dredging one must do to evoke an act of faith. If one can't do that, then one had better stay in bed.

Hope to have good word of you tomorrow. Our thoughts are constantly on you, and the strength we share—which is something far beyond us both—will sustain us, and what we are about. Love + peace.

In the Lord,
Phil

"There is no fact in nature which does not carry the whole sense of nature"—Emerson

Sunday AM, Sept. 12

Brother mine—

A glowering thundrous AM. Stood by the window last night a half hour as the rain started, straight down, gently, to such purpose that the flowerless fewer words were afloat in short order. 'Makes his rain fall on evil men + good.' It reminded me of Merton's meditation and at the same time was a stun reminder of things around + within. 1) I suppose an unprisoned rainfall will get to be rarer and rarer, and 2) I suppose it is one thing to be a monk with access to some hundreds of acres of unspoiled fields + forest—and another to be under (however mild) a turn of the screw.

The weather makes for a quiet lull. Fr. chaplain is back, which makes for another. It is good to chasten the memory in light of present and future needs. Not much trouble w- this; I think neither of us EVER got so stuck to the dolce vita we were leading, as not to be able to move on to other pastures. For me the hardest thing is patience, beyond doubt. I have concluded after 50 yrs of trying vainly to synchronize with other peoples' planets, it is simply no go. I shall have to lose, win or at least run the race on my own. Does that sound foolish? In any case your months here gave me the best run for my money yet. I had not realized how complementary we were—which meant different edges, as well as nicely joined ones. The years apart, the very different lives we led, had made a difference at least I had not reckoned on. That plus the really bitter adjustments I was called on to make in coming to prison at all—made for quite a time. But as far as putting a stone on a string and lowering it into the psyche, I think there was nothing quite so wholesome as our sessions tete-a-tete. I came out often feeling birched and steamed clean. And with more respect + love for you, even though I sometimes may have gotten to your apotheosis prematurely; so much of living and suffering still lying ahead for both of us.

I hope at times you may warm your hands at the fire of others' love for you.

You hit it on the head; we've got to make it, at least for another while yet. I've tried a few people at times half jokingly; I think last June 9, confirmed me in certain zen tendencies, as regards even death. I needed your 'right on!' and sometimes wonder if you had not been there, whether I wd. have wanted to survive badly enough to make it. Well, dear bruv, this lil review of conscience is meant only to share the present, in view of a future He knoweth. Someday all of us will sit to the board + crack walnuts + quaff mulled wine in the Kingdom. All, for the present, well! Everyone sends love. Some rumors are even beneficent. We'll wait + hope.

Daniel

[On September 9, a rebellion broke out at Attica prison in New York over living conditions and political rights, during which roughly 1,000 prisoners took 42 hostages. On September 13, Governor Nelson Rockefeller ordered the prison retaken by force. The struggle resulted in the death of 33 inmates and ten guards and prison employees.]

Mon. Sept. 13, 1971

Dear Dan—

We are just getting the first news on Attica. Appalling! Nine guards and 20 inmates dead—no count yet as to the wounded. And now the State will enter the scene with heavy indictments, adding to the despair of inmates. I'm sure many of those who will be most affected are long-termers. Jesus, Lord! The reign of the sword and bullet is a bloody and useless one. Eye for eye destroys eye and of course, I. But at Attica, there is quite a little history of violence and counter violence, beginning with conditions causing the uprising—and it will end only with the summary sentencing and/or execution of several inmates. Apart from the implications it has for other prisons. Am writing Bishop Baum a lot of things. Poor man—I hope he won't to be taken aback. Merely tracing the record of the American episcopacy in the Indochinese's war is enough to give one nightmares. And of course, no one is more capable of mishandling such a sorry fact, by getting self-righteous or by weaseling out. I read somewhere yesterday that no less than 32 have condemned the war as immoral. Isn't that cause for faith? After 22 yrs. in Indochina (1949 we began supporting the French) they are finally getting the idea that the war is immoral. And I delight in the statements two or three issued after visiting their priests in jail—"I'd visit any of my flock in jail. I was merely following a Gospel admonition to practice the works of mercy!" But it will be a torturously slow process—helping them see themselves as they are, petty bureaucrats who ape the State, and learn with cultural aptitude its worst lessons—from abusing conscience to the ruthless employment of power politics. And of course, they are scared and have little recourse to fall back on but empty formulae of worn out evangelism.

All the brothers here want to write you, but the consensus was that not a chance existed of letters reaching you. Want you to know also that everyone here—I mean everyone—was fully agreed on pulling out all the stops for you—work + fast to the limit—in order to secure your release. The difficulties were of course, the impossibility of getting your consent, the Harrisburg defendants (some of them), and general support. There was unanimity that we should have adopted such a course from the outset. Hindsight at this point is useless, but I tell you this to describe the love these guys have for you. Well, the saga at Attica has finished, huh? Bill K summed it up correctly—murder—why couldn't the state wait 2, 4, 6, 8 days if necessary? The fact is, that Rockefeller, or most of the other non-entities currently living it up in San Juan will not negotiate except from strength. Lives, guard or inmate, are inconsequential to these barbarians. At the very least, I hope guards learn what pawns they are—even as the police must learn. Those ruling the anthill's summit could not care less for them. Lord be merciful to the dead inmates and guards, but also to the Living Dead who rule. God bless—may we meet again soon.

> Love from all + Christ's good health + peace,
> Phil

Patience
that tedious non virtue
hangs around hangs around—
Pantheon, Cave of Aeolus
Plato's pad; the last hour
of Socrates. Wherever
the action is. Near hero
like near beer
money laid on the slow horse
history out of time and this world
(fool and money soon parted)
he's waiting outlasting
poverty programs, pogroms
skin and its trade.
A man hangs around.
Hangers on sidle up
2 stand beside—
dumb animals.
Raddled streams. Straw.
Stars. Flowers that
transmogrify the hideous
braving the world. Even us
it seems to me when men
make meat of us or less
the less is still the more
and crude at the core, our
patience
deflects the butcher's tool
hard hard, no resolution—
the con's infernal whine
the druggie's foolish tongue
intemperance, cowardice
the mirror held
corrective cruel exact
2 our own face. Day
after night. Night
imposed upon day
the universe waits on us
great patience on a lesser—
the prisoner's days run
his weeks a slow drawn pain
his years stand like a stone

> great nature is doing time
> hard time or easy depends
> on ill or benign will
> clobbering or tender hands
> jack boots, juggernauts
> consider the lilies—
> good news good humor, grace
> I had rather so live a few
> brothers assailed than mick mock
> whoring Caesar's strut
>
> the children live the children
> rise from the My Lai ditch
> who pays who renounces who—
> brings that new news anew?
> unheard of news—heard now
> seen now touched now
> I had rather—
> but how descry it? eyes
> flare like a lamp in rain. the children.
> the children live.

Thursday—16 Sept [1971]

Dear Brother, yours was a good solid basis for relief yesterday. Wrote the "pome" for yez all, feeble and approximate as it is.

3, yes 3 of yrs. arrived this PM. I will delay comment except for a thank you, until tomorrow, to get this into mail. Love yez. Thank much.

Please no worries from here, all reasonably well.—Daniel

Friday Sept. 17 [1971]

Dear Bruv—

A windfall of yours yesterday. A good week of visits and I suppose someone will be here today. And Jerry and Carol tomorrow.

But whatever else may tend to discourage us about our ranks or ourselves, it seems clear 2 me that from '67–'71, there is a lucid moral continuity in the Catholic sector of the movement. Whatever else. That is something for history. Obviously this has meant a lot of drudge work, the rejection of much that looked scintillatingly ad hoc, but couldn't stand up under the non-cult nonviolence we were trying to promote—But the rest is almost entirely spasmodic, amnesiac, or despairing. This is a great deal; we've lost headlines, adherents, etc. etc., but in the main I think the sombre warnings have not even been needed, except at peripheral consciousness; because we were determined to build slowly + stress community + live as tho we were in possession of the promise.

The Attica thing is horrendous; I think one element of the horror is the continual battering of liberal consciousness by the armed facts of the military life. How broken one gets when he bases his life on "decent" expectations; he would as well be expected to scatter his millions from the Port au Prince balcony where he stood w- Papa Doc. What people really long for I think, based on their non fragmented sense of good + evil—is that the big boys will choose to leave them alone; the hypothesis being that benevolence toward Americans rectifies everything; just as almost any evil, as long as it is exported, becomes bearable. The idea of regional payment, for any but blacks or the poor, is strictly a new one, not yet assimilated. But maybe the dead of Attica are helping a puffy liberal to get redeemed.

Cath. chaplains were interviewed in *Times* today; one from Attica. It is pure institution. And so instructive. One wants a 'revolutionaries' prison, tight as Alcatraz. He said "they destroyed 1) religion, 2) schoolbooks, 3) shops where men learned trades." I thought those were 3 areas most in need of something new. White religion, white texts, white slave labor. Thought it significant no chaplain was called in for mediating team.

I guess the real mediating is by blood, freely offered, for a long time. It's been a long time, since Socrates + Jesus, up to King. And then the redemption goes on, but only afterward. There's really some historic verity to that Catholic thing. I remember vividly the chaplain, when I went to say Mass for Harry Stevens, taking me back to his posh quarters for a posh meal served by a nun: he remarking on how all of them want to get your ear with their grievances! Item: the chaplain in NY state prisons gets 15 grand plus house + housekeeper. An economic analysis on the soul of a functionary and its changes, would seem in order.

Thank everyone there, for their thought of me. We'll make it.

Love yez,
♥ Daniel

IN MEMORIAM VICTIMS + HEROES ATTICA 1971

Sat. Sept. 18th, 1971

Dear Dan—
    Wanted to write you something of daily schedule. We left it flexible
from the outset, because personal reactions to a long fast are bound to
be very different, and because regimentation added to already present
tension might very well be destructive. For example, at one point, I
looked at those who would never help clean the place up. That did
no good, so we quietly dropped the subject, and allowed cleaning up
to remain voluntary. This flexibility applies also to a vast project we
adopted of writing Congressman and Judges (the better ones)—about
40–45, very long and tiresome letters. Some felt unequal to this, and
did relatively little. It struck me that while in the fierce grip of a community experiment like this, some young guys would suffer violent
enough changes without having a Clausewitz over them. But to get on
to a normal day, we lived in a cozy, two story wing (1st floor—some
setup over us), exactly 11 individual rooms and a common area. The
guards would wake us at 6:30AM—most of us would take a cup of
orange juice, ½ pt. of milk, and a little of the abominable coffee. Afterwards, most would go back to bed until 8AM, though a few news
hounds would catch the 7AM national news. At 8AM, most people
would go to the yard for ½ hr., to walk exactly 3 circuits amounting
to 3/5th of a mile, then to sit in the sun, and bask like salamanders.
Then, back we would come to lockup, to shine our quarters for
15–20 minutes—and then settle down to work—mostly letter writing,
personal journals and reading (the young guys read voraciously—I
learned very early that the fast affected my eyes. I had to treat them
very gently, despite exercising them faithfully). At eleven-thirty, we
ate again—more orange juice, another ½ pt. of milk. After lunch,
we would hear the news again, and then go to visits—the CCCO
[Community Corrections Center–Omaha] guy would faithfully and
daily see one of us, rotating with the anti-war people—or back to
work, or to sleep. Attitudes toward sleep varied, according to needs.
Some needed twelve hours a day—others, after beginning the fast,
needed less. Though lights went out at 10, with TV off, I rarely got
to sleep before midnight or 1AM. And so, I would catch an hour in
the late afternoon. The mail would arrive soon after four—always
an event—and then we would have supper—more juice and milk
and coffee. Following the 5:30PM news, we would get into our
rap, rotating on discussion leading. They usually went 1 ½ hrs—to
2 hrs.—at least half were interesting, some great. But they served
another purpose—they anticipated the minor and major irritations

and petty rancors that afflict people in close quarters, and subject to boredom and isolation. You could describe the process far better, but it had something to do with anticipating inadequacy, and instilling deeper confidence in those around one. It suffices to say that these men were never shaken from their resolve to continue on. Beyond these raps, and largely in addition to them—sometimes, we would literally spend 4–5 hours talking.

So closing for now, dear bruv, and as per usual, our love and thanks. See youse soon—it will be a reunion like few we've had. The Lord's blessings.

In Christ,
Phil

They forbid us to live like men, we shall at least die like men. Attica 1971

Sat Sept. 18

Dear Bruv,

Lots of people still need a symbol of some transcendence, some cable to the sea bottom. Some connection. I suppose a ghastly symbol is better than none. I'm not sure of this but then again I'm not a bewildered father or mother, price frozen, son in V.Nam, prideful, fearful, stuck in the pew, stuck in the job etc. etc. You try to keep something when everything seems to be getting unstuck; and (this is speaking for me) say, that celebrated rattail-chasing behaviorist Skinner, and all his brain clipping crew of destructors. Bishops have a use; mostly to deny Christ. It's an old job; Peter saw its potential so brilliantly. Thus they make sure in a perversely successful way, that He never gets out of sight. I say bully for them. Anyway the big Christheart, blessed by excellencies + pursued by laity, keeps everyone in a tradition, safe + orthodox—the 'movement' so to speak.

An educated or compassionate bishop over in Rome even for a few weeks might turn a trick, God said something like it about the search for a diminishing no. of just men—love how the Creator's hopes get minified as he became acquainted with the facts of life! He finally settled for 1: which possibly says something like: look, the whole thing isn't a body count after all (when big nos. don't turn up, we all get virtuously qualitative) it's to find if the truth took with anyone. And if so, why. Armageddon's off! Anyone who could bring himself down (having set the big show in motion) to so meagre a bargain in bad times deserves our respect.

I say a pox on all congressmen + their promises, roughly equivalent to their flatulence, which is awesome if inconsequential. But I am still sorry because they dare to raise hopes in good men.

Yes this self-congratulating air of ecclesiastics who visit us is nauseous. Makes one feel like the deserving poor, visited by the mill owner's chaste daughter. I suggested in a letter to some young Jebs that Fr. General lay his hoity toity care not to get Amer. dogs—in his heels, was really violating the supra-national word of Jesus and betraying the victims to the powerful. Once more, yet once more. The utter factuality of that tradition being its inability to give a new twist even to its sin, or to think up a different one than its counter-ape, Caesar where humbug at least doesn't have the keys stamped on it: BETTER BELIEVE OR ELSE!

Daniel

[*Phil was returned to Danbury in September, reuniting the brothers again and accounting for the lack of letters until Phil was transferred without warning to Allenwood, Pennsylvania, on January 13, 1972. Dan reacts to the news here, revealing a sense of adventure, faith, and purpose.*]

5:40 PM—13 Jan [1972]—George Fox (d) 1671; Ammon Hennacy (d) 1970

Dear Brother,

I learned of yr. going at supper time, so am in spirit commending you to the above 2 gentlemen who were fairly conversant with sudden death transfers of scene, and the sudden life consequent on this against all expectations of Herod.

We have had occasion so often to speak of the antiks of the Great Surprizer Upstairs. Never more so than today, our eyes meet wordlessly across the miles, our lips form a slow whistling O-oooo! Wow! Gazooks. What next?

The sense of wrenching and tearing has also subsided among friends, I think now there will be a steady purpose, after a more human farewell, a sense that seeing you about for a few more hours has made many things possible.

Could it all have gone better, given our fierce and beautiful world? I marvel and marvel; the karma is right because the people's hearts are sound. Now the next big struggle begins, so much of it will be a matter of patience in which all have been so well schooled, esp. in the past year.

You leave an incalculable void but everything of importance goes on. Much love dear brother, I will be able to have the Mass tomorrow as usual! Write a line soon!

♥ Daniel

Dear Philly (Sat. Jan 14 [1972])

Here's a kind of poem (out of recent resonances) for yez—

> The mind proceeds
> from cold turkey nightmare
> to cold truth.
> I invoke the latter
> paying tribute to the
> purgatorial first act
> The surreal is the leavening
> ingredient
> of the real—
> or a gypsy band
> bounding off at dawn
> phantasmagoric chimerical
> into western shadows;
> shivering chastened exalted
> on edge steeled upward
> we wait.
> The universe holds steady
> instrumental
> to maestro sun.—
> then Downbeat!—
> You are on earth rightly
> as liturgy or love
> You are prisoner rightly
> as thunder on the left
> You are lover rightly
> as the differential beauty
> of right hand and left
> possessing letting go
> that face that freedom.

Love brother,
Daniel

[Dan refers here for the first time to an ongoing case. On November 27, 1970, J. Edgar Hoover told the Senate that Phil and Dan led an anarchist group that planned to kidnap a government official (later named as National Security Advisor Henry Kissinger) and destroy pipes and electrical conduits in Washington, D.C. Phil was indicted and faced a maximum sentence of life, along with Liz McAlister, Pakistani intellectual and activist Eqbal Ahmad, and five others. Dan was surprisingly listed as a co-conspirator and not indicted. What became known as the Harrisburg Eight trial would begin on January 24.

Further, part of the evidence in the trial would be love letters between Phil and Elizabeth McAlister. They had married informally in May 1969 but told only John Grady, whose church they used, until revealing their relationship to Dan in January 1972. Grady was a close collaborator with the Berrigans and active in the Catholic peace movement. He would be a participant in the Camden 28 action of 1971 and had chaired the defense committee of numerous other actions. Dan was hurt that his brother had kept the marriage secret but supported their decision and witnessed the renewal of their vows in Danbury prison before Phil's transfer. Although Phil had no qualms about the decision to marry, he "bitterly regretted" not telling Dan.]

Jan 17 '72

Dear Brother,

Came on this by M. L. King, a sermon he preached in Ebenezer Baptist Church, Atlanta; "If any of you are around when I have my day, I don't want a long funeral. . . . I want you to say that day I tried 2 be right + walk with them. I want you to be able 2 say that day I tried 2 feed the hungry. I want you to be able to say that day I did try in my life to clothe the naked. I want you 2 say on that day that I did try in my life 2 visit those who were in prison. And I want you to say that I tried to love + serve humanity . . . I won't have any money to leave behind . . . but I just want to leave a committed life behind." So be it. R.I.P.

When I think of all you and the others are being asked to endure, my ♥ all but fails within me; but then I have only to reflect on the few peoples huddling under Nixon's big bang, to get perspective once more. No doubt there will be an accounting. A Christian form of conduct in the "meantime." I think that is the question; and that too is why I think we are right in *rejoicing* over what is coming down. "Every hour is alike to you, but my hour is not yet come." Truly everything looks alike to the unaccountable conscience, but for us the death of one child sets our universe reeling . . .

Dear friend + brother, good evening on this one, God bless + keep you cheerful, His Son, and our pride. It stays cold here, thought of you is all there is.

Daniel

[Dan refers here to the trial of Walter Dejaco and Fritz Ertl before the Superior Criminal Court in Vienna that took place from January to March 10, 1972. Both men were members of the SS and had helped design, construct, and maintain the gas chambers in Auschwitz. In typical fashion Dan points to the crimes of his own government, invoking the "tiger cages" in the US-built Côn Sõn Island Prison used to torture hostages in the Vietnam War.]

Anniversary Jan Palach resister in fire, Prague 1969.
19 Jan '72

Dear Philly,

Everybody here asks me every day: did you hear from Phil; I wish we had a way to speed up this damn mail thing. I keep wondering too what the details of life are like for you, whether fairly tolerable. Usually things are hardest in the beginning, until one can get to work out an 'arrangement' that will include a little humanity.

I see they're about to prosecute the gas chamber designers. When will they begin on the Tiger Cage architects, the fibreglass anti personnel fragm. bombs (un xrayable after the strike) the—etc. etc. I suppose the 30 yr. lag shouldn't dismay or discourage; but how come only losers pay?

Sometimes I guess it's only the vision which saves, in the sense of sanity, continuity, self-accountability? We were into these deep waters tonight in Castro discussion; a mixed bag but at least it seemed to me the desperate possibility of a Hitler is mitigated by the existence of a Bonhoeffer. Thus we are not left hopeless. . . . Which brings one quite naturally to the existence of you and the others there, for whom one can say only a DEO GRATIAS! and be silent.

And hoping for some word from you. And making it here, help of so many. And grateful every day for the work we have been given to do. In which let us pray, we may be found faithful, to the end—

Mucho love.
Daniel

Sat. Jan. 22nd (1972)

Dear Dan—

Your Wed. letter arrived this morning—I am so sorry no word from here has yet arrived. In any event, have gotten a daily scrawl off to you. Can honestly report optimum conditions here—my little cell, privacy, time to work, and later—permission for the brethren to gather for meetings. So as usual, the Lord provides what is needed. I do the exercise thing assiduously, and thereby survive the lockup thing with grace.

Currently, have toiled laboriously with an opening statement. It looks as though myself and a lawyer will do some screaming after jury selection, as the government's case opens. Later, as we begin our side, perhaps two or three more, a combination. The main problem is that there's so bloody much to say, and probably not too much time to say it.

Actually, looking forward to Mon. and the fiasco's beginning. Certain defendants still find it unreal—it appears they had clung even though late to the hope it would be dismissed. We are all very complex machinery, wot? Once it begins, however, we may hopefully expect a new birth of resolve, even security. I think that, despite preparations that from many standpoints were dismissal, we have enough in the reserve tanks to rise to occasions. People do know enough, for example, to dig deeper into the prayer, and to firm up communally. And that's a vast advantage.

We think of you constantly, and of your immense donation of yourself to all of us through the years. I would not be here without you, and this is as much a measure of your influence as it is of my gratitude for your love. Stay well and careful of yourself, give love to the brothers—adieu until tomorrow.

The Lord's love and my own,
Phil

Sun. Jan 23rd (1972)

Dear Dan—

A very good day here—statement for trial to finish and ponder, reading and praying to do. The chaplain here kindly dropped off a Mass kit last week—so I had Mass last night for the first time. Again tonight later. Needless to say, I missed you, and the celebrations we had that acquired such profound meaning. But I set up the communion between us, so the Eucharist had its own focus.

Administration out here tonight, supposed to be a big thing—everyone official uptight about it. Felt I had to share a few thoughts with our friends, but don't know if any of the lawyers will come in, or have the opportunity to try. Something like breaking out of the lockup that's this society by serious non-violence. Something about not focusing entirely on us, but using the trial as the occasion of building a movement—communitarian and continuous, a movement just groped at, before. Something about giving people hope and love—since that is all any of us need. Something like pushing back the darkness, just as Christ did.

Well, we begin tomorrow—I actually welcome it. Like jail itself—it's something to transform, wot? I honestly expect that we'll get into a tighter huddle as the fiasco progresses—that it will be a growing and toughening experience, as resistance itself was. In time, I hope, some of our friends will learn to value it. That's essential I think, so that they won't recoil—and retire.

The folks are outside, going through some lovely folk songs and hymns. Don't think I'll be able to wave hello tonight. Peace, brother, mucho love to you and all there. Oh yes! If you'll ask our legal eagle for that book on Gandhi—The Life of Gandhi, or some such. It's one I would like to keep. Thanks much. Love again.

In Jesu,
Phil

[The next two letters, written on the same day, react to the news that Dan had been granted parole and would be released on February 24. He indicates here that he plans on seeing Phil at the Harrisburg trial upon release. Phil's letter conveys a sense of how intermingled his faith is with Dan's fate.]

Jan. 26, '72

Dear Brother; still digesting your 3 course banquet of last evening.

I guess it is now possible 2 close a letter to you by saying, see you soon. That sounds hyper-surreal. Something like the dying busting their ropes + beginning a dervish dance. If I knew how.

I am sure it was another of those days in court for you. When the well is full we drink: when it is dry we refuse 2 curse. Is that what they call negative virtue? Or something.

Anyway I am happy that God who allows all kinds of purgatory now and again outside of books and hopes and nature, allows for another form of things. The joy of this day is because of you; and so is the sorrow, and both are feelings out of love; for you and the others and the Vietnamese—one Body.

Daniel

Wed. Jan. 26th, 1972

Dear Dan—

Am sitting in the marshal's office upstairs after another day in court. The judge has now narrowed jurors down to the final questioning—the greater part of the day devoted to questioning them individually. Several impressions emerge—one is the reality of neutral people, perhaps five or six of them, who have lived their lives on a no-see, no-hear basis, and who have opinions on virtually nothing which doesn't concern them directly. The assumption is of course, that they are neutral,—nothing could be further from the truth. Ah well, you know the story. Most of the day consumed however, and thinking of you and the hearing in D.C. and praying for a positive answer, knowing what that will mean for human dignity and justice.

Back at the jail. Was just settling into this when a delegation arrived—Bill C., Ramsey, Jogues, Liz—all of them hearing the great, great, great, Good News—like the glad tidings of redemption itself. Beyond the grins, they were quite speechless, even as I. We tried fumbling with a statement for the press, and for minutes at least, got nowhere. As L remarked, one gets so acclimated to bad news that one doesn't know how to deal with good news. In any event, I finally came up with a simple word of thanks to the community that stayed with us so steadfastly, plus a hoping that the sanity of the decision to release you might be applied also to those political people in exile, in prison, underground and of course, those abroad, most subject to the mailed fist.

Dear bruv, I am still imbibing what this will mean for the defendants, the family, the church, the country, Lord! What a glorious breakthrough. I curse my lack of faith now, and realize better, that you were friend and brother to others—and so, did not lack friends and brothers. And now the work of building true and lasting community beckons once again—a work at which you are unsurpassed. I remember this now with tears in my eyes (as you know, I'm not prone to tears) when ole Pluto beckoned last June, and you fought with all your strength to remain among the living; and then began the long fight back, the Lord had grand designs, and wanted this version of Calvary to implant clarity and courage in people. He wanted you back from that to speak of your undying hope, peace, sanity, guts—all honed sharp by Idiot Acres [Danbury prison], now to be freed for the civilizing of men. The thing was obscure them, and too frightful for overmuch reflection; but I see it now. So now we can sing the holy psalm together—and bless His Name. And I will fight harder not to be so unfaithful again.

I cannot write more. The defendants and lawyers will rejoice with me tomorrow—this will inject a tremendous infusion of hope into the dolorous proceedings—we will grin through them now, taking them as little more than bad humor. Peace to you, brother, and all my love. Our team is more intact than ever, huh?

Phil

[On January 24, the trial of the Harrisburg Eight began. Dan notes the support from Bishop Carroll Thomas Dozier of Memphis, Auxiliary Bishop Thomas Gumbleton of Detroit, and Brazilian Archbishop Dom Hélder Câmara of Recife.]

27 Jan. (72)

Dear mah fren' + bruvver,

3 bishops, Dozier, Gumbleton, + Helder Camara have issued excellent statements supporting the 8. Many vibs undoubtedly came together on this—unthinkable even 6 mos. ago; Liz's presence at Kansas City, the connection you mention w. D., also my old affectionate friendship with Helder—and didn't he meet you too in NY at one point? You'll recall the great PM I spent with him in Recife in '66, his deep understanding of why I was on pilgrimage there—+ then the subsequent snafu when the Unmentionable Eminence Wright (Wrong) foiled his tentative plan 2 come 2 Catonsville trial. So it goes, all quite mysterious.

What I feel is a measure of joy that others are rejoicing, an untidy and unverified hope, as I look over my sorry spread of resources, of offering something to the scene. We shall see.

I wish + pray you good days there, or failing them (they will fail) your unfailing Thing To Go On.

I hear the bread breaking even here. Keep passing the cup, friend.

Dan

Thurs. Feb. 3rd (1972)

Dear Dan—
Half of yours (Feb. 1) lost in transit, sadly enough. But I sez—half a letter from Dan better than a whole from most. Hope you're getting these—I know the variations on that and, famine and plenty stuff—I've continued writing daily.

Quick one. A day here which has one bedding down in faith—by necessity. Let's say the neutrality of the region grabs one after a while—after hearing it expressed in an infinity of nuances. Not surprisingly, we run into old school brethren of the faith, with religious even in the family—who will nonetheless, refuse to venture bias toward us, though it is resoundingly clear that coronaries would result if this kith and kin became that wild. So they bide their time, hoping to be included in the lynchhopper.

At this point, I began to ruminate on the confidence great men placed in the people—from Christ to Gandhi. This helped to revive me. If their common sense does not sufficiently register to question the divinity of contemporary divinities, then more time is needed. Anyway . . . another aspect to shore us up in the bowels of Christ.

Otherwise, more of the normal, dear bruv. Another note tomorrow. I cherish you, and expressively.

> Best love + peace of the Lord,
> Phil

Sun. Feb. 6th, 1972

Dear Dan—
Skipped you yesterday, brother—forgive me. The Trial of the C-9 will open next Sun.—They have some fairly opulent people in the lead roles, esp. the State's D.A. for the area in your part. He has vouched on TV that the role has him huffing and puffing over his values, and his life. It's a great educational tool.

Please extend our love and gratitude to the men there—so many extraordinary types who undertook with profit the baptism of fire that prison offers. I remember thinking—at one low point in my checkered career—if each year in prison meant only one good man. Yet how many good men have we seen? And how they tip back the scales of justice. Caught a little Emerson the other day, "If you love and serve men, you cannot by any hiding or stratagem escape the remuneration.

Secret retributions are always restoring the level, when disturbed, of the divine justice. It is impossible to tilt the beam. All the tyrants and writers and monopolists of the world in vain set their shoulders to the bar. Settles for evermore the ponderous equator to its line, and man and mate, and star and son, must range to it, or be pulverized by the recoil." Reminds me of Christ's words about himself as cornerstone. Good cheer, dear brother and comrade—I hope you found Carol + Jerry well. And that they found you well. Good night with peace.

In the Lord,
Phil

[*Camilo Torres Restrepo was a Colombian priest who campaigned for land reform and nationalization of industry, eventually leaving the priesthood to fight on behalf of the poor. He was killed on February 15, 1966—during Dan's exile in Latin America—after which Dan defended his legacy and criticized the church for rejecting him.*]

Feb 15. 1966 Camilo Torres [1972]

Dear Brother—

Such a gorgeous day for Camilo's anniversary. Our spiritual leader has offered me the podium at Sunday's Mass to say my farewells. There is almost an embarrassment of riches at hand to draw on—the temptations in the desert, rebirth, creation, prison, hail + farewell. So we'll see. I will do my slack-jawed best to say it for us both.

Since Mt. gospel says a trial lies at the end of things, you will be just about the best rehearsed mortal this side of Jesus. 4 of them! It wd. be truly Kafkaesque and impel one to the bourbon hemlock if he could not believe that each spiral of absurdity concealed a further purpose; I mean a further important connection of the trial to events at their deepest. No doubt!—I mean in the midst of doubt, which seems 2 infect purpose all around, purpose being rendered insubstantial as sow fat over the fire. For most that is.

You are a motor, and we move even
unto here,
♥ Daniel

[*Pete Seeger, folk singer, activist, and supporter of the Berrigans, played a concert for the Danbury prisoners on February 17.*]

Feb 18, '72 (Friday)

Dear Brother,
  This will be known for a long time as "Time after Seeger!"
  The poetry of last night! He sang the Joe Hill song which was all about not dying. Then some song of bells, about miners in England, an agonized lament in which he suggested the tragic fate of the men underground by the different voices of the bells in the countryside. Then "Little Boxes . . . all made of Ticky tacky . . . " and "Where have all the flowers gone." Ended with "If I had a hammer," which everyone sang along. We came out and had a great mix of slushy mocha in the stands and thought of you. . . .
  Pete proved to be all we hoped—he hummed + whistled and cajoled and made the kind of sounds that made me (and all) stand up and call for more. . . . Met him to say thanks at the end, of course he had everyone there in mind as well. What a man can do for others with those gifts! You get the impression of a very burdened unselfish decent man whose gifts keep him going and who wishes he could go further.
  5 days have passed in court, 4 you and the others. The face of our leader has flashed across the screen, like a trail of jet-soot, as they pump off to their latest fabricated distraction. A scene that would make a jackal scream. The distraction is precisely from you and me + the Vietnamese + justice and free breathing of sweet air by all God's sons. That poor mouthed sooty-eyed face is tribute indeed 2 the ruin of inmost spiritual pollution—that avid breathing of the foul bargains struck over the years; "all this will I give you"—All distractions, all a shadow. . . . Let them stick 2 their guns, lies, blood, glory, wars, gods, liberty bells, slave holds, unreal estate; we will stick 2 one another. And see who lives, and see who dies, and keep like the last mystery of unpolluted faith, the difference between.
  (PM) I feel like doing a chick-pee harvest dance, 3 of your letters (11, 12, 14) arrived in one swoop. Can hardly believe it. . . . Many hearts with you; mainly so we can do a mid air refueling from yez!
                              Love dearly.
                              Daniel

Tues Feb. 22nd, 1972

Dear Dan—
  Three beeg ones from you tonight—and I'm reduced to writing home, where please God, you'll soon be. Absolutely superb you

could hear Seeger before you left. One of the quiet (unassuming) and loveliest heroes of our times. Never quits, that man! I remember his generosity when I was in Newburgh, and his family taking their licks because he dared to oppose the war.

You must make it up to Freda for my forgetting her birthday. Cuss me! And someone reminded me of it yesterday, and I intended to have someone call. And then in the press of this idiocy . . . Ah vell, she'll understand.

The town emptying of young folk to be on hand for your release—they'll carry cheers and love and gratitude from this quarters.

Don't be concerned about my lawyers yesterday—it was all an attempt to go pro se, so I could speak. We even allowed Hizz Honhor to censor the damn opening statement—he found it unsuitable for the purpose. It was no more than the reasons why we were in his dock. But it may leave a point for appeal. As it stands now—I am constitutionally unrepresented, but since he refused permission to discharge lawyers and to go pro se, I'm still cornered.

The main point being to welcome you inside Danbury—it could never bury you, even if you did life there. But what your presence outside means to people, esp. those we love—you cannot guess this. Askings for you constant here—and people send love without reserve. As do I. Remember what I said—'72 is Easter year, one of hope.

> Peace brother—the kind Christ gives,
> Phil

[*On February 24, Dan was released from Danbury and headed back to New York, where he gave the fifty dollars provided to all released inmates to Dorothy Day at Mass. She sprinkled the cash with holy water, telling him, "Now we can use this." He returned that night to his Fordham residence to find his possessions dumped in the hallway and his door locked. He headed to Syracuse to be with family, where Phil here writes him. The "invasion of privacy" mentioned refers to the public reading of private letters between Phil and Liz in court.*]

Fri. Mar. 3rd, '72

Dear Dan—

It's the weekend—so an opportunity to catch breath and look around. And I'm grateful for it. Between us, it's the toughest week I've spent in my life—and I've had one or two. It's like standing by and watching oneself go into a meatgrinder. Others register shock at the invasion of privacy. I accustomed to that well enough—what reached me was powerlessness—no word possible, no response, no question. It helped some to read Mt's account of the Lord's exchange with James and John, and then the Passion, with utterly no one around him, and the thing happening with the cold decisiveness of billing in war. So I profited by the contrast.

Best love and gratitude, dear brother—to you, Carol, Jerry, Ma, the kids.

> In Jesu Lord,
> Phil

Mon. Mar. 13 [1972]

Dear Dan—

Yer first one since return arrived tonight, and I hasten to answer while eating my suppah. Your letter struck deep vibrations—it was like your visits here—so incredibly thoughtful and generous. You bring the mead, you bring yourself—we sit down as though 2 mos. and many events had not separated us, and we go at it. And I could see—it was the most obvious aspect of our visits, or of your presence here, that you came to share your great heart and head with us, because the endeavor is common, and because really, you're more with us than we are with ourselves. I've been reading Gandhi's appreciation of the Gita, esp. as guideline for action—something to the effect of detachment from the fruit of one's work, one's effort, one's pay up is the trick of accomplishment. And that being the utter key to everything we're attempting. And I couldn't help but read that without thinking of you, and the way you've done that, and done that recently for us. I also felt that you and I no longer need the slightest gesture toward one another—though we will make them with a kind of invincible love. What I mean is that a total trust prevails—I loved your coming and it meant immeasurably that you did come. But if you hadn't, I would know that you had something more imperative, and that that something was for us. That is why, when notice came through friends of your plans for Harrisburg—I exhibited no inordinate interest, though I was enkindled with anticipation. What I'm fumbling with I guess dear bruv, is this—I know you'll do the utmost and best thing and that will grant us more liberation than any other source—save the Lord.

Everyone talking of your being here—the vigil group last night, the defendants, the lawyers. And they are so damned grateful, only slightly less so than I. So in turn dear brother, I do love you hugely, and we will make it—with a flourish and with egg on the face. Of you know who.

> In the Lord Jesus,
> Phil

[March '72] Sat PM,

My dear—

I guess just want 2 say thank you, and say no miles could bring any separation in spirit from anything I saw this week in Harrisburg. Especially + above all, my visits 2 you. It would be evident 2 a dead man that everything we hoped for from the trial cannot happen, given human realities.

My hours with you were precious beyond saying. I needed them so much. I had never been sure of how I could take this latest turn in the road, always sure of you. Now I know more, see better and have more confidence.

It seems 2 B part of things that I am repeatedly saying goodbye 2 you in jail. This hits the flesh like a drop of acid on an eyeball. But I blink a few times + it goes away + I see your face again + all is well. Another way of saying thank you + I love you + we'll make it.

> Daniel

[Phil informs Dan about the maneuver to rest the defense rather than call the defendants to the witness stand in order to prevent the prosecution from asking incriminating questions about who sheltered Dan while he was on the run from the FBI.]

Fri. Mar. 24th, 1972

Dear Dan—

Well, it's over, and it went like clockwork. We had the leaks to contend with, but apparently, they did not get that far. About 4 P.M.—Ramsey stood up and said, "yerhonner, the defendants proclaim their innocence, and state that they will continue working for peace. The defense rests." Each of the lawyers representing us individually stood up and said, e.g. "The defense rests for Dr. Eqbal Ahmad." My turn came last, so in order to pressure to the pro se, I stood and said, "Since I've discharged my lawyers, I rest my own defense. Thank you!" It took them totally unaware—the fumbling and the mouthing was something to behold. Monday Leonard and Ramsey will present summation—we expect them to be on the extraordinary side—and Lynch will probably ramble for some three hours. Then the jury with go and deliberate.

Good wishes to the back—hope you got a decent board to sleep on. This comes with utmost of love and gratitude. You move it, bruv. The Lord's good cheer, good health + strength.

In Jesu,
Phil

[On April 5, a mistrial was declared for the Harrisburg Eight. Phil and Liz were convicted of the curious crime of smuggling letters out of prison. The conviction was later voided by an appellate court.]

Wed. Apr 5th.

Dear Dan—

Well, the flea circus has ended—to the considerable relief of all. Now, hopefully, people will face themselves for more demanding issues. Someone will call you tonight and give a good rundown. Until nearly 4 PM, we had heavy expectation of the jury coming around to the judge's mentality, or so their most recent questions indicated. Then they froze on Count 1—the conspiracy rap, and Cts # 2 + 3, the so-called threatening letters, and hung there, contenting themselves with convicting Liz and myself with 3 counts apiece 5–10. Which is mercifully carrying the comedy of errors to a strictly anticlimactic end.

The govm't saved face, and seemed content with that—they didn't contest Liz's bail, nor attempt to impose travel restrictions. They heaved a sigh of relief, as did everyone. Now we go at the appeal—no large chore—and hopefully, chew this contraband rubbish to ribbons.

Would imagine I'll be stuck here for another two weeks or so—awaiting sentence and a few other superfluities. And then back to Idiot Acres [Danbury prison], I hope.

Will close now dear bruv—Carol and Jerry here—Their own loving and loyal selves. I expect them in a few moments at the jail. Ma was never better—and Spring is coming. We have so much to be thankful for. I hope with all my heart that you are getting many long, invigorating walks by the turbulent sea, and mucho good chow, and mucho restful sleep and good grace for your gallant soul.

As for what happened today, dear brother, it signifies nothing—a little manure to stretch the nostrils and clean the head. Christ's good peace and love.

And mine,

Phil

PS—Liz took it all beautifully and strongly. No sweat! Everyone very proud of Her Nibs.

Fri. Apr. 7th

Dear Dan—

First one from Block Island. Thank you. Great relief to know all goes well with you and the brothers.

I am grateful, immensely so, for your time with Joe [Wenderoth]. The next day he came up, and we went at many things, gently and easily. Nothing esp. substantive, but then, I've found that my view of the substantive—awful word—is distinctly unpalatable to at least four of the defendants, which says something about them and about me. But I will welcome any opportunity to discuss this with Liz and yourself—perhaps we can get some mutual daylight, esp. in regard to the Scoblicks, Neil and Joe. I would prefer to think that the scar tissue of the last 18 mos. is not that serious, while knowing against my preferences that it is. And if my intuitions are correct, then we will all try as we did with C-9, though perhaps with greater perception and love. The human mystery still remains—one never knows how people will react to the oven. That is why this business of c.d. [civil disobedience] and surfacing strikes me as wrong—it provides too many escapes, too many opportunities to settle back for ego-tipping and self-congratulation. The accent rests on property damage (effectiveness), and not on community building. And now, we are finding to our dismay, that true community spirit is most elusive, because the primitive breakthrough was not agreed upon. People did not agree to the harsh regimen that makes a community person—public witness, conviction, jail, jail organizing and resistance. Does this make sense?

Yes, I would agree that conversation between us is crucial. For my part, I will always need your great wisdom and charity—and an insight into suffering—and experience with it—that I will never know. Except from you. To my mind, our greatest achievement in jail was learning our meaning to one another and trusting it implicitly. We are not done yet bruv—just beginning. I love you, and wish only that I could love you more. Which is to say, appreciate your worth. Good health, peace, love to the brothers.

In Xto,
Phil

[On May 1, J. Edgar Hoover died. When asked for public comment, Dan said he hoped Hoover received the mercy he never afforded others. Phil refers here also to his mother Freda's initial misgivings about his marriage to Liz.]

Thurs. May 4th

Dear Dan—

Quite a difference between this year and last—that bleak and harrowing crisis awaiting you at Danbury, and all the pain following it, leading up to your release, which I still maintain is the event of '72, and the augury of new and unforeseen hope, all embodied in you stepping out of those obscene walls in February. Including of course, the demise of poor J. Edgar, who made power, and control of many by the few, a way of life. God be merciful to the poor man. He never got to answer y'all, or any of his victims, because he couldn't. In a way he will never understand, he fell victim to the Vietnamese and to those struggling to understand their resistance. Just as his chief will, I sense, election or no election. Their propaganda and their technology will never perfume the stench they leave behind in the nostrils of decent men—as their chief and almost sole legacy.

Another great card from you today—thank you so much for breaking the ice with Freda. L will write her and I'm sure that will help. But in lieu of more advantageous conditions—it was exactly right that you do the groundbreaking. She is a great soul, equal to very nearly everything, as she has so amply shown us. So it may involve a little catching up, but that's all.

As for springing me, let me assure you that our legal eagles astounded me with their eagerness to confront that one—and I'm fairly used to their service and exploits. The issue is now a personal one with Ramsey, who loves L and has a certain devotion to me as well, I suppose. He will pull out all the stops once we know our ground on sentencing and appeal. He has confided to Jogues that he expects me out by summer. You might assess my attitude toward that—same as to your release—but I mention it to indicate his determination. So, with you and with them, I remain in very good hands indeed.

To return however to the purpose of this—I will offer the Eucharist for you, my prayer being that He will allow us more time together, mucho time together—as long as we can remain of use—to offer something to the Kingdom and to the worst of times, which by every indication, might get yet worse. Such, I would expect, will be the nature of our joy, and of our crucifixion. Love you, dear brother. Peace, love, joy.

> In the Lord,
> Phil

[Phil writes this letter as Dan prepares for a trip to France to meet with Vietnam delegations and attend the premiere of Gregory Peck's production of Dan's play, The Catonsville Nine.*]*

Mon. May 8th

Dear Dan—

A last card before your departure, and a letter from the plane, and in from California. Deelighted with the clearance to Europe—these things always have a significance when they break that way. (I understand you leave directly for Paris after Notre Dame.) The Lord is layin' down carpets for you, and then you get the beckoning finger—c'mon—as Pop used to give. But you can give, as no one else can, great evidence of love and solidarity to our friends—a little proof that some of us take them seriously.

Heard from Ma today—very short and hurt. She did her best to disguise it, but it was very apparent. I wrote her back immediately—strong on the gentles and diplomatics—with a little oblique explanation thrown in. Perhaps Carol can offer an interpretation. But she is great—absolutely great. Naturally, she would wonder about perfidy against the church, and damnation for my crafty soul. But she will understand.

Saw the 1st ad for C-9 in *Times* yesterday. You will yet shake thousands with that, comrade, even though it might not yet be as good as we would like. Will stuff this into the pigeon. Good + fruitful trip—much blessing, much love—give 'em hell.

> In the Lord,
> Phil

Tues. May 9th [1972?]

Dear Dan—

   Don't know if this'll catch you before you leave for Europe. Writing it as a safety valve as much as anything. I suppose—since it's a hard day, for sanity. It's not just a question of shame for this pathological country and its plastic cipher leaders—it's more for the important colleagues and decent people, who are very decent about their scented hides. I sometimes bitterly reflect—knowing it as a temptation—that nearly three years behind bars haven't changed that. In fact, there is perhaps less real questioning and resisting than when the C-9 were locked up, to start the only type of education we could to—with our persons. Ole Gandhi used to develop what he called equanimity. How! I'd like to see him practice it with Nixon.

   L was in shortly last night and today. She knows my moods and what causes them. Which is good for her—maybe it extends the field of choice.

   Ah shit! I'll be snapped out of it tomorrow. Shouldn't write such crap, but I know of all people, we can compare notes. There's one thing I can do, and that's pray more. I've even thought of sackcloth and ashes. But those prayers will ride with you on the trip. Convey to our friends that there is some anguish here, some shame, some sympathy with their suffering. My love and the love of Christ. What more can I send you or wish you?

Phil

Wed. May 11th

Dear Dan—

   Well. I've rebounded today—with the help of my friends. Some-times, I think the Lord employs these dark-night periods as a cathartic, and to deepen something or other in the trembling old soul. A friend dropped in to tell me of widespread and promising response which may surprise my cynicism and burgeon into something lasting. We can only hope—it's an infantile scene, which up to now, has determined to stay infantile. One of the things most unsettling is its silence about pitching us to the wolves—somewhat of a complement to the chief wolves' readiness to chomp on us. Jesus! and our peace friends speak of martyrs!

   Deelighted we can keep contact with Angela [Davis]. With the Panthers toothless, she remains about the only black symbol around.

One clutches at straws these days—ain't anything else. Sterling love to youse, dear bruv, you light minds and hearts around you.

In the peace of Christ,
Phil

Tues PM—16 May

Dearest brother—

I'm getting this off the side of the eternal Air France plane, this time between Nice + Paris. The Vietnamese have warmly set up an AM + PM meeting, and supper. Followed by a 9PM press conference.

I don't know if anything of the song + dance of yesterday reached you by any means. The movie showing was a mob scene followed by the largest (+ longest) press conference in history of the festival. The most excitement over any film of the year. (It also opened in NY on the same day so people are awaiting US reviews with some trepidation.) I was on French tv for 5 minutes during news—quite unusual. Over 200 newsmen + movie people from around the world were at the showing + p. conf.

Where will that little May morning of '68 ever stop? See what you started? and by the way when will you ever stop? (I won't if you won't.)

EVERYONE ASKS FOR YOU ♥ ♥ ———> ad infinitum.

Will you please dear one, make sure this chit gets to Jerry + Carol + Mom + Jim + Rosalie? I miss you all—but why? since you are always at my side.

♥ Daniel

Tues. May 16th

Dear Dan—

Want to get a little message to you daily.

The shooting of [Alabama governor and presidential candidate George C.] Wallace has us all unsettled—the gunman is presumably sick—little out on him yet. But despite all, it's a reminder how we treasure violence and follow after it. No word from any of the candidates, or brass balls about how Indochina reinforces centuries old patterns and contributes to material insanity.

I see a few scattered professors are risking—and getting—arrest. Now that's a new one, huh?

Long 2 hr. session with Liz last night on community-dev. and on the future. Told her most imp. to remain in touch w/ you—and of course, she will. Has offered to do anything possible w/ Freda—but I don't know if a trip to see the latter is advisable at this juncture. Adieu—we are praying for ea. and every phase of the trip. Best love—everything jake.

In the Lord,
P.B.

rue de Rennes 156 Hotel Unie
Wed, May 17.

Dearest Brother,

I'll attempt 2 set down a few foolish notions at the end of a long day, a glorious and painful one at the same time. I was called for, about 9:30 and brought 2 the S. Viet delegation in their suburban center.

Talk of the American movement, again "We have been accused of overestimating you; but we accuse you of underestimating yourselves," half humorously, half seriously. Tribute + challenge. An attempt 2 exchange with them some sense of where things are going, that would not be too devastating or negative. In the midst of their agony about the daily destruction of their people, they remain gently, totally nonviolent in attitude toward us, even as they convey a tough purpose that surpasses words.

That spiritual élan is what remains with me, in contrast with Fits & Starts Incorporated movement headquarters at home.

Anyway, a beautiful Vietnamese lunch and more converse and departure about 2:30 for hdqtrs. of N. Vietnam delegation. Here another great embracing welcome. And another atmosphere. More tension and agony than before, more immediate sense from the bombing, that ruin is overhead. I didn't do any weeping as I feared I might; but we had long silences together and that was as good + perhaps not as painful 2 either side.

There was the most profound spiritual understanding between our friends + ourselves. Only on their part, a humiliating sense that we were doing something real. "Your task is more difficult even than ours; while we are in combat, you must change the spiritual perspective of your people."

Will you carry loving thought 2 Jerry + Carol + Mama and hopes for good estate + glad tidings? And 2 you; you give us a center, a heart's desire.

Soon,
♥ Daniel

[Paul Mayer was a close associate of the Berrigans and a former Catholic priest who was also implicated in the plot to kidnap Henry Kissinger. Mayer died on November 22, 2013.]

Fri. July 24th

Dear Dan—

Mayer in today—typically, at 3PM. He has worked strenuously at impending liturgies and had a much more positive report. Apart from details, he made exhortation about reconsideration on the part of you know who. I can now see the point of some of your infrequent annoyance with him—he is not above giving a few heavy pieties, and even drawing the Vietnamese into his homily. I had patiently explained to him the decision, approaching it from multiple angles to little effect. Oh vell—in a sense, he's right. And in a sense, he isn't. But I think that you and I need homilies about as little as most. I would listen to one from Our Lord + Saviour, and from you. But from few else.

Nonetheless, I was most grateful for his energy and dedication. He hangs in there better than most. So gave him the loving treatment, and he promised to get news to us of the outside world.

Gotta rush this, dear brother. Consistently and suffocatingly hot. I figger we're in for a big storm soon. Too much of a low—we otherwise + politically. But the signs of hope remain. The brothers all send undying love and fidelity. One ea. crucifix arrived, so did the stipends for the impoverished towhead. He was properly and deeply grateful. Love you, man. Peace of the Lord. Thanks and affections to the dear brothers there.

In Christ,
Phil

Wed. Aug. 10th

Dear Brother—

Yers of Mon. AM at hand. Thank you from the heart. Always an infinite relief to know we're okay without having the least suspicion that we're not. Betty sent *America Is Hard to Find* [Dan's new book] and I began it today. As usual, what you write strikes immediate chords. I sometimes think that's because we share the same wave lengths. But then, I say to m'self, we have those wave lengths because of where we are. And others don't have them, because they aren't where we are. It's relatively simple. But getting back to the book—you're on target with a richness of expression. That is incomparable. Have I told you? I think you're the greatest writer in the West—west of Solzhenitsyn that is.

Saying goodnight, dear brother, bon chance, mucho blessing from the Lord.

Love + peace from the joke,
Phil

Mon. Aug 21st

Dear Dan—

I have devoured *America Is Hard to Find* at about three sittings, and feel a compulsion to write you about it. It is a magnificent book—keen as a blade, powerful, compassionate, flawlessly expressed. I thought to myself in reading it—Dan has always lived his ideas, has always paid for them in bitter coin, has always insisted on the truth—in a much more lofty and outrageous way than I have. And it shows. Your utter generosity comes through, causing a purity of insight, imagery, and power that is simply breathtaking.

Maybe I'm coming of age, and therefore, more capable of understanding you. I've long known you were a great writer, and that your talent flowed honestly from your great manhood. But none of your previous work has hit me as this one. Maybe it's because we were in the lower bowel of Leviathan together, or because we learned to suffer more together, and to love one another more, or because you, mainly, turned back death physically, to reflect the daily turning back of death you made among the denizens of the compound. Whatever the case, or because of all of them, thank you—with all my thanks. You gave the underground speech, and now it will live—to the assistance of many.

And the letters—to Thomsen, to the young Jebs, to our mourned director of the efff beee eye—well, something else. I suppose the sublime,
to be sublime, must also have its power.

This book will touch to the core those still redeemable. The re-
viewers we ought to ignore totally—have we ever seen one who can
understand? But from it, so many will understand that the life of the
spirit, the life of truth, is by no means, the worst life. How!

I was reading today how the Lord predicted a jaunt up to Jerusalem, and a few little disagreements with the authorities. And I
thought joyously that there are still a handful of Americans who
will take their own jaunts with results about as predictable as those
the Lord had.

So my prayers constantly this week. And my gratitude for you as
brother, friend, comrade—a man whom the Lord does not send to
every age, but only one like our own. Someday, I will appreciate you,
or if not, in eternity. But know that I am trying.

> Best love, dear brother, and the Lord's
> peace,
> Phil

Wed. Sept. 13th

Dear Dan—

Very good notes from Carol + Jerum tonight also. They wrote of
their 17th anniversary (Sept. 10th)—where the hell have the years
gone? Jesus Lord! we're a long way from the officatiation 'and the
praying' huh? But they're right in remembering their marriage and
reminding us. It was, and is, a great one—we've all been the beneficiaries.

Yeh! I wince with you at the campaign (McGovern's). One has
to scramble to find any hope in it. Everything remains warm and
vapid—like baby vomit. The Kennedy strategy might very well be to
preserve enough of the Democratic Party—whatever that means—to
give Teddy Baby a crack at the Throne in '76. Now, that's something
to wait for, isn't it?

Will scoot this off to you. Thanks for the great confab—everyone—
literally everyone—sends love from here.

> Peace of Christ,
> Phil

[Phil speaks of receiving news of his release, scheduled for December 13.]

Wed. Nov. 29th (1972)

Dear Dan—

Scootin' off a few notes to kin and friends. The news caught me plumb off stride, since I thought the mechanics would follow schedule. Natsherly, and like yourself—there was the onrush of mixed feelings— A people's victory—gratitude to the thousands who prayed, and to the handful that worked. Without you and the others that we know so well—immobilization would have been my lot, perhaps for a good deal longer.

And then there's thought for the men here—and prisoners generally. You know far better than me the identity that develops. But I'll carry them with me—both in their education of me, and in their pain.

Ramsey called—he was quite incoherent. I'll have better opportunity later on to talk with him, and to learn better where we stand. But unquestionably, he loves us.

So it goes—dear brother. The year opened with your release—it closes with mine. At appointed times, it seems, heaven breaks its silence. I'll see you Saturday. Best love, thanks, peace.

> In the Lord,
> Phil

Wed. Dec. 6th (1972)

Dear Dan—

One of [Thich] Nhat Hanh's fine cards from you tonight. Thank you muchly!

Somebody wished me Pacem in Terris in a letter today—evoked memories of ole Pope John, and those hopeful, unreal days. But maybe he'll help us write it through. Thank you bushels, bruv—we'll chant the Te Deums together.

> Love you—and every peace from Kid
> Brother,
> Phil

1973–1979

[The period from 1973 to 1979 concentrates heavily on the creation and activities of Jonah House, founded by Phil, Liz, and their friend John Bach in order to organize a community around disciplined resistance and radical discipleship. The letters reveal an initial struggle to find common footing; Phil thought others lacked the enthusiasm shared by he and Liz for resistance yet took advantage of the community's finances. Still, Phil and Liz organized systematic protests at the Pentagon and White House throughout the decade, which brought both death and new life to the family. Phil, Liz, and Dan would now add the memory of their mother to the reasons to protest America's militarism, and the birth of Frida and Jerry gave them children to protect from the nation's nuclearism. By 1975, Dan had moved into the West Side Jesuit Community on 98th Street, where he would remain for almost four decades.

The year 1977 ushered in references to something new, an "ultimate resistance" and "greater risk" that might be demanded of them. Phil, very much in the forefront of this talk, began to feel that he was not giving enough to God's kingdom and living too comfortably. He worried their nonviolence had become routinized and wondered if fasts were not enough; perhaps they only detracted valuable energy from a more faithful form of discipleship "beyond symbolic resistance." "We will be called upon by the Lord," Phil assured his brother, "in increasingly serious ways." It would not be until 1980 that they felt ready to set this new call into action.

Very few letters are available from Dan until October 1976, affording a focus on Phil in the wake of his release on December 13. Former Attorney General Ramsey Clark confided to Phil that Nixon ordered his parole "as a concession to the North Vietnamese," who were concerned about the welfare of him and Dan.]

Thurs. Jan. 11th (1973)

Dan—

Welcome home brother! I have tried calling you but suspect you haven't touched down yet. This morning got your long letter written en route to Paris—I will go over it again tonight. As usual, your vision and clarity shines through. And yer love, which I am cursed so often to take for granted—and yet which I attempt to return in my small fashion. I will continue to learn from you, as I always have.

Dear Lord! When you write, I get a faint notion of how damn hard you work, and all the sheer devotion behind it all. And what you accomplish! Have long had a theory, which I've crowed about from time to time, that you move more in an hour than some of the rest of us in 10. It's a matter of quality.

Just talked wid youse—abs. terrific. Please shuck the cold, and get plenty of rest. Love youse. Peace aplenty.

In the Lord,
Phil

Tues. Feb. 6th (1973)

Dear Dan—

Thanks for the hospitality, the good, direct talk, the love. Neither L or myself or the two of us together have been particularly successful in explaining our relationship. We must try harder to do so. I'm writing L to see you more frequently—hoping that both of you can manufacture the time. I think it would help immeasurably if you knew her better, and she you.

Please continue to level with me on the issue, bruv—I consider it another demand put upon your love. Thank you for what you told me—I think it suffers an adequate explanation—I hope we can give one satisfactorily.

Peace to you, brother and best love. You are light + leaven to me.

In Jesu,
P.B.

[Here, Phil refers to telling his other brothers about his marriage to Liz, as well as his support for Dan's short-lived idea about adopting a child.]

Sat. May 19th (1973)

Dear Dan—

Sitting here writing letters. Just broke the news to Honor + Tom. And I'll get to John when an address is available.

Thank you for your beautiful confidence on assorted matters, most of all, the question of adoption. To me—your thinking is solid, even flawless. You've intimated the loneliness before, but I could only guess at its depth. Certainly, the Society has been a whore to you—that infidelity weighs and gnaws, huh? I recall how you've never stopped struggling to realize those hopes of yours in the Society. I guess my abstractions saved me from that.

I would support the idea of going ahead while in Canada. And I would suggest that you give thought to joining this enterprise when the moment strikes you. Or that we join you. This doesn't necessarily mean that you plunge around the countryside, but that you place at our disposal your great heart and head. Wherever we are, we can fashion some privacy for you (even as we need it ourselves). And welcome the kid(s). And love you, almost as much as you would love us.

I want you to help me (Liz and me) to appreciate you more, stay closer to you, love you more. For our sakes. As you say, the selfishness gnaws imperceptibly, even as one works agin it. But you can save us—keeping a public (unselfish) focus on our marriage is a formidable task. If we can't preserve it—it will have been a mistake.

We can talk more. But please give the above some pondering, vague as it may be. Thanks for the bread dear brother, and all that you are (give). Peace of Christ.

> Love,
> Phil

[Phil and Liz legalized their marriage on May 28th, attended by Dan, who was fresh from meetings with Yasser Arafat on his trip to Jerusalem, Lebanon, Egypt, and Cyprus with Paul Mayer.]

Tues. May 29th (1973)

Dearest Brother—

Arrived here in the early afternoon, and immediately went to the sea. It is relatively unspoiled—nearly, fishing boats and sailing yawls ride at anchor. And one can walk on the seashore without encountering gobs of oil. I wish you were here with us.

To say what your presence or help meant yesterday would be doomed to failure. It was not so much the difference—it was fully as central as the presence of Liz and myself. That is very simply because—what you are about, we will try to be.

This afternoon, I reread Ed Guinan's book [*Peace and Nonviolence*], and esp., your essays from Danbury and prior to Catonsville. And they ring with the same vision and clarity now as then. And I thought—the spirit that inspired these is enduring.

If Liz and I remember—and I think we will, with God's help—what you mean to us—then our relationship will draw us even closer to you. Wherever you are. If these few days—as well as Monday—have any meaning—they will have that meaning.

See you in Boston. I love you—if possible, more than I did.

> In Christ Risen,
> Phil

[*The Josephites expelled Phil after he announced his marriage to Liz, and both were excommunicated. Here we see mention of a eucharistic controversy surrounding the continuing practice of Phil and his community to celebrate the Eucharist with no ordained and practicing priest present. He refers also to the Tiger Cage vigil and fast at the US Capitol from June 24 to August 23, in which both brothers participated.*]

1933 Park Ave.
Balto 21217
July 20th (1973)

Dearest Brother—

An answer to the cards, very gratefully read by all. And for your ministrations and kindness, I hope you'll end the fast at a week, and allow some of the rest of us to share it.

Just got back. LaCroce tells me he faces imminent suspension—the pretext being that he shares the Eucharist with me and Liz. The Bishop is a cro-magnon named Daley. It's my view that we should go to the press—with a lot of drum thumping. What thinkest thou?

Care for yourself, and best thanks for the $, for the love and consistent wisdom.

> In the Lord,
> Phil

Tues. [Aug. 1, 1973]

Dear Dan brother—

Thanks for the exquisite card, awaiting us on return from Syracuse. Sounds good—though I had expected an earlier date (Aug. 3) for release from parole.

In Syracuse only overnight—but good. Saw Freda twice, including a good, prolonged lunch. She is feeble, but chipper—and the lovely balance is there.

I'll try calling you on Thurs. night. Am off to D.C. and a telly show with Guinan + a Fed. Judge on c.d [civil disobedience]. Should get the latest from Mitch. Gregory arrested today—immed. began a water fast + went to jail.

Peace and love. And as Elisha would beg Elijah before the chariot bore him off—"a double portion of your spirit." Miss youse.

> In the Christ,
> Phil

[Michael Dougherty and Joseph O'Rourke raided the Dow Chemical Company in Washington, D.C., on March 22, 1969, in opposition to its production of napalm.]

Sept. 18th 1973
1933 Park Ave. Balto 21217

Dearest Brother—

So g.d. good hearing from youse today. O'Rourke and Dougherty up for sentencing tomorrow. The others got suspended sentence, so it shouldn't be sweat to them. Yesterday Liz, two nuns from Boston, Jim LaCroce, Brendan—all had the punishments dropped. Woeful lack of organization from the prosecution—no cases prepared. It appears that people showing up is an ounce of flesh—and that's all required. From the other end, folks concur that it's a bucket of fly shit. And who can fight that?

Big spread in *NY Times* today—on Liz and myself. So, so. The press treatment recently, has so reeked with ignorance and venom, that we tend to like this one.

Will write Jerry tomorrow—there has been a considerable silence from their end. And so, I hope all is well. More later, dear brother. Liz and the bros. + sisters send best love and thanks. So do I, doubly so.

> Peace of Christ,
> Phil

1933 Park Ave.
Balto 21217
[undated—ca. Oct. 15, 1973]

Dear Dan—

No less than 3 from youse today—all greeted with joy. At least 7 valiants here have by now read your kind words—and have been so heartened by then. You have that exquisite touch that comes from understanding. (Remember how you used that word at Danbury—and my struggling for your meaning? I think I know a little better now.)

Dorothy speaking in D.C. tonight at the Pax Christi. I thought seriously about going, but Tom got sick on the northern jaunt, and about everyone else is on the verge. But as for the Pax Christi thing—going would be a concession to Dorothy + Guinan—the remaining luminaries are hacks for my money. Though ole Gordon Zahn has made a difference with his scholarship.

More later, dear brother. You were light and peace to us—in fact, are. Mucho love from Liz and me, and all insurgents here.

In Jesu,
Phil

Oct. 24th [1973]

Dear Brother—

As Freda would say, a great lift talking to you yesterday. Sorry about the confusion on the checks. It takes about $1200 a month to run this place. Betimes, we run very close to becoming broke.

Liz will add a line. She is incomparably good, perceptive, strong. Recently, we discussed at length a perception I have of return to lock and key. The main thing—not the only—but the main thing deterring me are her and the child, good people to move with and a good scene of witness. I doubt that I can do my parole.

I know you sense this. Will talk more at Christmas. We all love you.

In Christ Jesus,
Phil

Dec. 24th [1973]

Dan Brother—

Complete uplift seeing youse. Does something for both spirit and digestion.

We had a great yak with Liz's mom, and then drove down in leisurely fashion yesterday. Now, we're deep in preparation for tonight, and tomorrow.

Two fine letters of yours awaiting us on return. Unfortunately, didn't get an opportunity to discuss peace prize thing with you. I think you're exactly right in reasoning that no peace—no prize. There isn't any peace, so why accept them? Moreover, I think there are various human ways that we can illustrate the liberal ambivalence of the peace prize givers. If they were truly working for peace, they'd have no time to be dishing out prizes—which contribute to peace in no way. I think our policy in jail was exactly right, except when an award (like the Nobel) would give us muscle to whack the warmongers.

Perhaps we'll have chance to discuss it at Christmas. thanks for the time, the chow, your great company, your love. Lord bless you. Christ's love, peace, joy from all here.

Phil, Liz et cabal

Jan. 16th [1974]

Dearest Brother—

Just read [James] Weschler on your dialog with [Hans] Morgenthau. Poor joker! Neither Morgenthau or Weschler know that much about Vietnam. Which is to say they don't know this country, and don't know Israel, its god child. Delighted about [Noam] Chomsky—consistency is a noble trait.

Have a coupla fine diocesan deacons nearby, living with the blue collars—one of them in a black neighborhood, the other in a factory. Anyway, they've gotten a priest from the Sons of Charity—a Fr. Canadian W. priest outfit with them. Lovely guy. He speaks—apropos of yes + Stringfellow seminary idea, of their candidates in a factory during training. And in a few pointed theol. courses at night. They will soon begin to work with us, hopefully. We like them very much, but their politics tends to be European/Marxist.

Will scoot this on with wishes for good trips. See youse I hope, around the 26th. You keep so much of what is alive in us, alive.

Christ's peace + love—ours too
Phil

[*A frequent character in the following pages will be Ned Murphy, S.J., referred to below as Neddie. Murphy, who died in 2012, was active in the Catholic peace movement, including taking part in the Camden*

28. Murphy went on to found Part of the Solution (POTS) for the homeless of the Bronx.]

Fri. March 22nd [1974]

Dearest Brother—

Wanted to send these on posthaste. The Nat'l Security Agency has to be the tightest place on earth. They wouldn't let us get 150 yds. from it. Talk about security overkill. Anyway, we dumped a gal. of blood (ours) on them, confronted them with our Lenten cross laden with symbols of America's blessing on the world flag of Chile, an oil can, truth in chains, and a Guernica like takeoff on a woman of Indochina—saw three people arrested, and then went home. The press was popeyed through it all.

Liz suffered prelim. contractions last night, felt okay this morning, and determined to go to the demonstration. We now have 25–30 hard corers who will show up for weekly demonstrations, and the interminable meetings. Please God, the more serious stuff will come soon.

Back to Liz—we're closer to the birth. I suspect within 3–4 days. She is fully and magnificently under control—a valiant woman, if there ever was one.

4 ex prisoners now in DC—soon to open their own house. Peace to you brother, and deepest love from me, Liz, Neddie, Mitch., Jan, Tesi, and other raggamuffins.

[Liz gave birth to Frida Berrigan on April 1.]

Easter Sun—Apr. 14th [1974]

Dearest Brother—

Liz and Frida + myself just back from DC and a celebration in Lafayette Park. Very nice, very hopeful, and considerable numbers of the faithful rallying around.

And three friends in jail—Mitch, Neddie and Debbie Daniel. Please tell our friends in Paris that they invaded the S. Viet Procurement Office in DC with blood, and sent the mercenaries flying, including an A.I.D. general, who opened his files for blood, and then waxed furious, much after the manner of the military in Honolulu. Good scene. Meanwhile, four other friends (on Good Friday, too) invaded the S. Viet consulate—mission to UN in NY Carol attempted a similar caper. Not that successful, but still arrested. So we are attempting some faint response to the victims.

Frida Danielle thrives and sends you burps and chortles of love. She is somewhere near 11 lbs. already. I'll save some space for Liz while assuring you of love and peace, all of which the Saviour promises us. Peace be to you, and to our friends. Be well and care for yourself. We love you.

> In Christ,
> Phil

[Dan's favorite place to retreat was Eschaton, the home of friend Bill Stringfellow.]

From Eschaton, Block Island April 15, 1974
Almost Sat. 15—Damian 1859

Dear Bruv—

Today I spent about 2 hrs. on a remote beach under even rarer sun reading short stories of Frank O'Connor. I think I had read most of them years ago but the setting + style were irresistible + I laughed aloud, rolled up my trousers + went wading in the surf which was so cold it scalded. Then walked home under the swaying dirt road that in places is about 2 plunge over the cliffs into the sea, the erosion being terrific. . . . Went 2 Mass about 4:30. We prayed for everyone in + out of sight.

Carol wrote 2day about initial enthusiasm on C'ville films in Cannes. They are invited 2 enter it + r preparing French subtitles, wh. I will have a chance 2 look at, soon.

The Angela Davis book is a road-trap of the 1st order, so bad it is not worth discussing. Quicky books being like bird seed, 4 bird brains. Very few corporate works qualify above 0. Our best testaments being letters of one or another—ie., Cleaver, Melville, yourself.

> Thank you,
> Daniel

[Phil asks Dan to send greetings to Thich Nhat Hanh, with whom Dan was living in Paris.]

Sun. May 26th [1974]

Dearest Bro—
    To recoup, in a measure, our past neglect. Just back from 2 hrs. in the country—at a prerevolutionary Quaker meeting house, ironically enough, named "gunpowder." A good discussion on prayer, and a liturgy. Everyone found it restorative.
    Yours of May 15th in yesterday. I understand you—one feels like dying (if it could only be constructive) in face of the terror and death around. It's almost as though every generation learns to ignore the blood soaked soil under their feet! The Holy Land and Europe—where has more blood been shed?
    Our Good Fri. friends face a 12 count indictment—2 of them felonies. The same old violent hogwash. I tell others that the only adequate response is to hit that rat's nest office again. Some may do just that.
    We have a couple of young guys with us—one from Chicago, and one from Albuquerque. It is I suppose, a quest, of 2 things—buying our elusive waves, as well as learning them. The last year has taught us much of the society, as well as of the primitive church. I'll leave space for Liz. We long for your return. Best love to Nhat Hanh and our friends. And esp. to you.

In Xto,
Phil

[Protesters, including Phil, created their own tiger cage that remained outside the Capitol until August 9. People from all over the East Coast chained themselves inside, fasted, prayed, and leafleted.]

"For your kindness is a greater good than life."—Ps. 63

Jun 3rd [1974]

Dearest Brother—
    A short scrawl, on the run. Am beginning to understand your love for the Psalms.
    We do a Tiger Cage thing in DC tomorrow, and then attempt to keep it going for a week. Next Tues., our friends try their Jesus defense, while concurrently, a liturgy similar to their own takes place at the selfsame site. Then we go home to see Freda for a coupla days while Carol, Jerry, and kids go to B.I. [Block Island]. Anyway, we try to keep a tempo going. Lottsa people coming through, we have

a young WRL [War Resisters League] woman from N. Mex with us now.

Every blessing for sessions in the Midwest. So how is it? We miss youse and hope you'll scoot this way on return. The little one chortles on the floor, and blows you a kiss. While Ned, Debbie, Mike Bucci, Mitch, Liz and me send warmest love + thanks.

> In Christ,
> Phil

June 15th [1974]

Dearest Brother—

The greetings from Thich Nhat Hanh arrived this morning, with your last observations in Paris and the Mideast. Also advice on the rice cake—typical that those Buddhists, beset by anguish for the folks at home, could think of us—already too pampered.

Please give us some advice—do you think it a good idea to send the Buddhists 2 thou? It can be from all of us. And can we send it through you? Let us know, dear bruv—we have nothing but superfluities.

So grateful you got the welcome at 98th. I feel in my bones that the Rev. piss ants will go very cautiously with you. The Little Fatso and Liz blooming. Everyone else too. We all collaborate in sending you beaucoup love.

> In the Lord,
> Phil

"For with you is the fountain of life; and in your light we see light."
Ps 36

Sat. June 22nd [1974]

Dearest Brother—The Lord's best treat in having you home.

We called Sarycuse tonight—Jerry claimed that Freda was stronger. Measures have improved her sleep and helped her to gather strength.

This little "kitt" has us pondering, I tell you. Daily, she grapples more and more with the human scene, and the environment. In a month, she'll be crawling all over these acres.

We are praying over the housing—and the Rev. authorities. Know that you have carte blanche here—forever or longer. As Debbie said, in the best remark of last night, "We felt we should honor him" (you). Well said. You are worthy of honor, and we would like to offer some.

So the love of all of us. And our gratitude to God for you. I often think of the low periods of old Gandhi, and how he picked himself up, and went on. Your return is an occasion for continuing—in the hope of Christ. Peace, dear brother and mucho love.

> Fraternally,
> Phil, Liz, Frida et al.

[ca. Oct. 1, 1974]

Dearest Dan—

I found the Conn. experience restorative in a sense—though they did run my _ss. But a change of pace, and of work—after a summer of slogging away here, it does wonders for the ego that one can be useful still on that circuit. There ain't anybody much—you and me? still speaking the truth. Guess the message got garbled through intermediaries. I think a useful ploy would be 8 of us, including only those capable of living the rarified thing (words and action) in order to do the constant of directions, symbols, solid nonviolent tactics etc. Even if nothing happens—I feel it will have valuable spinoffs.

As Peter Maurin would say, We are praying for the eyes.

Peace, love thanks.

> In the Lord + Brother,
> Phil

Give light to my eye that I may not sleep in death—Ps 13

[ca. Nov 15, 1974]

Brother—

A meeting rages upstairs in subdued fashion. Tough to fan any flames these days. Rather, people want to "talk." They have "questions." I heard one activist use "questions" four times in a 10 word sentence. Came across some wisdom from A.J. [Muste] recently. He advised that people had better make up their minds to act, lest limitless "talk" destroy any meaning attached to action.

Howsomever—loved your letter to [vice-chairman of President Ford's committee to draft rules for amnesty of Vietnam draft evaders, Charles] Goodell. Seems that once good guys—with no counterbalances—taste the dreadful dew of power, they're poisoned. Ole Charlie even has debts to Rocky [Rockefeller], who appointed him when Bobby was murdered.

That blurb came out in *People* magazine. Less bad than expected— though mention in that rag is a special humiliation, slightly less than *Playboy*. Anyway, out of it comes invitation to the talk shows in Chicago + Boston. So now we must make decisions on them—made more difficult by the fact that we can gas on what we choose.

Good trips around, dear brother. We too look for the weekend with longing. We all love you.

> Peace of Christ,
> Phil

Sat. Feb. 1st [1975]

Brother Dan—

Liz'll be writing more lengthily—but a scant word from this ole churl. Yer poem on Johnny Bread on our wall—can't tell you much about the asylum, so no need for comment. I will pore over it many times.

Cornell as you say, mob scene—turned away by hundreds. Of course, the kids have some smarts and remember the militancy of the 60's. Found the Gradys superb—no startling work, but good pluggin on a no. of human issues. I sense that they are priming up a base.

Waal, I came home Thurs. to big plans for Fri.—Liz and others planning a para liturgy in the Blight House, reading of Accords continuing, while a few planned to bloody up ole Glory in same Blight House. One toppled the flag over with an enormous clatter, and was promptly reduced horizontal by the guards, uptight from recent bombings. Liz went through her whole liturgy—no difficulty—the others hauled away. Through all of this, the lion hearted press censors itself.

We miss youse. Good luck in Houston and w. the housing. Peace dearest brother, and every benign gift from the Lord. Love you.

> In Xto,
> Phil, Liz, Frida, et al.

[March saw Dan and Liz arrested protesting President Ford's amnesty program together at the White House, where Phil was later arrested for chaining himself in a tiger cage. Phil speaks here of Dan's poems in his letters becoming wall decorations, their mother Freda's waning health, and Liz's pregnancy with Jerry Berrigan, born in April.]

Mar. 22nd [1975]

I greet you with Spring. Christ knows that any winter in this country is a long one.

Two pomes for our door. Liz has a full moon there. And we faithfully put them up—6 at this point. I will read and ponder yours on death—"I will imagine the way death comes." And perhaps understand Freda's letter when it comes. And that of the Viets, and Amurrrrricans, and my own.

Good show on giving Carol + Jerum a breather. As for Freda—she will go from intercessory role to intercessory role—she has sustained us. She will again. I have no fear for her, though I pray that she who endured so much, will slip painlessly in Abraham's arms. But she might be summoned to do the suffering until the last. For us all.

Liz great—though her time approaches. You should see the big one (Frida). She now walks officially—and belongs to the scene proportionately. A blessed Easter, and the Resurrection's hope. We love youse. And all send love.

Christ's peace,
Phil

Mar. 25th [1975]

Dearest Brother—
We're finishin' up details on the K and S thing. I think we'll touch some nerve ends on it. And maybe open up further dimensions on this horrifying nuclear thing. As it stands, the silence makes the whole world an asylum.

We are very affluent, and so will probably send Nhat Hanh and his folks two thousand this weekend. The young guys have broken into the painting game—we have pretty well broken down the welfare state nature of this shebang, if'n yew know what I mean. Lord! it took some n. viol. ass chewin' to accomplish that. Despite the rhetoric, our young friends were all for the bourgeois, and a rather comfortable patriarchy.

Liz flourishing—vibrantly strong + active. The doc sez that heart beat indicates a boy. But we will rejoice at either. We send you Easter love, joy, peace, gratitudes. We need His hope, huh?

Love you,
Phil, Liz, Frida—the whole sheebang

Apr. 7th [1975]

Dearest Brother—

Saw many friends in Philly—numberless devout ones asking fer you. Of course, nobody is/does anything, but rather congratulate themselves on hearing one like us at bargain basement prices. As usual, we become the action. But it reminds me of your observation—"the moral consequences of genocide." We're reaping them now, and those who have escaped number about as many as those who got out of Sodom.

We're wrenching heads on reaction to distraction/diversion by refugee and orphan in Vietnam. Did you catch [N. Vietnam prime minister] Pham Van Dong's condemnation of our rip off of Veet kids? Right to the point. As Tesi told me—"we kill their parents and then get sentimental orgasms over rescuing them." Only slightly less atrocious than napalming them.

Liz still waits—no rhythmic pains yet. Pains, but nothing irregular or sustained. It could happen tonight—or within a week. Liz somewhat longs to be 1 person again instead of two. That's natural enuf, I guess. Anyways, we'll call you when the Kingdom's heir arrives.

In the meantime, great luv to youse. The Savior's blessing, grace, peace. Everyone sends that.

Phil

[Liz gave birth to Jerome Berrigan on April 17.]

Sat. night May 31st [1975]

Dearest Brother—

Fresh from a shit session (here at Jonah) mostly a rationalization of 3 steps backward. (We have forgotten the 2 forward—too buried in memory).

And the rhetoric says—"This is a resistance community." What bird is it that sticks its head up asshole to get the next flight plan? I remember a classic metaphor of yours.

I've tried to come back to the theme of some splitting and leaving the nest. That bounces on the floor like one of Frida's turds. One sage sagely remarked that our trouble rose from differing notions of community—some (including me, I suppose) not accepting community as end in itself. That's the Roman heresy, it seems to me.

So the issue remains open, so they say. We have a "resistance" meeting tomorrow, and I'll suggest a serious action on my part. Have gone over it with Liz—her remark, "That's what we're supposed to be about, isn't it." She's a Christian woman—I can compliment her no better.

Anyway—Jerome has come and I would like to challenge the parole thing (inter nos) before it ends. Moreover, as you know dear brother, I think it basic to say lovingly "up yours" to the hucksters and war profiteers and misanthropes. So have vaguely thought of a caper for Aug. 6th, with some ex-prisoners, or whatever. Will try to give it more flesh in the weeks ahead. Please tell me what you think—I value your estimation as no other.

You are light to our feet, and power where it counts. Luv youse.

From all—in Xto,
Phil

Mon. June 9th [1975]

Dearest Brother—

Back from a fine two day stint with Freda and the Maywoods. Our mother came down Sat. night, ate a hearty meal, and enjoyed the antics of the two little creatures. The intervening months have exacted their price (the stroke etc.) but I thought her excellent, all considered. Maria and Carla [Berrigan] took excellent care of the small citizens. And it was so good to do a solid yaaaak thing with Charlotte and Jerry. As usual, they bust—as for us, in a truly loving way. And sent us home loving them more.

Still working at planning the summer's protest. It goes typically slowly (given the times) yet with some hope and effort. We have looked at AEC facilities (appalling!), and have taken a tour through a huge Johns Hopkins research facility—the largest campus effort of its kind in the country. So something may spring—but presently at least, the outrage is not there. Or should one call it perception? In a sense, the more our people master the roots of rhetoric, the more they arm themselves against it.

The smallest heir emerges with more and more of his own character. He is very strong (rolls over at will) and watches things with hyperinterest. Thank God—we are very blessed.

We think of you constantly, and are waiting for a first hand and recent report. Liz goes up to Rochester for 2 days tomorrow. She will take Jerum along. Peace brother, and the bestest and mostest of love. From all sisteren and brethren.

In Jesu,
Phil

[Every day between July 1 and August 9 Jonah House brought models of the atomic bombs Little Boy and Fat Man to the steps of the Capitol.]

Happy the people whose strength you are. . . . They go from strength to strength.—Ps 84

July 4th [1975]

Dearest Brother,

Liz and the kids down to a vigil at [Secretary of Defense James] Schlesinger's house. And others go to Ft. McHenry tonight to greet Ford on one of his patriotic jawbonings. And then, after, we will do the effort on the capitol steps with Fat Boy. A little life, not a helluva lot, but a little.

One can predict the regimen down to the wire—people up and down, in and out. I must in addition think of Liz and the children with this group of friends. None of them are esp. together, and/or blazing torches. They range from the very young to the shook. By and large, we have a common denominator, for the most part, drab. To risk a good stretch on ice under these circumstances may push faith too far. I dunno.

I know you understand from the talk the other day that implicitly, you're invited. Would never attempt anything w/out sharing it with you, share it under any circumstances. As for me, I rely on your superb sense of what is best—for me and Liz, for you, for everybody. And I know that any decision of yours is perfectly in accord with your discernment. Peace to you, and love in large measure. From the Lord, also.

                              Phil

July 13th Sun. [1975]

Dearest Brother—

Waal—A tough, ambitious, paint job for four days—with the community striving mightily, if sometimes ineptly. Now we must prepare for the BOMBS on the Capitol steps. Liz does superb work with graphics—we have one Bomb nearly built in our cellar already.

Both Alber's office and the Capitol Police have called to assure us of all welcome and cooperation. When it comes to us, the b_stards are surely educable. When it comes to their own crimes, not so surely so.

As for Aug 6th—we apparently have the people, and now need to do some work. I got in touch with [Daniel] Ellsberg + following the phone call, wrote him the scoop. A friend from Nat'l SANE [National Committee for a Sane Nuclear Policy] will try to do some interviews with leaders in said office, trying to get geographical layouts. And this week, we will circumspectly check approaches and accesses, and huddle with the Hartford folk this weekend. Other details will appear in the course of reflection—but we should have, with God's help, a clearer panorama for when we see youse.

The babies thrive like young marigolds—so much to thank God for. Just back from 4 hrs. before Schlesinger's house in the teeming rain. Reports have it that the bizarre so and so is hyper with the Cross on his front lawn, and quiet, determined demonstrators. I cling to my thesis—that if we could do such a caper around the clock for several months, these spooks would go bananas, and police would drag anti-war people away. We pray daily for youse, and send mighty love. So to the brethren also, to Bill + Anthony. And Christ's good peace. Write us and have good weather at B.I.

Phil

[Phil hints at the tendency for others in Jonah House to live off community money without taking seriously the commitment to resisting injustice he and Liz shared. It would be a persistent frustration they faced in building and developing Jonah House.]

Aug. 16th [1975]

Dearest Brother—

A relief to hear from youse—yers cheered us mightily.

Good news this morning—Ladon Sheats and his sidekick Jay will return from Vancouver and join us. This after long confab with Shelley + Jim [Douglass], who agree on this as the best course. Both are excellent prospects—good resisters, sensitive and intelligent. Moreover, they have imagination + initiative—something we are not notorious for, outside of the vets like Liz and me.

Others apparently wish to go their own way, and to use their own means. Once we saw this as inevitable, Liz and I gulped and tried to salvage something by avowing support for their consciences and their efforts. So it stands, with thank God, no great bitterness or breach.

So it is Joan Cavanagh, Joan Burds, Ned, Liz, myself and our 2 friends from Georgia, who will arrive in some 2 weeks time. I thank God we have trimmed some fat from the lean. As for those who leave, we can only commend them to the Spirit, assure them of love and support and hope they will rise to a challenge of sorts. But the darkness seems to encroach, doesn't it?

Will send this home. Wish we could join you at Maywood, but must scramble with too many items, including the everpresent one for bread. As I mentioned to you—those who prove most unyielding and self-centered are invariably the most expensive. And they exploit the community and its exchequer to promote their own desires and directions. They love community when it suits them.

But I mean all this to be essentially hopeful. I must come to NJ for a coupla talks on the 14th and 15th of Sept. Could we arrange for a palaver? Liz indomitable, the babies spurting, we are all well. And we love you, send you the Lord's peace and His every good gift. No—God has not turned from us—He's just unusually soft-spoken. Not as long as such as you go to the vineyard daily.

> In Xto,
> Liz, Phil, et al.

Fri. Aug. 22nd [1975]

Dearest Brother—

This'll miss you on return from Syracuse. So grateful you could have time with Freda. I can imagine what it means to her.

A week of scrambling around for painting jobs—and painting. A coupla pissers in fact. Figger if I can still hack it on the business end of a 40 ft. ladder, then not quite ready for the bone heap yet.

Got a very nice letter from ed. of *Cath Worker* in answer to a request that I be able to write for them: Sorry! Dorothy etc. etc. Very kindly, but very clearly stated. But Dorothy loves us, and that's the main thing.

Hope to see youse brother, before you leave. Could you come down for a day of rejoicing? Love you—we'll pray for the sem's retreat. The kids send fierce hugs + wet kisses to Uncle Dan.

Peace, love, thanks.

> In Xto
> Liz, Phil et al.

[On October 6, Phil and twenty others were arrested at Pratt and Whitney's fiftieth anniversary air show. He told the press their actions, described below, were performed to "break through the frightening amnesia of the American public so they can remember the meaning of these planes."]

Fri. Oct. 10th [1975]

Dearest Brother—

Thinking of youse. Scrawling this on return from Boulder, and Ludwig's scenario. Up and down, in and out scene. Some reality and a lot of academic, abstract flotsam. Ludwig does what he knows best, and no faithful departure from that. But I think this—what would the Boulder scene be w/out him? Bad as it is, certainly worse.

The confrontation in Hartford last Sat. and Sun. got all over the country. Of course, per media, the name Berrigan went central, which has elements of truth and elements of ambiguity about it. Afterall, sez I, who has taken (within the ranks of demonstrators) more of the sweat and tears than usns? But the action itself once more proved to me the prime importance of spirit and resolution. Security was tight—they had Marines, Air Force GI's, Pratt and Whitney security men, local cops and God knows what else there. And that didn't discourage nor deter us. I operated on the first plane with Joan Burds and Tom O'Brien, a tough young New Jerseyite arrested with you on March 1st. He got a bottle of blood into the cockpit, stone in front of the Marine guard, who seemed befuddled by what he did. Meanwhile, Joan got up on a rear wing and sprayed Death on the tail before being dragged down. I worked on the mid fuselage, and when grabbed by a civilian after DE, went for the nose, and got the same DE there before security men throttled me and muscled me off. They were furious and rough—one threatened to "use that spray can in your G.D. face." Others practically propelled me through the crowd to a waiting cop car, handcuffed behind the back, jamming the cuffs to their tightest notch. The others got similar signs of endearment. Then the cops sped us off to the E. Hartford police station. In 15 min., the second jet went down, and the treatment got rougher. And a mob began to form. Ladon Sheats had to dodge several blows; John Bach got kicked in the head and ribs while on the ground; another young guy lost his glasses as his face was thrust into the ground; the cops and civilians badly manhandled two of the women. They arrested everyone—those merely in death costumes, those leafleting, those doing nothing. Sheats told me (he worked on the third plane) that he thanked God for the

Marines and cops who protected him (and others) from the mob. This much is certain, he said, the mob would have beaten us badly, if not worse if it had not been for the cops and GI's.

So it went—those assigned to the 4th plane wisely waited until some rage subsided, and then, on an individual basis, sprayed the 4th, 5th, and 6th military jets.

Treatment in jail went very well—the cops settled down and gave us notable consideration. Some immediately went on a fast. The State's Bond Commissioner showed up, set low bail on us all, and we all promptly rejected it. Since the E. Hartford jail had no capacity to hold us, we non-cooperated with a move to Hartford jail (and the women to a women's prison near the coast). Outside, the press were stumbling over one another white-faced and awed. I got a few remarks to them as the cops carried one to the police van. Over in Hartford (the jail goes back to 1870, and is packed to its mouldy rafters) they put us in deadlock (indiv. cells in a max. security section) and we settled in for the night. Back at Pratt and Whitney, they swiftly cleaned up the planes, but fearing another wave of demonstrators, and influenced by the adverse publicity, closed down the military section of the picnic. On Sun., they let us out twice to talk to one another—the food was decent and we caught up on sleep. I felt abjectly grateful for the whole crew—they were superbly self-controlled and non-violent in jail and out. Liz getting the word around and calming fears. Where does one find her equal?

On Mon. morning, was scheduled to speak at Colo. State in Ft. Collins on Mon. night, I determined to stay in jail if the judge didn't let us walk on our own recognizance. Against likelihood, he did, and I spoke to the press, raced to the airport, missed a plane, and caught another at 4 PM. I found the United Airlines folk strangely cold and uncooperative, and remembered that both they + P.W. were subsidiaries of United Aircraft. They could have perhaps gotten me on the plane missed. In Denver, they had a light plane waiting for us, and we got up to Ft. Collins and the campus in ½ hr., where Ludwig held the fort with eloquence on Civil Religion, the Berrigans, and readings from your poetry. Spoke at 2 campuses in Denver also.

Hope there is something from you waiting at home. We will presumably now go with the mine shaft idea, hypothetically taking a bust on the White House side of Pa. Ave. and another group digging a mine shaft (or grave) in Lafayette Park. We commend you to Christ and His Spirit. And this comes with maximum love and remembrance—

In Xto,
Phil

[On November 17, Phil and Dan were arrested as part of the Disarm or Dig Graves campaign, digging graves on the White House lawn in reaction to a plan to build bomb shelters. Earlier that month Phil was arrested for painting "Disarm Now" on the British, Indian, and French embassies. This letter was attached to a note, reading, "Dear Warden—Please let this letter get to Father Berrigan—I've heard of censorship of mail to prisoners—This is just a note of friendship—so, don't worry about its content—Thank you for respecting freedom."]

Wed. Jan 28th [1976]

Dan—

Waal, brother, the young 'uns left this morning. So we look to your trial tomorrow, and news of you. Did some solid praying today, and you were uppermost in heart and spirit.

Have gotten down to a regimen of prayer, writing, reading and exercise. Some more good books arrived today, so that cup brimmeth over. And the brothers continue to care for me.

The chow remains superb, plenty of mail, plenty of time to tune up the spirit—it is really a privileged existence.

We will think of you tomorrow, and pray that the outcome will serve the Kingdom. You will certainly see to that. Thanks for the great visit yesterday. Know you will care for the back zealously and well. For the sake of all of us. Love you, brother. And Christ's good peace.

P.B.

Tues. Feb 3rd [1976]

Dearest Brother—

Fine visit with Liz—she has trial on Fri. and faces it with characteristic aplomb.

The poems too go on the wall. Love the equation between 10,000 words and the one deed. The Balto. one was read me at the marriage of Mike Egan—Amen! I'll have a first class wall before release. I've shared some with friends—not right that I should have a monopoly on them. Seems to me that your language—like your life—has deepened over the years, grown more incisive, wise, humorous.

Just killed another fly—they all have blood in them. Whose could it be but prisoners' blood? If only more folks could see the Predator State as we've seen the flies of D.C. Jail—gorged with people's blood.

Getting so I can turn off the noise at will. And slowly, the brothers grow more cordial. Scandalous what an easy time the life is for me. The grace comes in giant doses—grace won chiefly by you and others of the specifics of Christ's Redemption of me—you, Liz, Freda, Carol + Jerry, the community at Jonah, the little ones, the books and sacraments, the Soup here—the list could run off this page.

What else? We're praying for a good Fla. trip. I love you. We will make it, one way or the other. Mebbe with the Lamb's mark only. But we'll make it. Peace, brother mine!

> In the Lord,
> Phil

Fri. Feb 6th [1976]

Brother Mine!

Waaal, looks like the pomes go back on my wall. Had things tidied up against the possibility of enlightenment from the Judge. But alas! The ole boy wanted 1. a promise not to break the law again and 2. contrition. All of which struck me as non-negotiable.

Anyway, we had a nice chat—the old reprobate and me. When we began to palaver, no one was in the courtroom. But during the profound exchange, Frida came to stand next to me, all unnoticed. Ran into a very human and friendly marshal nonetheless, and on the way out, was able to speak to Liz, Joan C, Joan B and give the little ones a hug.

Lord, the mechanics of going to court are a form of deterrence in themselves. One starts at 6 AM and spends the greater time in that old Amurrrican institution—the bullpen. I was particularly fortunate in being back by 3 PM—others will be in at a time resembling ours of the first day 11 PM plus. In the future, we all ought to be particularly wary of lawyers' motions.

Will try to pilfer an envelope for this. Davis brought more books—I'm well stocked with necessities, and more. And the measure still overflows.

Thanks so much for recent poems—esp the one written on your return to NYC. Your love and consideration continues to astound me. And for the visit the other day. Care for the neck and spine—for the sake of the Kingdom. And despite the pain, please do the exercises. Love you, dear brother. Every peace and good grace.

> In His Name,
> Phil

Tues Mar 9th [1976]

Brother Mine—

Jerry writes that Freda has become more stable, and stronger. Bless her great heart—she doesn't yet want to leave her boys, or this world to her boys.

Good meeting today. We decided to do a dual action during Holy Week at the Pentagon, and at [Secretary of Defense Donald] Rumsfeld's home—c.d. at both places—the latter a dig-in. It'll stretch us because the vigil prior to Apr. 15th damnit, I see that's Passion Week + is a 24 hr. affair. Maybe 3 days prior to the action. But the spirit is good, and I'm sure that friends will respond.

How's by you, and how's the back? Wish sombuddy was at hand to get you over to Doc Rose. We love you and send you much love. And as always, Christ's good peace.

> In Him,
> Liz, Phil et al.

Wed. Mar. 19th [1976]

Dearest Brother—

We feel for yez at Haaaavaaahd—that may be the worst campus in the country (world). But it's credit to youse to walk in and dare the Prin. + Powers that infest that place. Suspect that the climate will be lighter—there just ain't that much energy, even with Roman Zionists.

Jerry writes that Mama has returned to solid food and strength. Astonishing! I had thought we will soon gather for her funeral. Shows how little I know her and her temper. She will I expect, go suddenly sometime—when this or that hits her with force. But the steady declines she comprehends utterly—and makes provision for them. And she recoups.

We thank youse for that last great letter. And Lee Griffith writes a fine piece on Christian Resp. toward the BOMB, using Barth's contention that it threatens everything, because it threatens the faith of the Church.

We'll keep you up on Holy Week. If you miss it, don't fret. There'll be others. Smacks from the children, love from all, best thanks, peace. You're always with us.

> Christ's peace,
> Liz, Phil, everbuddy

[From 1975 to 1977, Jonah House residents dug graves outside the Pentagon and symbolically poured blood multiple times. Here, Phil writes from jail after one such action.]

Alexandria City Jail—Monday May 3rd [1976]

Dear Brother—

Waal, as they say, history is cyclic. This joint would remind one of Balt. County jail in Towson—5 two-person cells with a shower and rec. area outside. The food is fair, and I find them a fairly decent, amenable crew. Despite 24 hr. lockup crap, one has better control over the noise and human relations—a departure from DC Jail. "Count it all joy" as James' NT book would say.

The demo went well enuf. We saturated the columns again—caused huge confusion and anger, and were duly busted. They got the cleansing operation going in split-seconds, astonishing their alacrity. They don't want such a festival photographed, and communicated.

Would have gotten this off sooner were it not for lack of commissary. But wanted to observe your birthday, dear brother. Early May always has heavy significance for me because of it. One has at least, the annual opportunity to reflect on a great truth—that everything concerning us—and because of us, conc. Church and State,—began with you. If you had not had the faith + guts to go with the Jebs—Lord, where would we be? I suspect that mediocrity would have defined us, especially me. And it appears, dear brother, that an initial step (yours) explains so much. It has dominated subsequent decisions—again yours—and these decisions have freed countless others, notably me.

I reflect now that some of the early options—civil rights as well as anti-war—tended to be solid and therefore irrevocable, simply because I had a tradition of justice that was immediate, "family," coming from you. A living example. Guess every example tends to erode if it isn't immediate, personal.

So I guess dear brother—through all this rambling, that you have been chief grace to me—greatest save the Lord. Or more accurately, the Lord's through you. I'll try to forget less. And to remain true to Him and to you.

Hear you brought home a snafu back from California. Please give the bones a better shake. We gotta guard ourselves as precious real estate. There ain't hardly anybody ready for some truth—12 in the country?

I've had the luxury here to sort out the agonies as you call them, of the past weeks. To discover that they weren't so monumental at all. Of course, now it's hindsight but the fact remains—I coulda done a helluva lot better with them. Maybe I've picked up a grain of wisdom or two. One is the realization that I'm so immeasurably blessed to have this community—Liz and the rest—and the resistance that does come from it.

Love you. They give one good time here, apparently. So I should be out by the weekend. Fare thee well.

> Peace + love from Big Brother, Head
> Honcho,
> Phil

Tues. June 1st [1976]

Dan—

The contact with Carol + Jerry + Freda good and refreshing. Freda maintains a lucid calm and peace so characteristic of her. She understands well when we ask for prayers.

Your McSorley letter excellent. What, one might ask, distinguishes G'town from College Park or Haavahd? Nothing substantial, it appears. In fact, less pretension with the latter?

But now we get ready for the Pentagon stew, and I hope, Mr. Rumsfeld. Thass abooot it—must get upstairs and help get out Year One. It is a so-so issue. Jerry sez the back is improved. This comes with more than thicker than blood—a love and unity in the spirit.

Oh yes, an offer from *Viva* (as it calls itself, the internat'l mag. for women) for interview w/ Liz + myself. To contrast, if you can feature it, with Calley and new wife. We will decline mostly for reasons of *Viva*'s trashy substance. It is mostly garbage can illusion. Love you.

> In Christ's light + life,
> Liz, Phil et al.

[ca. June 15, 1976]

Dan Brother—

Back in the paintin' business to support the summer's work. My draggin' ass has an embarrassing connection w/ a limpin' mind. Know you'll understand. Gettin' a little old, bruv. Don't bounce back with the same Indian rubber facility.

Had a nasty little scene last Fri. night. Hold up. Two nasty young punks invaded us with drawn .38—trying their hand at Terror. I jumped the one with the gun in the cellar, but wasn't quick enuf or sumpin! His buddy helped him and they kept the Sat. nt. special secure. They got us for about $40 and in the process ripped off the house and car keys. So we've been alternately changing locks and giving thanks that no one was hurt. Hopefully, we can take some n.v. measures with the neighborhood to erect a little vigilance against such local Kissingerisms.

Liz her indomitable self—the kinder puttin' us through changes—delightful ones. Little Fatso won't walk. We all miss youse. Is the Lord treatin' yew well? Tell us if He ain't. His light, life, peace. And our love.

Liz, Phil, et al.

Sat. July 17th [1976]

Dearest Bruv—

The friends in DC—thass a saga. On Thurs. they dumped ashes—to which we will all be antiseptically reduced—(lots of them, 2 hundred lbs. on the W. Dept. steps) with adequate explanation. 5 arrested, Ladon included. All released, including Ladon, inexplicably. On Friday, they had ample enuf time to put in a neat vegetable garden (brought some fine plants), and 7 arrested. Nothing daunted, 5 more returned in the afternoon and planted again—all arrested. This became a little much, so the poolees ended up by holding 6 and letting 6 go on personal recognizance. Jay and Ladon now in the slammer. Tom Lewis busted, (deelighted at that (long moratorium)).

So we are puffed up with pride. And thank God for the spirit that He keeps alive among us. Know you will rejoice also, and pass on glad tidings. Everyone here loves you.

Peace of Christ,
Liz, Phil, et al.

Bridal Dance

The man hangs around
idle as a man
in frontier town at noon

hangs around
he looks, first glance, like an idler
a nark, a tout, a drifter
an unreconstructed character
taking his ease
ease! he's choosing his own death
month day hour minute
executioners instruments
he shifts on his feet—
sublime, subtle shift of history's sands
grain on grain
of golden behavior
or a bride, choosing her
trousseau, making much of this
Unrepeatable Great Day
models materials colors weaves
fugues processionals
For all time the bridal dance
goes on goes on goes on
his translucent marrow bones
move in the world's close spaces
his flesh like wild roses
his bones like the hops of roses
his eyes an impossible communion
his skill, to make the oppositions one
his beckonings beginnings
his his his perpetual
ALLELUIA
HIS HANDS FLEXING LIKE WINGS
a moment before flight
can it be can it be can it be be be be
his limbs emotive as a cloak his
garments the tegument of a flying squirrel
his joy the astonishment
of unrewarded humanity
his awe an open supulcre
and HOLY HOLY HOLY his perpetual
self praise universal praise
miraculous enclosing his body
and his cosmic body
his wounds bound up & he binding

in healing exhaltation all wounds up
& the dominion of fools extended who in the world's
    estimate had no place
    & the cup of gall transfigured; come taste
    you who are without money
    then
    let the poem go nowhere as our God goes no-
    where
    the sanctus of the non self
    sons and daughters come
    there will be room
    for all who come
    MARANATHA come lord Jesus

[ca. Oct. 26, 1976?]

Dear Brother (Tues PM)
    I had a good visit with Mama, she is what they call "stabilized"—a helluva word for much improved. I recalled to her how she was so congested and barely breathing a couple of months ago. She listened, no comment.
    Think I'll get down by yez next week, weighing things that seems easiest, love 2 get a little quiet time w- you + Liz above all!
                            Love brother, at your side,
                            Daniel

[Phil details plans that would result in their arrest at the Pentagon, refusing to leave the premises while dressed as a beggar (Dan) and a ghost (Phil).]

Mon. Nov. 8th [1976]

Brother Mine—
    Jes back from Atl. Life Comm. retreat in York, Pa. Liz gave a superb presentation of where we stand with the BOMB. Some 60 folks there, unfortunately however, some drifters, star gazers and retread hippies. Dunno how we can restrict these affairs to serious people—ready for personal change and some risk. I would hand-pick the roster but I think such a measure would sponsor howls of anguish.

We'll open hostilities at the W. Dept. for the 3 days prior to Thanksgiving. Wed. we'll have an inside action as well as busts on the steps. Could you possibly make a portion of it?

Looks like we picked up a sterling couple from Toronto—Margaret and Ken Hancock. They'll come next summer hopefully, with their tiny daughter Rachel (3 mos.). Very impressive people—we like them thoroughly.

I'll miss you on the 17th—but we'll hope for Thanksgiving. Miss youse, dear brother. Every grace and strength, and best love from all.

In the Lord,
Phil

[Freda Berrigan died on December 22, age 91, with Phil and Jerry at her side. Phil's homily at her funeral on December 24 expressed his "incapacity—or the incapacity of anyone—to appraise a life like Freda's. In such a life one can only explore the mystery of themes, of meanings and markings. And then strive to remember, to learn and to grow up." Because their mother knew God, and knowing God means knowing justice, her death is an occasion to struggle "against the bombing of the innocent, against victimizing the weak, against the put-down of women and blacks, against imperilment of everyone by atomic wrath." He concluded, "We of the family wish you her memory—which is to say, her peace and her life. We wish you the same breath—the Lord's last gift to us—His peace and His wounds."

This poem was sent from Dan to Phil, attached to a newsletter that read, in part:]

January 1977

Dearest friends,

Our mother Freda died on December 22 after a long twilit interim. Toward the end, the only sentence her wasted body could form was a simple I love you. We who love her will never hear those words spoken in such a way again.

Philip announced at the funeral that three of us, he, Jerry and I, would honor our mother's memory on the steps of the Pentagon on December 28. Accordingly, on that day, some 75 people from east and west, gathered there. It was the day of remembrance of the slaughtered innocents. We were denying Herod his historical prey—here and now, the children of the world. Twenty nine of us were arrested for pouring our blood on the pillars and chaining our selves to the portals.

Many of the Pentagon resisters were given heavy sentences; among them Elizabeth McAlister, 6 months, which she is presently serving. At this writing, Philip is also in jail for the grave dig-in at the Rumsfeld home.

> One night
> while poor daft souls
> gathered moon moss scavenged in dark closets
> or hopefully
> died
> you
> rose from bed
> combed your
>   waist long hair
> quietly, quietly
> (children asleep
>   in the house)
> from room to room
>   went
>   touching
> the moonstruck
> faces of children
> then
> opened the door of the house
> —which of itself closed—
> stepped into
> and were
> that
> light

> Freda Berrigan
> 1886–1976

[In addition to the arrests Dan mentions above, Phil was also arrested on January 8 for raising banners outside President Carter's home in Plains, Georgia.]

Thurs. Jan. 13th [1977]

Dearest Brother—

Waaal—here we are again. Who was it? One of us I suppose—who said we'd be in and out of jail for the rest of our lives. An easy prediction to make. Supposing that the "rest" of our lives is not abruptly terminated by mass suicide.

From our standpoint—this rehabilitation center ain't half bad. Apparently, Montgomery County is rich enuf to shake a few bucks loose for a tolerably decent lockup. The food is good; prisoners friendly; staff considerate. Ran into a case worker who knew us; "respected our efforts;" and did his level best to help.

Mebbe we didn't say it that often, but profound and repeated thanks for that return from the W. Coast, and for your presence, great humor, wisdom. Thanks to you, we'll make it with elan and laffs—giving the lames a race for the goal. See youse on the 21st. I get out the next day—we'll celebrate. Luv to youse, gratitude, peace.

From Brother Jesus and
Brother Phil

[ca. Jan 26, 1977]

Dear sister and brother,

I keep thinking of you all, the chilluns, and Freda. Liz put it so well in her letter, it gave me a lot to ponder. When I think of Freda, it's with a rush of gratitude for her life; together with immense relief that the long loneliness and near death are over. And I know too that that lovely outreach of the oldest to the youngest, will go on, better than ever, more.

Please be well, more later,
♥ Daniel

Sat. Mar. 5th [1977]

Dearest Brother—

Lottsa mail awaiting me—very heartening. Out in Ky., the Presbyterians and So. Baptists ate me alive. Or sucked me dry—by Fri., they had me on the ropes. Can you picture it—the So. Bapt. Seminary has 2,300 students—many of them tough, earnest, poor, Bible-lovin', red-neck kids. I found their sincerity very touching. They would come up and wring my paw and voice—"Thank you fer comin'!" All they apparently wanted was some Bible applied to the horror scene. I think something may come of it. If they ever cultivated a real dislike of Big Brother, it might well prove interesting. The mountain kids among them have a populist side.

More later. What you did for us during the 30 days will see light in life and in witness. The whole crew of Jonah will thank you eventually. We owe you—so much, so much. Thank you for your brotherhood as well, for your love. I return it as well as I can.

Christ's peace,
Phil

Tuesday [March 15 1977]

HERE COMES THE AMERICAN MESSIAH OF THE WEEK

Used to talk as though words
were salvation birds. Saw his words plucked
out of mid air, throats wrung; corpses or slogans.
Resolved then on silence, which in principle
couldn't be debased.
    No?
    The National Election Campaign
cast up an inspired deaf mute. He raced for the throne
under a banner that blazed, sunrise to sunset;
And the hands of his followers fluttering like inven-
    tive apes;
HEAR NO EVIL SPEAK NO EVIL
In one year, tongues were branded. Two, ears were in
    village stocks.

[Phil and Liz received sixty–day sentences for their December 28 action, during which time Jonah residents Ladon Sheats and Joan Burd took care of Frida and Jerry. Trying to reconcile their jail time with the meaning for their children at home, Phil journaled, "Do it to remember the dead, but to fight like hell for the living!"]

Tues. Mar. 15th [1977]

Dear Dan—

Greetings! The books came, two packages. Will do level best to share them w/ Liz, though I suspect you made provision for her also.

Liz and I can write intra jail now. And we have our 15 min. phone + plate glass window every week. Leave it to Liz to ferret out these obscure regulations and to get some mileage from them. Waal sez I, they owe us a few tiny privileges—even on the level of quid pro quo.

Librarian showed me a *Wash. Star* article. Tass the Russian news agency, in counteracting Amer. rhetoric on violation of human rights, cites Liz and myself as current victims of govm't repression. Reference to fed. treatment during Vietnam era, and now contra arms race. Pot calling kettle black, huh? Ludicrous!

Care fer yerself. Don't cast any anxiety this way—am tip top, never felt better. Much love to you, brother, grace and peace.

                                        In Xto,
                                        Phil

Tues. Mar. 29th [1977]

Dear Brother—

A quick one to acknowledge yours of Friday—all to the good. Notice you keep up the hectic schedule.

This morning we had a rhubarb on the food during inspection. I told them that most of us returned to our cells hungry—3 times a day. They went up the wall, and since, there has been improvement. I inquired around our cell block discretely—how about a day's fast? One said okay—the others hung scared. I was not surprised.

Had about 45 min. with the old Sheriff this morning. Wrote him about an interview to discuss his jail and he responded. Found him a pretty open, fair minded old veteran. Everything I brought up was discussed fairly, and with no trace of defensiveness.

Liz has run into some rocky times. There was a blow up this morning with some of the women, who tend to be quite damaged types. Anyway, Liz spoke to them bluntly about their bullsh_t and it wasn't gratefully taken. Three of them threatened her with some heat. So she decided some changes were indicated—tried to get back into Alexandria (full up); tried to go to solitary (full up); and tried Len Rubenstein (lawyer) about possibilities with the Judge. There it rests.

It's a little bitter to swallow—Liz has been thru so much. But tempers cool, and Liz is resourceful. I'll try to see her tomorrow and get it all close hand. So please don't worry. Once it gets out in the air, there's usually a marked improvement.

Outside of that—all well. Thinking of you, dear brother, and sending you much love.

In the Lord—

Phil

Tuesday Apr. 12th [1977]

Dear Dan—

Liz and I spread out your gift (poem) and read it slowly last night, marveling all the way. What an exquisite "release" gift for Liz! Signs of your spirit and great love are all around us. Would that we could say thanks adequately to you.

Clark and I went to the produce terminal this morning reading your Psalms and commentary along the way. What a stunning exhibition of truth and perception.

Well, we meet tomorrow night and then get on to the Blight House and Pentagon on Thursday. C.D. on Friday. It'll be low-keyed—but the best manageable at this time.

So brother, we know you will move people there, if they can be moved. The gangsters are making death warrants of the blank checks. "Peace be with you," as the Lord says. And best love from us, from the little people, from all hereabouts.

In Big Brother, Big Lord—

Phil

[This letter was attached to another, explaining that Dan was declared "an Undesirable Alien by the Canadian government" for an incendiary pro-life speech in Ottawa. "Just for the record," he wrote Phil, "when the trip was rudely interrupted, I had intended to say the following; it made little sense to protect the unborn and to abandon adults; to poverty, to malnutrition, to death by capital punishment or war. That the real question was the building of a national and world order in which no one need die rudely or live despairingly. That there was room enough, food enough, world enough, for the living. But not if the military continued to stake out the world for its brutal own. That in any case, I was not ecstatic at the legalizing (or illegalizing) of a question which lies outside the competence of the law; belongs in the hands of a loving community. Of which communities we had few alas examples, whether in Canada or at home. And so on."]

May into June [1977]

COURAGE

> It is not an invention of the gods, in fact they are
> > afraid of it
> > nor of the so called godlike who have at their
> > > command
> all the paraphernalia—noble profiles, headlines, public
> > fealty.
> > I was once told to seek it out—so and so had the
> > > formula.
> Alas. He had perished, the circumstances hard to
> > uncover.
> > A few friends told me he died well
> > Life was torn from his side like a heart.
> > Uncomforted, I thought this a clue.

I'll be in Syracuse Thursday PM. Have 2 leave Sat PM 2 preach in R. Island.

Thinking of you on retreat, get good prayerful waves from you all.

I had 2 rush up to N. Hampshire 2 see Bishop Colin Winter who has had a massive heart attack. I would not give him much of a chance of long survival, think exile is killing him.

Love + soon!
Daniel

June 17th [1977]

Dearest Brother—

Again, thank you *de profundis* for your visit, for your presence here, which always lends us fresh perspective and renewed courage.

What hit me most deeply I think, was not so much the "mistakes," but my infantile doubts of you. Thank God, your great heart weathered even those, allowing me to learn from them like some sullen and backward teenager. But then, on wider reflection, it was always your love of the Gospel, and the magnanimity with which you shared that—that gave any meaning and direction to this poor life. I remember your saying once that we all need a teacher. Well, you have been my teacher—as well as brother and dearest comrade. And had I not had my teacher, nothing would have moved, nor happened, nor "emerged"—as Tony would say.

The above doesn't say 1/100th of it. But at least, a brother's love and I hope, permanent gratitude and sense of debt. I'll try to be a bit more worthy of you.

And we love you—Liz, the kids, me, everyone here. Every gift of Pentecost.

Phil

[For a number of years Dan volunteered doing menial tasks at St. Rose Home, a hospice facility in New York City.]

[ca. July 1, 1977]

Dears,

Rudy my 35 year old sea captain died last night at St. Rose's—brain tumor. Sister said his growth was unbelievable; toward the end like a second head. He had 2 little daughters, we used 2 talk + hold hands a good deal when he had a good day. He was beautifully gentle + uncomplaining.

Love ♥ Soon
Daniel

Friday 2 [Sept 1977]

Dears,

I was grateful for the couple of hours in the fields, grateful for the kind reception, the great dinner, for all you were able to put together in a short time, alone almost. . . . I'm torn as always not being with you more.

No need to say the 'ultimate' resistance discussion left me awash. It is one thing to sit down with Nhat Hanh and talk about these terrible things, another to have them on one's door, brought up by the nearest and dearest in the world, yourselves. But let me try the following. (I don't think by the way, I'm writing out of panic. I think I live in the mind, as do you, with the doomsday cloud very close, and the necessary question out of the gospel, what can we do? And of course one's own death and the deaths of others, including our family, is always part of this, both fact and hope; and to be faced.)

But I don't think what I said yestiddy will change much. To ask what do we do if the mads throw the grenade, is at least two edged. On the one hand, will there be anything to do? If there is, a group at the Pentagon, ready to pray, vigil, throw blood, do what has always been done; how crucial! On the other hand, what can we know? It all may develop so fast no one has much more time than an act of contrition or some immediate relief work would consume.

But if we're agreed that a long fast takes up more important work, depletes energies etc., what is to be said of this thing? A finality, to say the very least. And then the maligning of one's good name; which of course is no new or big deal as far as any of us is concerned; but it is the opposite of communion or agreement, and has to be taken into account, esp. in the Cath. community which despite all, is still our own.

I would think that the reality of 'greater risk to match greater crime' ought to be along the lines of former experience, i.e., nonviolent felonies.

I've been reading the prison letters of Gramsci, whom Mussolini locked up until he died. And that brought to mind all the thousands of others who paid and pay such a price. The cold comfort I guess is that without them, things would be even more bestial than they are.

In any case, I love you, and try to stay with it. And this is enough for now.

Daniel

May the future be better because the present is resisted.

[John McNeill was a Jesuit and close friend of Dan. McNeill was dismissed from the Jesuits in 1987 after refusing the order from the Congregation for the Doctrine of the Faith to cease speaking on the issue of homosexuality. A theologian by training, McNeill wrote a landmark book in 1976, The Church and the Homosexual, *and also was among the founders of Dignity, which ministers to gay Catholics and their allies. McNeill died in 2015.]*

Fri. Sept. 30th [1977]

Dear Dan—

Gotcher letter and thanks for the $. I suspect from yer note that they're trying to put the ouster boots to [John] McNeill. Whatta they got on the guy besides being gay? They're like the bastids in the Pentagon—they never rest. Ole Apollyon keeps kickin' their asses into motion.

We're goin' to Jimmy Carter's church this Sun., gonna hit that Pharisee both inside and outside, Schuchard was down casin' the dump last Sunday—like Jimmy, they're slick and superficial—combining the worst of revivalism and Madison Ave. From 10–11AM Marse Jimmy's up in de choir loft teachin' de Book of Revelation. Now ain't that a howl?

Finished up a paint job on Thurs. We'll try another on Monday. Our landlord in DC has not pried loose a house, so it appears we'll winter here.

> Peace of Christ, and every grace.
> Phil

Thurs [Oct 1977]

Dear Dan—

The folks just back from the Blight House, and a demo on the BOMB. They left the driveway just before arrest. We've agreed to do this twice a week. And then of course, go back to Jimmy's Church. The great man up at Camp David over the weekend. Ed + John went to the sanctuary with banners, and got very rough treatment from ushers presumably trained by Secret Service. Anyway, we stayed there for a full 2 hrs. with a good leaflet, so the great man will know about it.

The cops will be there this weekend, so the minister threatens. Friends will have to carry on w/out Liz + myself, who will be in Syracuse. They will go w/ banners again, reinforced by a statement from the bowels of the congregation. That ought to prove a gem for the muscle bound ushers.

Loved the cross you sent, your pome as much. Leave it to you to expend yourself. My thanks has to be insufficient, and it shure as hell is.

Will shoot this off. Wished youse could be with us this weekend. We'll hev some joy-juice fur yur cause, and persun. Love you—everyone here does. Christ with you.

> Phil

Sun. [ca. Nov. 6, 1977]

Dear Dan—

Ole Beantown seems to be waking up. Met many fine people there. B.C. even has a handful of promising students—wonders never cease.

Saw ole Tom Lewis and went to the new C.W. House which is booming with a fine young woman named Jean Fazzino.

Had an arraignment Friday before going to Beantown—trial Dec.
16th.

Talked turkey with "Caroline" [name changed–eds.] this morning.
Seems there was a party here while I was in Boston, and Frida was
outside on the stoop, it being a warm night. A black guy from across
the street, that we know well, crossed over and began to make a fuss
over Frida, in the most innocent and well-intentioned fashion. He was
holding her hand—so "Caroline"appears, rips Frida away, and drags
her howling into the house. A couple more stunts like that and we'll
be shit in this neighborhood—after 4 years of being neighbor.

It develops that "Caroline" "feels" she has as much value as a piece
of ordure. Exhorted her to get out, get exercise, get to the Eucharist at
a local church, and get with the New Testament. We've located a nun
who does counseling and who has contacts with shrinks in town. So
between her, us, and mebbe a shrink—we may be of some use to her.

Have to go to La Salle this week. Suppose between the teaching,
the hospital and speaking yer busier than the proverbial wet hen. Let
us know how you are, please.

Thass it! We love youse very much. The little pigeons send the wet
ones—all of us big hugs.

Peace of Christ,
Phil

Wed. afternoon—[ca. Dec. 14, 1977]

Dearest Brother—

Your letter (meditation) arrived—I've read it twice, and want to
hasten with this. You open up limits of reality that I (we) have not
explored. And I can only say—thanks so much. You are faithful as
few can or will be.

I find myself immeasurably sorry—I know this isn't the issue—to
have caused you such suffering. Sensed this before broaching the subject—that it would leave you with a nearly intolerable burden—but
thought, "we owe one another the harsh renderings too, even on the
level of such left-footed speculation." So went ahead, even though
the meanderings in the dark were decidedly primitive—perhaps even
unsound.

Liz read your letter with the same measure of anguish. And asked me to repeat to you something I intended to anyway—namely, that we're foundering, searching, wondering if there is a loving dimension beyond symbolic resistance, or more precisely, the symbolic resistance that we (you included) have done. Are these times, and the Lord, and the victims esp. the kids, calling us to something more truthful, more compassionate than that done in the past?

In these areas, my doubts come in. I have it soft here—a good home, a great wife, a very good community, a great brother in you, Carol, Jerry, and on and on—two beautiful and healthy children. It seems to me that I must seek further for non-violent means to protect Frida + Jerry and the other children.

That's what the talk was about—it arose from the realization that we weren't giving that much to the Kingdom, the victims, the kids. You raise heavy objections—they can't be discounted, some if not all of them. But I guess the exploration must continue, huh?

Perhaps we're presently and sufficiently responsive to Christ's Spirit now—perhaps we're compassionate and courageous enough now—speaking of me and/or the community. I don't know—but I doubt it. Perhaps the course is to be more loving and prayerful, to work harder and more self-sacrificingly. I don't know. Perhaps.

The community here hasn't voiced that much reaction to what I propose. It seems there was an initial, well-controlled shock, and then some deep pondering. Liz hasn't voiced any reservations—she would admit however, a community needs to explore a more insightful and compassionate mode of witness.

It'll be better seeing you, and conversing. Know in the meantime how we love you, and how we thank God for you. That sums it up.

Peace of Christ, brother,
Phil

Sun. [ca. Dec. 18, 1977]

Brother Mine—

Thanks for the note, and for that great poem.

I'm sure elements of impatience enter from our side—there's a routinizing of the actions and busts. But much more at work, at least in my own case, is the impression that n.v. is circumscribed by the Powers, and that a point may come when the symbolic is greeted by no arrest at all. Or if arrest, no jail. Furthermore, I must ask my-self—what is the Cross for me? I can dimly intuit that it is resistance/peace effort, but beyond that, what? I suspect dimly, that the Cross is not this scale of offering, and I think that grace, you, community, experience has prepared me for more. But what? I'm sure there are elements of spiritual weight lifting in all of this, there is the arrogance that sacrifice will communicate a sense of the peril of the BOMB. But those factors I must live with, in some confidence that main motivations have to do with oblation and the Cross—the "hour" that the Lord addresses.

Liz understands this, and from all I can gather—we've talked of it frequently—shares what we've conveyed. Maybe in times like these, the old sign of Jonah is the only one with significant meaning. And not necessarily when the cataclysm approaches, or when the pharaohs breath heavily over their buttons.

Anyway, perhaps we can talk of it more at Christmas. In the meantime, we'll do some more praying, and seeking for light.

At Carter's church this morning—we greeted his exit with a good chant. At least, they'll know we're there. Thank you for the visit, and as the Prots. would say, for your ministry to us. Liz away in California 5 days speaking. I go to Atlanta on Wed. Sarah makin' it a little better. Everyone well. We all love you. So does the Lord.

His Peace,
Phil

Fri. Feb 24th [1978]

Dearest Brother—

Thank you for the fine shirt—though it would fit you more aptly. And for today's communication.

A few court appearances next week—we'll tell you of anything noteworthy. Read from the Bk. of Daniel last night—litany of the 3 young men—and Frida asked, "Is uncle Dan named for Daniel?" Well said, yes! There's still a prophet in Israel. Love you, dear brother. Everybuddy here does.

Peace of Christ,
Phil

[Phil was arrested on February 24 for pouring blood at the Pentagon with Dan.]

Wed. May 3rd ('78)

Dear Dan—

In sending the blurb on, I forgot to mention your birthday, in my ordinarily obtuse way.

This is a poor way to celebrate it with you, from jail. We would both prefer to down a flagon in company, and have some fellowship and laffs. But there are always the friends—and we will celebrate on release.

What can I say about you're being 57, and myself 55 soon? We're passing more firmly into middle age. But it seems to me that the fact of deepening age suggests not a run-down of the clock or declining powers, but more renewal—better husbanded energy, more "effectiveness" in the true sense, more firmness in the long haul. This is especially true of you.

It seems further to me that the better fun is yet to come. And that we will be called upon by the Lord, summoned if you will, in increasingly serious ways. What this means God alone knows, but perhaps its broader outlines are already somewhat clear. The death mangers and the BOMB will be quite probably at the center of it. The former have no capacity to withdraw, even if they desired. And the latter symbolize not only the powers of darkness but all their corollaries—the world, the degeneration of institutions, public numbness and fright, the tedious emergence of even the best people, the empire on the skids. And an artificial permanence to all of these.

Good health, dear brother, grace and peace. I love you and I thank you. May the Lord give me sight and strength to appreciate you more.

[Phil refers in the following letter to the sentencing for an action on March 24, in which twelve people, including Phil, were arrested at the Pentagon. He received a six-month sentence at Allenwood.]

May 3rd 1978

Dear Friends,

On Apr. 28th, Judge Oren Lewis of the Federal District Court, Alexandria, Va, sentenced Esther Cassidy, Ladon Sheats, John Schuchardt and myself to 1 yr., six months suspended, 2 year's probation. We joined in prison Ed Clark, with a similar sentence, and Carl Kabat, OMI, serving 1 year. All six of us are from Baltimore's Jonah House Community.

Lewis forbade a statement at sentencing; gave us the above jail terms, despite concurrent dropping of charges for exactly similar offenses in his own and other local federal courts; and disregarded Esther Cassidy's pregnancy of 3 months, her incomplete recovery from a serious Easter auto accident, and her first-offense status.

The specific witness leading to imprisonment went this way: we first shared a litany of repentance, asking God's forgiveness for the main elements of American warmaking, beginning with the Manhattan Project, Hiroshima and Nagasaki, and ending with the new doomsday weapons systems—Trident, cruise missile, Missile X.

Then we poured our blood on the pillar and floors of the Pentagon, revealing bloodletting covering three decades. And we scattered ashes, as a symbol of mourning and repentance, and as a warning against a world in nuclear ash.

We said at Catonsville that genocide in Indochina stops here. Now we say that preparation for mass suicide stops here. (To prepare for mass suicide is to be guilty of it.) We will not pay for the conspiracies and mass destruction weapons of this government. We will not contribute our silence. Rather, we will testify against official waste and madness, simply because the price of complicity is unconscionably high. If physical freedom is bought only by complicity, then we will reject complicity, break complicity law, and go to jail.

The court sentenced us purely because we broke the law. But in our estimation, the law legalizes the State's lawlessness. If we are cremated in mass nuclear destruction, we will have the consolation of knowing that it was all legal.

Perhaps our imprisonment—in my case, added to 44 months already served for non-violent resistance to war—will give weight to the following reflections: if we want peace, we will have to pay for it. If we want peace, we will have to stop making war. If we are silent, we are making war. All this government needs to lead the world to nuclear ruin is an irrelevant note every 4 years and a sizeable slice of income for war. And silence.

We trust that sisters and brothers will awake, as the Gospel entreats. And respond in time.

Fraternally in Christ,
Phil Berrigan

Dearest Brother—

Liz visited last night—indomitable woman. Everything A okay. Reading *Little Dorrit*. Ole Dickens is a genius—incomparable! Thanks so much for getting him to me. I hope to become addicted to him. You are very much with us—in fact, your spirit is palpable. And I love you and thank God for you—even momentarily.

Sat. May 13th (1978)

Dear Dan—

Tried to call you from MCC downtown, but the long distance phone was tied up, and the local phone a pay phone and me with no money. You can imagine the frustration. Spent overnight there and arrived here via bus on Friday at noon.

You wouldn't recognize the place—a full fledged day (and night) care center. One prisoner told me, "the guards don't guard us, they babysit!" So it seems. On the positive side however—the prisoners are embarrassingly generous and decent. The fruits of canteen are immed. placed at one's disposal—the food is excellent, and some exhibit surprising—for today—moral and political sense. One came up and asked, "Did you read that demon at Leavenworth in '74?" I admitted to being out there. And then, he told what that meant, and how the Adm. reacted to a couple of hundred people outside those terrible, forbidding walls. So there you are. The euphoria will wear out undoubtedly, but there appears to be much sincerity and decency here.

We all anxiously await youse. But in the meantime, have no concerns. I am relaxing in the beauty (trees, flowers, grass) and friendliness of the place. And my only concern is getting down to some steady writing and praying. It's a little difficult on those counts—people want some rap. You know the scene. Love you muchly, brother. And pray daily that the Lord be with you even more powerfully.

Christ's peace—
Phil

Mon. May 15th (1978)

Dear Dan—

Pretty much into the flow of things here. We've had several days of rain, which shuts most people in, displaying the inadequate level of facility for bad weather seriousness a la Danbury, or most places.

Anyway, the old moss-back chaplain—he's a fascist Oblate from Carl's order (delicious irony having them in the same institution) called me aside before mass last Sunday and told me that he couldn't offer me the Eucharist. I assured him that was okay, and went anyway. But consequently, we've decided to worship Sunday morning, and then pray together on Wed. Out of that hopefully, will arise talk about keeping this lollipop acres under scrutiny, and how to conduct ourselves in a n. viol/resistant fashion. Everyone very agreeable and cool, but nonetheless, green to these nuances.

> Prayers with you, dear brother. And best love. Plus Christ's light + life—
> Phil

(Monday May 15)

Dear Brother—

Sunday was a sermon at St. John's Episcopal, where you had preached + Liz had spoken. They're good folk w- a good record on VNam + now open 2 nukes, interracial, sending love 2 you + the Jonah House folk. Lunch w- about 20 of them following Mass, then a PM with some Immaculate Heart sisters.

Today was an hour's class and 2 hr. discussion, students at Loyola Marymount, tonight is supper + meeting with old friends of Harrisburg committee. All week it will go that way, a trek we're all familiar with. The weather is superb, the people kind as pie, much concern 4 East Coast acts + jailings, but always an onlooker's distancing, esthetic or compassionate case may be, but very seldom questioning where it goes now + here. . . .

Wednesday is the 10th anniversary of Catonsville. Mische is a city father of some stripe or other in St. Cloud. Melvilles in Texas. Mary M is under. (Art Melville + wife has split, he has a PhD in you guessed it, psychology, is 'into' (ugh!) occult religion + about 2 marry again. Kathy works in a health food restaurant.)

Of all of us, your life shows the undivided self in Christ. You have help from some of us. I think given everything our family is a great strength. But you, as I tried 2 say clumsily in NY when you came up 2 talk, are our (my) north star. That is your place in our firmament, fixed and bright. Thanks are redundant, but yet never so. Thank you brother.

> Much love dear brother 2 yourself + brothers there!
> ♥ Daniel

[Dan's letter here touches on his longstanding disagreement with the use of violence that irked some liberationist Catholics in Latin America, notably recorded in his letters with his friend Ernesto Cardenal.]

Dearest Bro (Wed. [May] 17)

Today if I mistake me not is Catonsville 10 years.

Monday night was a supper of Unitarians, so 2 speak. I went 2 a rich house somewhere. Blaise Bonpane extemporized—a very spate. He advised us urgently of our bounden duty 2 support any + all gun wielding Latins, from Father [Camilo] Torres, thru Fr. Ernesto [Cardenal], to (get this) "Father Fidel." Literal words. Well. (Of course this was all aimed my way + yours.) Come my turn, I passed. Not a word, fury freely confessed. The prayer went on, various people otherwise unheard from, said big brave words about loss, courage, liberation. Again to Blaise, another flow of folly. Which I at last interrupted 2 suggest that since 1) there was no tribute here 2 those in prison for non violent activity, + 2) we were being harangued, no discussion, —> good night 2 all + rose + departed. Big B yelled after me, "Too bad you can't face these things!"

This afternoon at UCLA, tonight with Immaculate Heart Sisters. It's a busy often frustrating, exhausting time, but some good faces alight in the dark. I think of you, first thought in the AM, last at night. And in between a frequent prayer, mostly gratitude, sometimes 4 yr. great courage, for the bretheren there, for Liz + the children. All of us. God be at our side!

♥ Daniel

Dear Brother (Thursday) [May 18]

Yestiddy at UCLA. This topic was 2 be, "A Nuclear Perspective." Afterward this young fellow with a Latino look came up 2 me; "You were in our home in Caracas in 1965." So I was. It was Christmas day, I was invited courtesy of a Jesuit there. The mother stayed aloof and after festivities and an incursion of students from the local Catholic University she asked if I would walk in the garden. Which I did. She broke down + said her husband (daily communicant etc.) was really there to subvert students, name of C.I.A. And what was she 2 do? Told her she indeed must choose between a lousy marriage and her own life . . . and conscience. Now I'm told Daddy works for the "oil interests." Such recognition scenes are boggling, maybe they occur only in late empire?

Going to call this done, off 2 FOR [Fellowship of Reconciliation]. Thinking of you, thanking God for you first and last. You give a rare substance 2 my being out here in Fun + Mad Comic Land—

Love, brother!

May 20 Saturday PM

Dear Brother,

Off 2 airport and San Diego for early breakfast with the Presbyterian FOR. About 600 in attendance. Their church is in convention there for 10 days, in deep throes about gay ordination and other assorted non questions, so it goes. I tried 4 a bit of realism on CD and nukes, and a bit of it seemed 2 stick; as dado wd. say. God knoweth.

On the bus back to LA today, was able 2 meditate again on your beautiful birthday letter and its implications, an occasion 4 thanksgiving. The longer I'm out here the more it seems miraculous that so much has been accomplished back home.

The citizens here are between draught + heavy rains, a great deal of prahpetty collapse. That plus the earthquake faults + nuke installations sittin' pretty on Vesuvius, makes for a good solid symbol of Amurrica. The idea seems 2 b shove a dynamite suppository up the ars + then have a retired general push the plunger. This is called Saturday afternoon games on the village common. Jes as old, mebbe, as witch hunts or frogs leg pulling.

Luve yer brother,
Daniel

Love to all brothers there, as 2 Liz + chilluns!!

Dear Brother (May 31),

Main thing is to say that the visit to you was an oasis of the heart, you are coping as well as one would have expected, knowing you, which is to say, so well it sets the heart going faster. . . . I found myself quite at sea for the first part of the picnic, the sight of you on ice isn't the easiest in the world for me, and then we had come from Jonah and Liz and the children, and it was very much for one dose, or even two. But that passed and I found myself at ease with your ease. . . .

As for the June 12 sit in, I'm joining about 15 from the Catholic Worker for an 'affinity group;' which simply means, I guess that we try and support one another and the newcomers, and try also to work out common strategy with regard to bail etc. etc. I'm trying to find out if some folk will also consent to repeat the act if we get away with it the first time. But we'll see about these things. . . .

Let me close with a sense of things, obscure but what the hell. I think the deepest meaning of these months to me is that you are in the ideal spot for suffering contemplation; I wince as you do at the phrase, one wants above all to be modest when so many are in the noose and parrot's perch, but still. The reminder (to me) is the deep spiritual roots that have to be nourished if we are not to end up on the stones, thorns, wayside. Where nothing occurs, stalemate. I thank you for that, the deepest and best thing of all.

♥ Daniel

[early June, '78?]

Dear Brother,

I'm off to S. Norwalk tonight to read some poetry and talk about Bombs and other assorted fauna and flora. This is gotten up by some local poets there, I seem to sense some measure of awakening among artistic and literary types about political realities.

I won't dwell on the snake pit of our leaders' minds these days. They have a kind of hideous Nixonian consistency and cynicism; not even to pay a passing tribute to events in NY on disarmament, they set up their NATO bickerings at the same time and use the occasion (improve it, Shakespeare would say) to rattle sabres and big guns once more. . . . Reminds me of Johnson after the 67 arrests at the Pentagon announcing to the nation that the war would go on, we heard it in jail and it was chilling indeed.

I often think of Mama these days. I know that in her perfected joy, she is thanking the Lord for you and Liz and the children. And standing with us all as well.

All the best love brother, and may the Lord stand with yez and the brothers there.

Daniel

Mon. June 5th (1978)

Dearest Brother—

Elated you'll be present to them young C.W. types. It'll be great opportunity for them. We'll pray that the previous presser at the U.N. waxes into a clear-headed and a determined presence on the 10th. Your participation will lend spirit and quality and strength. And above all, integrity.

Will take well to mind and heart your remarks on suffering contemplation. Like yourself, I dislike the term. For one thing, I don't suffer that much. I suffered when Freda died, in an utterly unexpected fashion. I'd suffer if anything happened to you or Liz and the children, or Carol or Jerry etc. I'd suffer if the BOMB fell, even as I suffered when Nixon went berserk over N. Vietnam. But mostly, I endure, dogging along in rather churlish fashion, as Pop would say. But the contemplation side of your remarks are right on target. The demons keep coming back, the vacancies of soul are constant reminders. Lots of cluttered geography, lots of idols. The time in the morning with the Psalms and NT helps—so does the writing. So do prayers from others.

But one lives by community and grace, huh? And I have that, to a completely gratuitous degree.

Thank you, dear brother. And best love to answer your constant love.

Peace of Christ—
Phil

Dear Brother; (Tuesday, [June] 13, ['78])

I hope you are receiving some books regularly, today I sent Flannery O'Connor a coupla books of pomes. Plus Simone Weil. . . .

Yestidday was pretty good. We had some 400 arrests, the poolice were on their best behavior. Citations for 'disorderly conduct.' I marched with the Cath. Worker, who were in full force. Prior to that we had a mass at a good Franciscan house for street women on 40 st. It was jammed, just like the ol days.

I met Dave Dellinger. I had written him regarding the invisibility of you and the other brethren there in his *Seven Days*. He was apologetic, as usual seemed quite harassed, but good as gold. He wants an interview or article or column on the doings at Jonah House. I think it more fitting if Liz does it, maybe by phone, Dave will be back to me.

Media coverage here was good all TV stations and the *Times*, national TV also. Went back to Mary House for a meeting after everyone was released, couldn't get any enthusiasm for returning to the Doggerel palace today, everyone quite exhausted evidently. But maybe something later; they're now talking about a return toward the end of the UN session.

I blew my stack on return here last night, no one supported the day in any way, nor was there interest (except for Keck who called the CW) about my so called fate.

Well in spite of all, it was good, folk from all over the country.

Love,
Bruv

Fri. nite, June 30th (1978)

Dearest Brother—

Guess I don't help much with the scene here when you arrive. Like yourself, am somewhat tongue-tied—think it's mostly that I am so damned happy to see everyone. Then too, when the ord. climate is this, and the extraord. climate is you, it takes some time to adjust. As for longing to be here, I understand that perfectly. You would not be Dan Berrigan if it were not so. And if you were in, I would hope too long to be with you.

As for this time, as well as others, I think a certain Providence guides it. Let's say that I have the luxury of doing a stretch once a year. But I don't think you do. I have the luxury, or so it seems to me, because generally, it is the best contribution I can offer. Not so with you; you have so much more to give, or you have a wider diversity of gifts. You can help people more—those struggling to grow up. I've done a little writing; I've worked at it—not at all as you have, but some. And then I read your stuff and say, my God! Look at my slop and look at Dan's. And it's not just style, it's content. It's knowing the Bible, or life or politics. It's a spirit that I can only acknowledge and hail and thank God for. Another gift you constantly offer that I will never have to offer.

Will shove this off. Hope you found the W. Coast FOR's somewhat hopeful, and the Carbrays and Douglasses well. Peace to youse. All seems well—a lovely day and some good chit chat. Love you, brother.

Christ's best!
Phil

Aug 15—'78

Dear Brother—

A weird anniversary, entered Jebs in '39, now 39 years in! Practically a lifer but as papa wd. aver, No regrets!

Many many thoughts of you + the brethren perdure—won't be long now! Much love, dear bro—

Daniel

Aug 15—PM

Dear bro Philip

Liz called tonight 2 say happy anniversary.

Yer letters normally take 6–7 days 2 arrive. I presume mine are similarly sent along by land turtle.

I keep thinking of your remaining month. Suppose you hit a plateau about this time, that coppery taste in the mouth, a downer. The biggies seem gigantic, the true folk so inert or helpless or few (or all together). But this is the subterranean growing + building that will make all the difference for 'things 2 come.' I have never had any least doubt that your 'status' as ward of the Cosmic Cruncher was the exact + truthful one; and that these foul episodes, crunch crunch, were the times of epiphany, for those who could stand in the circle of shining. It is something to offer a gift 2 the future, when most cannot even so much as lay out something day by day—something that speaks sense 2 their own souls; let alone the victims + victimizers.

Thank God for it all, thank God for you and the brothers there. It may be scant comfort but where is real comfort—or what but scant were we promised?

Please believe the weight, gentle lesson, beckoning, heart in a heartless time, good logic, courage and right conclusion—your lockup has for us all.

And love above all—
Daniel

Aug. 17—

Dearest bro,

Yours of 12th came today. 5 days isn't bad. Dan Ellsberg called yesterday (Wed.). He was in usual haste, leaving town by four. I couldn't cut loose but we had good confab by phone. His 4th arrest at R[ocky] Flats, consequences getting heavier, he fully expects some jail time beginning in November. Hopes to be out till then though they're setting prohibitively high bail on repeaters. He said he got a lot of press (in Japan, not here) by announcing on Hiroshima Day that we had nukes in Japan in 1970, both on sea and land. Sounded very cheerful + up. I don't know if you saw young Bob E's [Robert Ellsberg's] jail diary in *Catholic Worker,* thought it had masterful moments. . . . Well dear bro, Jerry + Carol here tomorrow, we'll talk of days + days when you'll be with us!

Won't try your eyesight further. Liz called about sentences. Savage!

Sat. Aug. 19th (1978)

Dearest Brother—

2 of yers (Aug. 15th) tonight. Thank you for all the good words, and for the unquenchable spirit behind them.

Please forgive me for drawing a blank on your anniversary. I just happened to be a dim bulb on such things. But reading your letter got me reflecting on those 39 years in the Society. There aren't many who can, in all fairness, look back on such a history of teaching and witness, "loyal endurance" the Bk of Rev. calls it. You know where you stand, and what you've done. And millions are the beneficiaries— esp. me, and those close to you. I shudder to think—it could well be nightmare material—where I'd be if it were not for you. So in all truth, you can say—NO REGRETS! Amen to that!

Thanks for you, dear brother. And much love. We'll muckle thru— we always have.

In xto—Phil

[Dan here mulls over his willingness to return to jail despite his health issues. The letter reflects what Dan holds dear: the Jesuits, Phil, Liz, the kids, Jerry, Carol, and "divine logic."]

Brother mine, (August, 24; Thurs.)

Wanted to get yer reflections on a subject that's inevitably reared its head, *nempe* [namely] jail. What with the workshop drawing near, of course the possibilities loom. And then the sentences seem to stiffen as

our judges "emehhhje" for what they are, subprefects of the principalities. So what's to be done? I'm trying to mull the alternatives. There's
question of the eyes, which are stable, help at Rose, diet, and lotsa
vitamin supplements. There's no questions without these, they would
worsen. General health would also take a beating, esp. as a matter of
months in either co. jail, or wintering in Allenwood.

On the other hand—the call. Which is a mystery and respected
as such; and otter at least mitigate the above and put it in place. No
question that all through your months in, I've felt the deep divine
logic of your stance, being there. Right as crystal or the timing of
the sun. Right for me too. This remains unshaken, a matter of gospel rightly grasped. I feel also (you know this) no great stake in this
world whether in the Jesuits apart from a few friends, or the writing
or carooming about the country. My real stake is in you and Liz and
Jerry and Carol and the chilluns; and I have you, given one or another,
given jail or at large. So that's not in question.

I would like to consider myself spiritually prepared to gulp hard
and leap in; what else can one do?

This is about the closest I can get to a confession these days. The
rest I don't have to grovel over with you, you know it all anyway,
knowing me better than anyone. Bless me.

I guess what will happen will be that I'll try to absorb what comes
down during the workshop in DC, and go from there. Undoubtedly
a powerful current is always generated during such days, which cre-
ates its own lucidity, momentum. Going with the spirit. These scrawls
are the hieroglyphic doodlings that precede a good moment; walk!
or Do it! (or on the other hand, Don't do it). In any case, we'll see;
it won't be dull.

Would appreciate any reflections that occur to you. You're a good
teacher in a good school room (!) I can trust that. The Jesuits will
give me a kind of marmoreal respect, whatever the outcome, that
reminds me of the pantheon of saints around St. Peter's square; they
look elevated no matter what passes by; being statues they're not
required to join the rag tag procession. So here I hover waiting on
Godot.

I pray you are well and that the days do not seem too long, too
many. They sometimes (your days that is) seem very long and very
many to me. But that's me, trying also to count your days; or as the
poet says, let me count the ways. . . .

Love to you, dear brother and friend,
Daniel

Tues. Aug. 29th (1978)

Dear Dan—

Lord, if one could go Madison Ave., and have thousands of Religious listen to your Lk's temptations? Now, that's Amurrrrican thinking, huh? As the "believers" used to say to the Lord, "you must manifest yourself." Nonetheless, it would be a great blessing to go over another suppressed text with you.

Thank you, dear brother, for the "confession." Remember I shared a conviction once that you were the best judge of you. I've never encountered any sloppy or indigent thinking from you about yourself. On the contrary, your view has been unvarnished and gravely honest and unsparing. Your letter was another example of this.

But a few reflections, none of which promise to be of much help 1. The injustice is still random—Ellen gets 6 mos.; Paul Hood and Ray Torres 2 + 1 mos. for the same thing.

2. Arrests continue to be sloppy, charge sheets sloppier, esp. when folks move in concert and with relish. And so, some are not arrested and some have charges dropped.

3. Maybe my sense tilts slightly toward the probability of short jail (30–60 days) or no jail. But even the former bodes ill for the back and eyes. So it's back to your judgment and the intangibles that faith must engage. I think you're eminently right in going with the Spirit, and the community. If in a sense, the back or eyes begin to rage intolerably—then a court appearance will get you out, though I know that's more bitter than gall to you. I wish that I could share more of the health difficulties with you. I remarked to Carl and John tonight that if I had your back and eyes, I'd be doing less jail than you're doing. Most of my courage comes from a strong back.

Liz sez that when you come, you will be badly needed. Well, dear brother, you're badly needed everywhere. I know you'll inspire and find there some good, inspiring folk. Good rest—the grace is a short. Best love from the cabbage. All send likewise.

> In the Lord—
> Phil

Sat PM 2 Sept.

Dear Brother,

Two letters from you make one in return a big bargain. This is scriven in the B'more bus station before return 2 NY.

Well it all went off like a Swiss watch or star passing star. The die in was breath snatching, the lock out went mixed as 2 effect, river entrance so so, other mall one a 1 hr. slowdown in corporate death. There were powerful sonic prayer boomings in the stores of the stalking dead on both Thursday and Friday. And a good liturgy to close the workshop, Thursday PM.

After the busts + release, it was a return 2 Jonah, late supper and later talk. Then Liz gave me 2 latest from you, which sang me 2 sleep. Your reflections on the projected bust, read after the fact, were deliciously accurate. It is so nice 2 live the event you helped prophesy. We have trial date. I believe 13 or 14 of autumn. I'm awaiting with a gourmet's drool, the taste of religious + academic howls—when they learn I'm not coming 2 talk resistance, but locked up 4 doing it. You know that goings on so well.

Your work continues 2 start fires. 'The prisoners' are not only in our prayers but in our veins.

Thassabout all 4 now. When you get out, no one can really feel captive. Least of all me. How good it will be. And how soon!

Love,
Bro Dan'l

Wed. Sept. 13th (1978)

Dearest Brother—

I had no idea that the crud laid you low following return to NYC. Guess exhaustion had something to do with that—giving yourself unreservedly to folks everywhere, most of all those at the W. Dept. and at Jonah—to mention merely the last of a list.

Going thru the folder of "separation" here—they tell me I'm expected to contact a parole officer within 72 hrs. after release. I'll get a reading on that at home. And I'll see you at Jonah tomorrow night. Then we'll see what the unjust judges are handing out on Friday.

A certain grim logic at work—I get out, you go to trial. Well Fidelity is the watchword—you've been astoundingly faithful thru the years—I've learned and tried to follow. So have hundreds of others. One day, the full truth will be known. The Lord will see to that.

Love you, dear brother. We will have a better day together. Thass fur shure.

Every peace and grace from the
Throne—
Phil

Love the earth and sun and animals, despise riches, give alms to everyone who asks, stand up for the stupid and crazy, devote your income and labor to others, hate tyrants, argue not concerning God, have patience and indulgence toward people, take off your hat to nothing known or unknown or to any person or number of persons, go freely with powerful uneducated persons and with the young and with the mothers of families, read and reexamine all you have been told at school or church or in any book, dismiss whatever insults your own soul—and your very flesh shall be a great poem and have the richest fluency not only in its words but in the silent lines of its lips and face and between the lashes of your eyes and in every motion and joint of your body. (Walt Whitman)

[1978 — early October]

Dearest brother Philip,

They say there's some chance we may all be together to celebrate your birthday this weekend, I sure hope so! It would take a helluva lot more than Walt Whitman to say what you mean 2 all of us—a gift which like life itself keeps me in wonderment.

How many take their measure, the place where their soul is or is not—or ought 2 be, from you two! This is a great thing in a society that robs us of martyrs + confessors and saints and dumps on us (as its triumph) a church of xerox humans. What a thing you do for us, keeping to the line of fidelity + holiness and good cheer under duress.

I saw the Jesuits yesterday AM at Detroit U pushing their golf bags ahead of them to a car, off for the day. It was a fractured scene out of the 40s or 50s. I thought, there but for you, went I. What a blessing to be beckoned along so gracefully + gently—yet irresistibly too, like God's own nudge.

For standing while others wilt + whimper + waste it, for speaking up while others hum along—thank you dear brother, and MANY years!
Daniel

Thurs. Dec. 7th (1978)

Dearest Broth—

Bit a draggin' goin' on from this end. Some of the prelim crud, I guess.

Yers most welcome, as usual. The interdict idea a fine one—we could slide this desecration to a halt if'n we had one. But the Church—alas! Did I tell youse that no word from Gumbleton or Sullivan or Hunthausen from the Bishop's Conf.? Two of them had said that they wanted to talk while East for the Bishop's Conf. then we waited and waited. Carl talked with poor Gumbleton at the Pax Christi fiasco—his Lordship was properly vague, probably waiting for a "summons." McSorley sat in on the exchange—Gumbleton said it would probably be the end of his Bishopric if he went c.d. McSorley agreed, seeming to advocate a different morality for Bishops.

The young 'uns, 8 of them, on trial in D.C. for Aug. 6th at Carter's church. They're going pro se. It'll probably drag on. They'll get their punishment, somehow.

Are you getting some rest betimes? We love you. More later. The cherubs superb. They are budding, and thass an understatement.

Looking to see youse, dear brother. All best love, best grace.

> In xto,
> Liz, Phil et al.

Sun. Jan. 28th (1979)

Dear Brother—

We got a chance for a new place—closer to D.C.—in fact, near the Beltway—7, 8 miles from Sodom. Acre of ground, and a big house. The monthly tariff will be near $550, which is a hellova lot to give to any landlord, but he's a friend of McSorley's, and seems a decent guy. So maybe we can work out some negotiations. All in all, I think we're right in not getting into the real estate scramble, and owning property. We're seeing it tomorrow, and will let you know.

Think we're getting to ole Ladon a bit. You know, perhaps even more than us, the Prots seem notable for blind spots. He's got another big tour planned, which will take him away for 5 weeks. And he has holy indifference to $, he simply leaves the filthy lucre to the rest of us. That and the major part of the shit-work here. Anyway, he ponders what we say, when we come in ultra gentle. So goes Christian community.

[B]rother—we love you. The little ones ask for Uncle Dan more times than I can tell you. And Liz, Ellen, Carl, myself send you the Lord's grace + peace.

> Phil

Mar 10 [1979]

Dears,

There's damn little as you know better than I, that the academic piss can't dampen.

Our group had about 12 for prayer and discussion on Wed. It grows slowly. Dorothy Sölle and husband joined us. I don't know how many will actually show for holy week, but we'll see. I have a sneaking feeling in the marrow that this will be a biggie, no doubt. Everywhere I go there's interest and some sign ups.

Off to Boston tomorrow to read poetry for the C. Worker.

Did I write Jim Forest wants me to come in late May for 3 weeks, to go to about 5 countries on the nuke question. I've decided to go; Jerry and Carol will be in Italy for a week, then will join me in Ireland for a few days; it's in the nature of a celebration of their 25th. Of course I'll be on hand for holy week, at least the latter part, will cut clear here after Tuesday night class; by Wednesday. I'm trying to do a little fasting fasting in league with the big leagues.

> Mucho love + prayers dears!
> Dan'l

Mar. 12th (1979)

Dear Brother—

Am off to Minn. Fri. for a week—Benidji, Duluth, St. Paul-Minneapolis, St. Cloud, Moorhead etc. Heard you just been there. Waal—with the 2 of us, we should have the Pentagon assaulted by Minnesotans come Holy Week.

Spoke last Fri. at the No. Capitol community's "clarification" session. The fasters pretty well wrung out—there is little energy for anything except to fast (I still don't dig this experiment—but the hope is as far as I'm concerned, that so much will be learned, that nothing similar will be attempted again). Anyway, the crowd (over a hundred) was typically Washingtonian evasive. As you would say, very civilly obedient.

The date for Trident's launching—Apr 7th—has come in. Most hereabouts seem determined to go and take a bust. And then, we have Holy Week coming up the evening of the 10th. So it will be close. I'll stay there and attend house—Liz doing c.d. at Groton and during Holy Week.

Thinkin' of youse, bro. and lovin' youse. Hakkum you ain't written? Suggest youse is on the road. Care fur yurself. Best love from us all—

> Peace of Christ,
> Phil

May 12th (1979)

Dearest Bruv—

Sorry we've neglected you so sorely recently. Hope this awaits you on return. We discussed Joan Baez's effort last night and came down precisely where you are before your letter arrived today. We wouldn't sign anything going into the *Post* or any other Trilateral bombastor w/ out some illuminating of the imperialist's effort to choke and to topple the new regime. We had a grave resp. for pol. Prisoners before Apr. '75, and we have same today, I would guess. So Liz is writing Joan tonight.

Long session with Jim Wallis and co. today. Good! They're trying, and inching forward—trying to carry the Prot. Establishment with them. They're working on Billy Graham before his immortal statement. They're good as gold, but it seems to me, short on smarts.

Thinkin' of youse and hoping for a real reprieve for you on B.I. And a resounding effort abroad. Love you dearly.

> In the Lord—
> Liz, Phil, et al.

[Phil reports that Mary Moylan of the Catonsville Nine turned herself in after evading capture for a decade.]

June 20th (1979)

Dear Dan—

Mucho welcome. Joy to hear from you—from these predestined shores.

A few news items: Frida has a broken arm—rather a troublesome + dangerous break—in the elbow. Got it from a fall—kid's slide. Has a good bone man (poor people's clinic) and she's gaining her zest back slowly.

#2 Mary Moylan has turned herself in. Did it very quietly, and has refused interviews in Balto City Jail. Tried calling you last night about it. Mische suggested a statement, so I wrote one and gave it to the locals. Supposing interest from the news mongers—their flaccid curiosity tempted by a "lone, lorn" woman who stay[ed] out of the acid clutches of the FBI for nine years. One reporter sez he was "awed." Well, as we know, it ain't romantic. We can only hope that Mary has learned some wisdom, as we hope the same for ourselves.

When we gonna see you? I hope sometime before Summer sessions. Are you well? We all love you and thank you. The Spirit's gifts in the Spirit's season.

Liz, Phil, et al.

Sun. July 1st (1979)

Dearest Brother—

Good effort on the Baez thing. Liz and I found her slightly intransigent and defensive, and of course, refused to go along.

Liz, Ellen + John S. start the 1st hoedown tonight—I know you'll remember them.

Frida has adjusted well to the broken arm. But she counts the 2 wks. remaining of cast and limitation.

Tom Lewis is in town and will see Mary Moylan tomorrow. I got one letter from her nibs, in which she exhorted support for political sisters imprisoned, and 3rd World people. The word around is that a motion for reduction of sentence has been filed—Lewis sez the govrm't did it. If true—how about that?

We haven't gotten close to that idea—'80 at the Pentagon. It offers limitless possibilities—but outside of here, folks react tepidly in the sense that they aren't battering down doors to work on it. And it'll take a hellova lotta work.

Write Mary at Balto City Jail. I need to do that too. Ladon has a hearing on Tues.—they may lock him up again. Will greet youse with booze and hugs, in reverse order. Love from all around.

Pax Christi—
Phil

1980–1989

[The 1980s were, for the Berrigans, a decade framed by tragic results of American imperialism. The letters open with the possibility of Phil visiting Iran for diplomatic talks amid the Iran hostage crisis, and they close in 1989 with the news of the Jesuit martyrs in El Salvador, assassinated by US-trained soldiers. The talks of "ultimate resistance" in the 1970s culminated in the first of the Plowshares actions, inspired by the quote from Isaiah to "beat their swords into plowshares." Plowshares became a model that others would follow around the country and beyond. Phil called the act "a 2nd Catonsville," and the appeals process would span the entire decade and force a word from the Supreme Court.

The appeals made space for more resistance, and these letters find the brothers, particularly Phil, in jail time and again. It also afforded a chance to take advantage of their renewed celebrity, accepting invitations to speak around the country, appear in movies (one of which was based on the Plowshares Eight trial), and, for Dan, to publish a lengthy autobiography. But behind the headlines and publicity was the quiet work that challenged and sustained them. Phil and Liz resumed the struggle to build a dedicated community at Jonah House while raising children, and Dan volunteered at hospitals treating AIDS and cancer patients, doing thankless jobs and witnessing the passing of many patients.

Death was a reality that gathered around the brothers during this period. On top of his hospital work, Dan tended to his friend Lewis Cox for the last years of his life amid the constant flow of news about their friends growing old and ill. Reminders of mortality struck the family as well, with one of their older brothers being hit by a car and another suffering a stroke. Dorothy Day, whose Catholic Worker "found a place of honor" in their home as children and who

163

Dan honored as no one outside his family but Merton, died in 1980, months after Archbishop Romero's assassination and only days before four nuns were raped and killed in El Salvador. Reagan's policies further disturbed them, and Dan left for San Salvador to see the killing and destruction the Jesuits there had to endure. And as the Plowshares movement reminded those who listened, they saw in nuclear weapons the planning for death.

The first letter points to the fifty-two US citizens and diplomats taken hostage in Iran on November 4, 1979. Phil speaks here of plans being made to fly him over to negotiate a release, as Dan did in 1968 in Hanoi, referring to a possible meeting with Ayatollah Ruhollah Khomeini, leader of the Iranian Revolution that ousted the US-backed Shah in 1979.]

Mon. Jan. 14th (1980)

Dearest Brother—

Just called Eqbal [Ahmad] about meeting w/ him on Iran. This is in the works. Anyway—Mitch and other CCNV'ers [Community for Creative Nonviolence] did 2 occupations of the Iranian Embassy with an eye to setting up a people to people dialog. Both ended in arrest and quick dropping of charges. The second occupation's charges dropped because of word from Tehran—"release them; they are our friends."

Out of this, Mitch met with the Chargé (Amb.) in the company of Tom Ricks, Georgetown Prof., Middle East expert and recently in Tehran w/ clergy (after Coffin, Gumbleton et al.) Snyder claims that the chargé wants you or me to go to Tehran and open up palaver between Iranian representatives and American justice and peace people. (We were apparently the overwhelming choice—they know us, our rel. convictions, our resistance. It fell on me because I'm more available.) Ricks apparently will go again at a moment's notice. I would prefer Eqbal, knowing his competence, and trusting his judgment. Snyder also claims the Iranians will pay my tab—I wouldn't go under any other circumstances.

By way of projection, the hope is to meet the students in the Embassy, members of the Rev. Council, the Ayatollah, and lay some basis for serious exchange with an eye to taking the issue out of the hands of the pharaohs. Then, hopefully, another delegation could come—you, Dellinger, Liz, Paul Mayer, etc. etc., possibly John Bach—and return w/ some of the hostages. The appeal to the Irani would be a gesture which would empower Amer. just. + peace people against our official cutthroats. Some openings vis-à-vis Afghanistan are also envisioned.

So I will see Eqbal and ask him to come. He has his own competence, reputation and conviction. But, according to Snyder, the request is unequivocally for us. They are rel. revolutionaries and want to open it up with religious radicals from this country. So the line goes, and as far as I can see, it has some substance.

1980 goes famously—a fine double c.d. by the first group last Friday. Three arrests—all for blood pouring. The young law students are in center stage this week.

Of course, cf. above, I judge in this scene much more for your perception and acuteness and experience than my own. But for reasons of expediency, mebbe I should try it and then let other better people take charge. I got much aware of the volatile nature of affairs in Iran, perhaps more so even, of the ruthlessness of the warmakers in D.C., and of the yellow character of the press. So be it. We will trust in God, and in those of goodwill.

Best love, dear brother—I know you'll pray for us.

Much love—always in the Lord,
Phil

Thurs. Jan. 17th (1980)

Dearest Brother—

Waaal—saw Eqbal + Stuart Shain on Tues.—they briefed us for a coupla hours—non stop. Eqbal, one could say, rose to the occasion. Questioned whether he should go—has a few enemies on the other end. We'll see what Ali Agha (the charge) sez. Timing may be imp.— The general elections happen on Jan. 25th, + Khomeini comes out of retreat on the 27th. It's a can of worms—there are all sorts of evil checks + balances on both sides. But the "yellow" American Press has been kicked out—I see the Afghans have followed suit.

Eqbal sez he will go only if the Charge asks for him—and the Charge will ask for him only if he has orders to do so from Tehran. So we had no illusions about the clout of the Embassy crowd—they hold the towels, and not a great deal more. That leaves Tom Ricks, the G'town Prof.—a good guy, accomplished and knowledgeable—but no flaming torch.

Just finished another job. So we keep sloggin' along. And thinking of you. Love you brother. I have finished your Dante, and will do it again. Now thass spirituality for the times! A beautiful piece of work.

Thank you for all of us—and thank you again. Whatever you offer has meaning, guts, reality.

Peace of Christ,
Phil

[The following letter to "Friends" and the message to Phil written below it were sent with a New York Times *article reporting that the government would not prosecute Dan and fourteen others for a protest at the Riverside Research Institute in New York. As he mentions, this freed him to head to California to teach at the Jesuit School of Theology in Berkeley. In the following letter he refers to his activities there.]*

January 1980

Dear Friends,

The gospel excepted, good news is always ambiguous—especially when the government decides for its own sordid good, not to prosecute.

In any case, the news herein appended makes possible my fulfilling a teaching stint on the west coast. There of course, anti nuclear work is already underway—and then some! I will be teaching two courses—one in the book of Revelation and one in religious non violence.

This, I take it, is a chance to offer biblical and personal evidence as to the tragedy impending, the terror and glory of the human calling, under the nuclear cloud.

As Philip says, 'In such times, we are either in jail or out of jail.' Good landmarks indeed. May 1980 find us not stuck in an Orwellian nightmare, but courageously announcing the nuclear-free zone of humanity itself.

Love to you all,
Daniel

Jerry described the magnificent action. You set the heart blazing. Maybe I can carry some borrowed fire westward, at least I'll try. Much love. I carry you west. That's a luggage that gives wings.

♥ Daniel

Fri. Jan. 25th (1980)

Dearest Bro—

Thinking much of you. Them folks must be driving you hard—because we've heard from you but once. No complaints, dear brother—merely hope that you're well.

The elections in Iran today. And more c.d. at the War Dept. today. I've seen the Iranian Amb.—With Tom Ricks (from G'town) and Mitch. We'll probably go this week—though Eqbal thinks we may be pushing it—possible runoffs (elections), too soon after them, the Imam in the hospital etc. (this week means Mon. Tues. esp.).

Nonetheless, cert. things "emerge." One is that the pitchmen in D.C. have decided that they need the Iranians more than the Iranians need us—for their oil, and as a buffer against our "enemies." Next, Ricks has gotten to Jimmy Allen, a So. Baptist mandarin + class friend of Carter's, to approach Carter on a "deal"—3 of the ill hostages for a full exposé of the Amurrrican track record in Iran, which hopefully, will be aired on Amurrrican prime time. Ricks is to pick up today, at the Blight House, a letter from Carter agreeing to this. Eqbal has x reasons why this is impossible, and all of us, I think, are well tuned to treachery on the part of Carter and/or the mainline media. These are the bare bones—we go to the Iranian Embassy tomorrow to discuss it with the Chargé D'Affairs.

It's a can of worms and it's impossible to predict that anything at all might come of it. I feel esp. for those hostages in ill health—if anything happens to them, the consequences could be dire, given our cutthroats.

Wish you were here to offer your wisdom. Hope to hear from you today or tomorrow. Best love—think of you constantly—in heart, mind, person. All send love.

In the Lord—
Phil

Dears—(Thurs PM) [Jan. 1980?]

Phil's good letter today reminded me—if I needed such—of long peregenations and tardiness. I'm now in my 3rd dwelling since arrival; successive snafus kept me living in a bag like an undersized mole, until on Wed. of this week this place, 2 rooms + kitchen, opened up. Hear eye yam.

Wed PM some 300 Milleniarists showed up 4 the nonviolent opening. I came on in my panda suit + was deafeningly applauded. Much
mellifluous Californian shite continues 2 hit the fan. Whether anything
substantial can be built one must continue 2 question (+ build). I invited the multitudes 2 a lounge + coffee + seriosities after class; Wed.
some 50 or 60 came + we went for another 1 ½ hrs. at a good level. I
have inducted 4 or 5 young Jebs into helping me break the class into
small groups 4 the second hour. These youngers are first rate + one
can see where that goes.

Today 60 for the Revelation "seminar," same sequence, I blatt for
an hour, then groups. We'll see. There is much disaffection on holy
hill, the Jebs + others are now faced with an outpouring of folk and
different footwork; their style is the immemorial bonhommie pipe
puffing inconsequential banalities of the 60s, 50s, 40s, 30s, etc. I
think they'll just drag out the armadillo sleeping bags + crawl in.
But maybe not.

I sure think of all of you w- all my heart every day. The last summary was a whiz, what a sequence of events 2 stop the heart! I'll sure
make use of it all 4 classes!

> Hope all chilluns are thriving. Some
> bones shall live!!
> ♥ Daniel

February [1980]

Dear Friends;

The work here is underway, two courses, some 200 students, all
denominations, coming from all over, going where the Spirit listeth.

An action being planned here for Ash Wednesday. Our thesis, passing strange, is that theology and the Bomb (the one having lost its
capital letter and the other gaining it) cannot easily coexist. We have
Bible study and prayer together. They are coming to the Pentagon in
April for a week's witness.

May the jails and courts be too small for our numbers in 1980.
They are our true seminaries—in there our theology will be forged
and our God worshipped.

> Daniel

Tues PM [early Feb., '80]

Dears,

We've got a little righteousness going 4 Ash Wednesday. Ellsberg starts us off, there's worship + a homily (me) then 2 the prexy's office where some ashes + I hope some blood will hit the spot. Then we'll sit there. It's about Livermore death trap. I think some folk are getting serious.

I was at Carmel in Reno, walked in the desert + had many hours with great sisters who are laying it out + want 2 go further. Every sister including one 75 and one 84 is a dropout from lousy prison. One group of 4 came from Jersey to Reno in a tubercular old trap, including the prowess who was then 68. I loved every minute with them. Then off into the Sierras + snowstorm. Gathering that night, eucharist, long palaver. Fri. I tool up 2 the Redwoods 2 meet with the Trappestines Merton loved + made his last stop with, before Bangkok + the kingdom.

So it goes around here. The Jebbys lie low but 4 a few who help out + seek out. What else is new but the few? The rest lick their neuroses + stroke their diplomas + call it livin'. I can snuff 1 of their term papers a mile or 2 away, the same perfumed brimstone that puffs out of Livermore after a quake. Howzzat for a history of the order: "After the Quake?"

You're in prayer of petition daily.

Our little boy died at St. Rose after 2 years of comatose. Say a prayer for the family.

Love yez,
♥ Dan'l

13 Feb [1980]

Dears,

We're moving right ahead for ash wed. Looks like McAfee Brown will join us in the sit in in the prexy's den. We're going to ask Dan Ellsberg too. There are some 20 of the seminarians ready to go; and I think practically all the schools will call off classes and take some part in the day. Teach in, fast, liturgy, march, and c.d. We're also going to spread some ashes on their immaculate toes.

There is much stirring in the dovecote here. Also a reprise of the 60s, no? I fear that if Carter hadn't invoked the death lottery, there wouldn't be much stirring yet on the nukes. But mebbe just mebbe, the peanut vender pushed the peanuts too far and fast. We'll see.

So it goes. With infinite hopes all are well and anti pentagonal juices are flowing and healing. . . . Buss the chilluns wetly fer me.

Off to LA and Zwerling and CWs and Immac. Heart friends on Sunday; also Chapman College. Never dull thanks be!

Happy Heart Day!!
♥ Dan'l

[On February 20, Dan's Ash Wednesday liturgy for peace at Berkeley, drawing attention to Livermore and Los Alamos nuclear labs, resulted in his arrest at a sit-in.]

Fri. Feb. 22nd (1980)

Dear Brother—

Praise be! Reports have it that you and the Ellsbergs and Rob't M. Brown and other valiant souls did it! From every indication, magnifique! Must have been a sterling witness—mebbe it'll set the stage for more resistance against L.L. Labs. Profound thanks from all of us! A few more friends heard from means a few more that will be heard from. Right.

Tuesday some trials, incl. Mary Lyons, Liz and Emma and 2 young women convicted on Thursday for Blight House, Holy Thurs. 1979, sentencing later; today Mary West, Juli Lolsch and Kathy Cooney convicted but no jail. Liz expects ~ 3 mos.

Thass about it, brother mine. We have to cover 1980 ourselves next week, and I must do a retreat in P'burgh for the Thomas Merton Center. So we keep sloggin'. The little ones superb and gushing life all over this place. They send ecstatic hugs. And best love from us. Peace and thanks to you, dear brother.

In Our Lord,
Phil, Liz, et al.

[This letter is the first explicit conversation about what would become the original Plowshares action on September 9, when Phil, Dan, and six others would enter the General Electric Nuclear Facility in King of Prussia, Pennsylvania, and pour blood on documents and damage the nose cones of nuclear warheads. Knowing the FBI had intercepted his mail in the past, Phil here refers to the site as the "toy assembly line."]

Tues. Mar. 4th (1980)

Dearest Brother—

A lovely, invigorating word from you today—backing up the phone call last night. Thank you so much. You give us heart and spirit. Another action or arraignment day would indeed throw down the gauntlet. So we'll remember that—and keep it in prayer. Mar. 20th—right?

About the matter mentioned to you on the phone—it seems that quite nearby and we hope, accessible, lies a noxious toy assembly line (toys of the 80's) to which stalwarts may gain entry for an admiring view, and perhaps, for something more. A floor plan is available and more distinct info. is being sought. The name of the community is even stunningly fitting, inspiring reverence for Prussians, Junkers and other bloodletting notable that Kissinger, for one, holds it all. Pentecost is tentatively chosen as Time fit for obeisance and for personal touches that will alter their design and engineering. (I'm sure they'll operate better with rudimentary and personal blessings.) After all, Bro. State has charged us Cath. w/ personal and unctious blessings on such handiwork.

So from the above oblique ref. we ask you—what do you think of said adventure (one has called it a 2nd Catonsville) and its timing? And secondly, dear brother, would you consider its possibility, evolution, emergence with us? We thought tentatively of 11 or 12, sterling citizens, somewhat, or not at all, reminiscent of the original band to whom our Advocates descended. Including women, of course,—we will make a strong approach to them. Two women from this address, and myself, have expressed interest. Everyone has huzzahed at prospect of the toy reviewing and alteration.

But—we surmise—one goes from the toys to the oven. That's an expected prospect.

In any event—will pursue the contingency, and keep you informed, in gobbledegook of course. And ask you to keep mum as password, for obvious reasons, save mentioned to a likely sister or brother. Yew know what ah mean. The flavor of the band is of some consequence.

Leave yew w/ this morsel to let yer wisdom chew on. We are okay, and thriving. It may you be the same. Peace and grace and more young Turks daring to listen to you, and to work with you. We love you.

> Liz, Phil, Frida, Jerry, Mary L.,
> Mary W., John S., Louie, Ladon,
> Carl Kabat—everybody

[Phil speaks here of actor Richard Cusack, who was Phil's roommate in college.]

Thurs. May 15th (1980)

Dear Dan—
    Just left Chicago and now, flying to B'more. Was in Minneapolis last night to speak at (gasp!) The U. of Mn.
    Had its ironic overtones—one of the Christian ministries at the U. brought me out—they're in a loose community, have a considerable center on campus, several Christian "frat" houses. And business— they're all for business—two restaurants, and manufacturing co., a construction co. They've found Jesus and the system, too. But there is beginning, it seems, the faint realization that the system ain't the Kingdom. I don't know where that leaves Jesus.
    I don't look for them to be storming the Pentagon soon.
    Called [Dick] Cusack in Chicago—he's back from off B'way and a week's early closing of the play. He's properly unflappable—had a fine chat w/ him, the first contact in several years. Like most thoughtful people, he's scared as hell of the present Nixonian/Hitlerian gang, but hasn't yet arrived at a realization of what we're trying/doing.
    Great seeing you, brother—always a time for clarification and strengthening for us. Thank you for your full and inspiring years in behalf of all us; thank you for your great hospitality and kindness to us and them rascals. It's of such stuff that marks the Kingdom. Liz sez she'll take the Kairos people when they arrive—mebbe we can help a bit with them. And we'll be praying for new efforts at community. Love you.

Christ's Spirit and every gratitude,
Phil

Mon. June 23rd (1980)

Dear Broth.—
    Just back from the ALC retreat in Media—lovely old Quaker Meeting House ours for the weekend, and the elderly Quakers welcoming and decent. The exchange so-so—as usual our people, Bach, Hammer, Lewis, Belate carried it. Lottsa young folks, hopefully "emergin."
    The Pa. caper revivified and looking fairly good. Two problems— enuf "casing" to warrant feasibility, and enuf good people. We have 3 now clear about taking it as far as seemingly possible—we don't

know if we can get in to do it—and 5 more praying over it, and in the process of deciding. All are good people—Mike Wehle (just out of jail), Bob Smith, Anne Montgomery, Elmer Maas, Dean Hammer. Will talk more of it when we see you. So far, Molly Rush (Merton Center in P'burgh), Schuchardt and myself clear on doing it if it's feasible.

This should do it—let us know when you're coming our way. The Lord's peace and constant love and thanks from us all.

Phil

Sun. July 6th (1980)

Dear Dan—

Anne Montgomery here for work w/ the effective group (some 15 of them). It appears that she will withdraw from consideration of the Pa. caper. And that, on reflection, is probably wise—since she has interior "blocks" to it that she doesn't understand, and has never been in jail more than overnight.

Molly Rush, the fine woman from P'burgh, is here for more palaver. She has a bad family situation—a husband who will perhaps never accept c.d. + Jail for her, and 2 little sons, about 10–12 yrs. Moreover, she will remain alone, since we've pretty well exhausted the women resisters that we know, and none seem inclined to take the plunge—for one reason or another.

In short, that explodes one hope that we had—that a strong contingent of women be included. Well, we tried . . . .

But we're all well, and looking to see youse. We miss you.

Peace, love—all good gifts from the Liberator.

In Jesu—
Phil

Sun. (July 1980)

Dear Bruv—

I instinctively have grave misgivings about leaving Liz and the children to the infants we've been living with recently—infants both young and old.

More of this when we see you. Good cheer, dear brother, grace, peace, our love.

In the Lord,
Phil

[Dan left on September 4 to make a retreat at Thomas Merton's Geth-semani monastery in Kentucky.]

Sat PM [1980—early Sept]

Dear Bro—

This is lamentably brief. Good things are gathering slowly which seems the true pace of life. The Maritain Merton thing was mixed indeed but today (Sat.) we passed at the hermitage + monastery. Some of the monks remembered our retreat + visits + seem inclined to un-derstanding—which is a switch from the semi mad semi comatosed academics.

A good moment at Merton's grave suggested we are OK. This has 2 do with both executioners + perennial weepers. There is keeping on 2 be kept on. You all do it. I love you.

Daniel

[After visiting Ireland to visit IRA prisoners in August, Dan and Phil carried out their plans with the Plowshares Eight on September 9 and were held at Montgomery County jail. Four of the eight, including Dan, accepted bail to organize support for their cause, while the oth-ers remained in jail. Dan had written to Jesuit Superior General Pedro Arrupe asking for more support for his actions, and Phil here refers to Arrupe's reply, which Dan had shared with him.]

Thurs. Sept. 18th (1980)

Dearest Brother—

Just got the Arrupe letter to the bros. We all highly approve—it was excellent. May create all sorts of openings—perhaps a quality of support that will give the local hangmen pause.

Spirits remain very good, very solid. The difference, I suppose, is the daily meeting on Mk's Gospel—a good hr. or more. It's a lifeline, I'm sure.

Fine visit w/ Liz—she's def. on top of things. And everything going smoothly at home—the kids diggin' school, and a good spirit pre-vailin'. Your visit meant a great deal.

Get y'self some breathin' space. Since Ireland, it's been hectic. Prayers for the back and a general spirit/health. We miss youse, but

know absolutely that you will move it outside like none of us can.
Much love from everyone—many thanks, many prayers.

Peace of Christ—

Phil + the other outside agitators

"Listen to the groans of the prisoners, and by your great power free
those who are condemned to die." Ps 79

Sat. Sept. 27th (1980)

Dearest Brother—

Bless youse for thinking of us, and writing so freq. Had a half-ass
strike that the brothers called. I say half-assed because ill-prepared
for, with nebulous demands. Anyway, the bahstids handled it master-
fully—cooked + served breakfast, locked us in, closed the peep slot,
picked off and shipped the leeeders—and got the chicken-hearted
kitchen crew back to work. All phone calls + visits suspended. At
supper, there was nothing but grinning guards and new faces spoon-
ing out the hash. They shipped 19 bros.—pretty much everyone with
his heart beating. We preserved anonymity + diplomatic neutrality,
and it is well we did, for word had it that they would have split us
up to the compass—to add to the woes of trial preparation.

We are considering the change of venue thing—and are remaining open on it until we hear all arg., incl. yers and the women's and
Glackin's. Our caution is dictated by 1. this possessed County might
need word on G.E. + the fed. Psychopaths most. 2. Brandy wine
would have better support in G.E. resistance. We think as well that
the faith that made Sept. 9th possible must be called to and perhaps
intensified—though the possibilities of trying us are greater in this
county.

We stay with Mt's Beatitudes and St. Mk. in the evening. A great
source of light and strength to us. Have no anxieties, dear brother,
we're in great shape—taking this piss hole easily in stride. Praying
fer you in Ky and at BC. Mucho gratitude for the efforts you alone
can make, and make so well. We love you.

Christ's justice,

Phil and every buddy

The Lord stops wars all over the world; he breaks, destroys spears, and sets shields on here. Ps 46

Sat. Oct. 4th (1980)

Dear Dan—

Your birthday card and poem splendid, for all its being unwarranted and undeserved. No one can approach you for consideration and delicacy—it's part of your great spirit and heart.

I don't have you included or on my visiting list—for obvious reasons. That leaves you with a coupla courses—you can phone McCoy, the ass. Warden and ask him to come—bloodline, defendant etc. Or you can come clergy (with Carol + Jerry) and attempt to bluff + bluster. Or, you may choose to wait, until defendants can meet. The first course is prob. the safest. Or the third, except we don't know when that will be. I'll leave it to you—you'll make it, one way or t'other.

The Phila Inquirer sez today the feds won't prosecute—they don't want to give us "publicity" because "that's what we're seeking." The bastards! Of course, I don't believe them. They could change it overnight, esp. after [election day on] Nov. 4th, when 1 cipher might replace another cipher. Ain't that sumpin? After $millions, untold "energy," and is zillions of blah, blah, blah—the poor, pissant country starts with zero and ends with zero.

Nightly, for 1½ hrs. we ponder Mk's Gospel. The presentations are invariably fine, and we dig up some fine pearls. I'm gonna try more faithfully, to jot some of them down.

Are you feeling okay? The brothers greet your letters with the same loving relish that I have. Much love to you. Care for yourself.

> Peace and life from Christ's Spirit—
> Phil

Tues. Oct. 14th [1980]

"Your constant love reaches above the heavens, your faithfulness to the skies." Ps. 108

Dearest Brother—

So great to see youse—so delighted. And rejoice that the health is tolerable, if not better. The time was absurdly short—and I winced at the struggle of Carol, Jerry and you to get here. But sufficient to touch base, to have some good hugs, and to go over some of the essentials.

Just finished your [*Ten Commandments for the Long Haul*] and passed it on to the bros. upstairs. I've already said what I think of that—splendid, just splendid. I'm not one to compare your books—to say this or that one is the best. But this one is magnificent—absolutely superb. Know this—for those who have some hope in them, your writing is clarifying, inspiring, strengthening. As the Script. says, it helps them to explain the hope in them—more, it builds their hope deeper. Thank you with all our hearts. Elmer is now relishing your MS on Apocalypse—both books will get readings and re-readings here. Will Seabury have sense enuf to take to it?

Luv you, brother. Every best from all the brothers.

> In Our Lord's peace—
> Phil

Wed. Oct 22nd [1980]

Dearest Brother—

Yers this morning the fullest version of what's happenin' w/ the women. Thanks much! Another lesson in what/whom one can count on. We wrote the women again this morning. But, John S. got one to Anne returned, marked legal mail. Out of that, somebody speculated that the women have been switched—Molly S. of P'burgh; Anne to Lebanon County.

Hope you aren't driven too hard. Yer right—the Bishops are professional obfuscators. They keep the people on pacifiers, pablum and pre-school programs. Now Pax Christi can attack K of P (Eileen Egan + co.) as "violent" for the next 10 yrs. If we have 10 years. Love youse, so do the brothers.

> Phil

Mon. Oct 27th [1980]

Dearest Brother—

2 from you today. Thanks so much for the constant solicitude, information, ideas.

Molly has been moved again—last we heard, she is at Mercer, Pa. near Gettysburg. I doubt very much that the Warden here, who has jurisdiction over the women, will allow a reunion in Washington Co. Jail—he wants no resumption of problems in the warden's club—too much mail, too many visitors. Meanwhile, no word from lawyers—in fact, no certainty that they know of her transfer.

Which helps to illumine the problem w/ trial preparation. From that standpoint, the situation is unconscionable—it couldn't be worse, virtually. We've lost a month in getting ready to face these bahstids. The mail's tampered with, Reading no solution, and that even worsened by split up, transfer, and transfer again (Molly). During this time, nobody can get to them except isolated supporters—us, you, the lawyers, none of us able to maintain contact.

I reflect that even the crummy feds did better than that at H'burg. They put up roadblocks—sure—but finally let the defendants in once a week, gave us a room etc. But this crowd—wow!

So where does all this leave us? It seems to us that if the habeas corpus is not granted and they aren't cut loose, and if the bail set isn't within reason (they'll probably ask $50,000) then the habeas corpus should be appealed, and we should contemplate total (verbal) non-cooperation at the trial, simply because we can't reasonably prepare for trial. In that eventuality, we'll have heavy grounds for appeal.

I could confer at least a partial switch. Like yourself, I thought trial prep most important, and worthy of unusual measure to get ready. But now I see that the current injustice, sep. vis a vis the women, make trial prep—as we envision it—practically impossible. That, it seems to us—considering of course, the consciences of the women—the overriding and first order of business.

Take it a bit easy on yourself, please. We're all excellent, and battling hard w. prospects. Much love from all 5 of us—peace, every grace.

In Christ, Brother—
Phil

[*On November 4, Ronald Reagan was elected president over Jimmy Carter; Phil here expresses his displeasure.*]

"Even before I speak you already know what I will say." Ps 139

Wed. Nov. 5th [1980]

Dear Bro Dan—
Well, the sidewalk skit is over, and the Actor will lead the emperah downhill—ever faster. Really hard to discern what our noble "countrypeople" had in mind in shoving poor Ronnie into the slot. I confess to being puzzled. It'll take this poor wretch 4 yrs. to learn

where Iran is—let alone get the hostages out. Well, I'm trying to draw something positive out of the fiasco—mebbe this Bad News will get a few friends moving.

Still have 2 N.T. sessions a day—for a while we had 3.

Hope you ain't worn to a frazzle. Please give yourself some infreq. consideration—you're our most precious resource. Know how we love you, and our gratitude for yourself and what you do.

> Peace of Christ—
> Phil

"So great is the regard of the law for private property, that it will not authorize the least violation of it; no, not even for the common good of the whole community." (Blackstone's *Commentaries*)

Thurs. Nov. 6th [1980]

Dearest Brother—

Like you sed—"we should be able to level with one another." We met last night re your letter on bail for all, and will do so again and again, as the need arises. So let me fumble with the guts of our discussion.

1) Acc. to our best appraisal—trial in late Jan., early Feb.

2) We attempted, as well as we could, to imagine the last 2 mos. for you—your anguish at the women's status, being a chief spokesman for us all, chief idea person and organizer—the aloneness and incessant, hard work of that. (And our sense that you're prob. working too hard—for all of us.) Out of this came the imperative of listening closely to your appraisal and suggestions, and doing our best not to do hide-bound to this side of the experiment.

3) We understand that you will meet w/ many friends today, and that out of this will prob. come some full time or partial help. By the same token, the bail hearing of Anne and Molly will clarify somewhat the help available to you—or to us from the outside. In turn, we've approached a couple of trusted people from here to do the shitwork in Norristown. The local parish has offered living space—and prob. working space (rally or anti-trial space is still an open question).

4) We would like to hear more re a focus on the anti-trial, building on the assumption that we ain't gonna get far w/ the courtroom Junkers. We don't think last Fri is a paradigm of the whole scene. Every one of their fascist blunders is an expose—many can be turned

against them by alert, determined people. Moreover, in a worst case view, we can non-cooperate, or we can take the stand. So—until we get more clarity, we'd tend to regard the trial as imp. as the anti-trial. (We must prepare for trial, since we don't know at this point how they will react to justification theory, internat'l law, higher law, Nuremberg, etc.)

5) Finally, we're trying to understand the contribution of jail witness—we believe it to be a constant testimony against them. Carl put it well, "I believe that I speak more loudly to folks from here than I would outside." (This is entirely apart from our suspicion that we have a good thing here—the luxury of one another, time to read, pray, work w/ prisoners.) I suspect that the jail factor is something of a consensus—that we'd be open to one or two coming out to help more directly, but that the rest should stay in. Personally, I incline toward staying in, but I certainly want to hear more from Liz and yourself on that. Don't want to freeze in any position.

Thinkin' of youse always, bruv, and me and the brothers sendin' much love. Thank you for being that touch and that beacon for us.

Christ's peace—
Phil

10 Nov. [1980]

Dear Brothers,

A funny thing today when I returned from Riverside. A letter from our Handsome Harrys of Norristown, peremptorily ordering appearance at trial, Dec. 3. I called Glackin, perplexed; not to worry, sez the counselor, that's their ploy to make sure the application for continuance is in our hands, not theirs. . . . So it goes, no day without its little ticks and roaches.

Messages reach us about youse not wanting to consider bail. OK by me. I'll await word directly to know your own thinking. Meantime this is just to fill you in on good folk who keep on keeping on because you do. Much much of that unkillable non degradable non electoral commodity.

LUV,
Dan'l

Fri. Nov. 21st [1980]

Dearest Brother—

First—Dean will have bail hearing w/ Molly + Anne next Tues. That much seems clear—though we're not holding our breath. Object—support the women and work Norristown.

Second—Howard Zinn showed up, and sat w/ the rest of us and listened. Then came the blockbuster—the Judge + DA went into their threatening routine—they don't want a trial, let alone a long one, they don't want people from elsewhere in, they don't want the expense, they are getting scared and are showing the fangs. So—plea bargain—that's the solution to every difficulty. Plead guilty, or we'll stonewall you in court and send you to state pen. If however, you go guilty—we'll let you have statements, and might even let expert witnesses in—devote a whole day to it, that sort of thing. The women (2) are costing them $100 a day ea.—usns more here, and they blanche at the idea of a long trial. They're not set up for it, the country is cheap + stingy, they don't want their "thing" disrupted. Precedents are dangerous. Hence the bared fangs.

We're gonna try to hash it out—we have roughly 2 wks. to decide. I'll write Liz tomorrow.

It's a challenge, brother—a substitute for bars and go-go girls. We'll muck it—do some prayer and deep pondering. And perhaps we can hope to see you on Tues. the 25th.

Love you. Warmest best from all of us. And Christ's peace.

Phil

Sat. Nov. 22nd [1980]

Dearest Brother—

Last night was another example—we were discussing the court's "offer" i.e. to cap a plea—and about all that was initially said was on the level of fervorino + moral rectitude. We've finally decided to go at it comprehensively and discuss all aspects that occur to us—legal, moral, the communities involved, family, defendants etc. etc. It'll be good—but it's like putting on thumb screws.

Zinn was his usual fine self—we were moved by his generosity in coming. He'll come completely w/ our decision re plea—in fact, he advised us to go along with Cirillo and the scoundrels—but apart from that, seems prepared to do some real work. Which is refreshing to hear.

That's about it, dear brother. Apart from the roller coaster imposed by the bahstids—that's good for us too; life gets too normal here—everything hopeful and good. Mebbe we'll see you next week or in early Dec. Much love always. Great to be aboard with you.

The Spirit's largess,
Phil

Sunday 23

Dear Brothers—

Glackin phoned last night about the bail hearing this week. Thanks to God as the Chermanns say. I expect 3 of you will be hitting public adulation & wall about which there are practically no laws or regulations, except that every apple falls and everything that goes round comes round. And that seems to be enuf.

The "plea bargaining" is a thing that will bear a little appraisal on my part, a bit of sharing, as well as of history.

To make matters even more interesting, Glackin informs me that we will probably have the same judge that reigned supreme during my bail hearing. The best of a bad lot. And that two things have been made abundantly clear already by hizzoner. 1) There will be no futzing around on HIS turf about such irrelevancies as intent, etc., and 2) He will look with jovian benignity at a plea bargain. Now I submit this is spoken like a true servant of GE and the corporate kingdom of Babel. And otter be received as such. Enuf.

As to myself. (And I promise this is the first and last time I will burden you with the following. It is offered to clear the air, and is difficult for me to give even this space to.) I'm probably as aware as anybody of the unpredictable character of my frame and its functioning, having inhabited same for over a half century—with mixed results to be sure. I go into this next phase probably knowing less than anyone else of eggzaktly how it will turn out for me. But that was part of the bargain from the beginning. And any turnabout now would strongly imply for me that either I haven't been sensible from the start, or was now panicking. Neither of which happens to be true. I still get that subdued quizzical look from Jesuits and others that says; you're out on bail for health reasons, and you think you're going to survive years of same??? All of which is the sort of "planning" that builds basilicas and museums, but doesn't build much conscience. Anyway. I feel and have for months, quite strong in the sense that we are all together, that we have the sense and stamina to realize that big to-dos about the future are immobilizing and paralyzing, and that all we are asked to do is to see the next day or few days through, and as human a way as we can well manage. And let it go at that. In my case, if some sort of crisis arises at some time, we will cope as we go. But for now and for what lies ahead, I wanted you to know the foregoing as a sign of warmth and solidarity, the bond that endures.

> Love to y'all—and then some—
> Daniel

Satiddy 29 Nov. (1980)

Dear Brothers—

I'm sittin pretty here, baskin in all the good letters that have flowed forth from yer parts of late. Thank you, most restorin' to the spirit. . . .

I'm off to Block Island for a bit. S'Fellow [Bill Stringfellow] is not well, I'm gonna try and shore him up on the project of Dr. Rose to go to the Bahamas and get some natural treatment for his worsening circulation. The alternative is bleak; they want to carve him again, and Rose assured him he would lose both legs if something like his proposal weren't done. Trouble is, Bill is by now really addicted to conventional (killing) medicine, and something like this is such a radical departure he doesn't know where to carry it. Say a prayer.

Much love, I'll write from the Island. But expect mails to be damn slow from there.

> ♥ Dan

Monday Dec. 1st (1980)

Dear Sisters/Brothers,

Dorothy Day and Harry Brown both died Saturday. Mebbe we can put things under so distinguished a patronage for the immediate future.

I wanted to raise a few questions which have come here (!) quite forcibly during the past days.

1) Particularly painful to me is the growing unanimity among our 'inner circle' of friends here. I mentioned earlier that Paul was in last week, he has undoubtedly by now visited the men as well. And he speaks for and with Eqbal, Jake, Jack Egan, the lawyers. In fact those

who work hard here, our old friends. There is another 'circle', consist-
ing of those who in general, leave things to our own conscience and
sense of things. That would include, for Phil and me, our family; and
for Anne [Montgomery], as she mentioned, her superior general. This
of course is a lifting help, but is not to the point here; which I take to
be the fact that a we-they situation is developing. Within it, as Paul
and Jake and others make clear, they will continue to work as hard
as they have, but under duress and sorrow about missed chances, ar-
bitrary punishment, and health hazards; and finally, political waste. I
don't have to tell anyone this is a division which is not only painful
but dangerous. God knows the movement is riven enough without
another spectacular from us.

2) Speaking of political waste, the developments with Jay Schulman
introduce a loss of some moment. (I risk going over things people are
perfectly aware of, just to get them down in some sort of agenda.)
We had been led to believe that through Jay there could develop a
public education that just might change the atmosphere of the trial;
and more than that, make a public contribution, debate, cross wind,
whatever, in that dreadful golden blog. We (I) had envisioned numbers of volunteers canvassing, leafleting, discussing, building access
to media, preparing profile questions about prospective jurors (which
qq. would then form the basis for an 'ideal jury' a la Harrisburg.)
Need I say there will be none of the above? According to Charlie,
any questioning of jurors will be done at the discretion of hizzoner,
by himself not by lawyers. About as effective a selection as, eg.,
Catonsville. (Except that at Catonsville, we had days on the stand,
and a full story gotten out.)

I am looking for a spar in this boiling element. I think of the B'more
4 trial; is that the example I ast myself? Which is to say, 4 great &
good people say in the teeth of apathy, snarls, objections, and plain
old Amurican purblindness; the thing stops here. In other words, is
this present episode a prototype of faith in which one says; we go for
broke, others will come along (which they did). . . . Or is this one in
which we yell the gospel, yet no hearing, and shake the dust?

–Can we reasonably conclude at present, as to whether a trial
would be harmful or helpful to the cause?

–Are we taking the sense of our friends seriously, their feeling of
being included?

–(Paul brought this one up.) Are we counseling one another, not
merely respecting or going along with one another? I think this is a
tough balance.

I wanted to include Ramsey and Charlie in this sweat house. I think
they qualify as friends. And in every sense, as hyper delicate about our

diameters. John said something about the plea proposal not having come from prayer; that hit me hard at the time; then I reflected, maybe we shouldn't make such distinctions, since everything, esp. friendship is providential, a gift.

I'll get this scraping into the mail. I've left the Block I. telephone with folk, sos we'll have a life line all week.

Everything here's copacetic.

> We love you muchly,
> Daniel

"I will make right the measure, and justice the plumb line." Is. 28

Mon. Dec. 1 [1980]

Dearest Brother—

As for Dorothy Day—mebbe she'll endow us with a double portion of her spirit. I suppose, in typical fashion, the mediocrities who ignored her in life will try to provide all the claptrap at her death—like they always do with the truly great. Well, she will elude them, and will do for us in Abraham's bosom what she did for us here. That and more. It's no coincidence that she dies when we're all in Caesar's clenched fist. She knows what that's about.

We've drawn up some rationale for not plea bargaining, and not taking bail. We'll send it to Dean and ask him to get it to you, Molly, Anne for approval. Then mebbe it can be circulated to communities and lawyers.

Liz came yesterday with the children. We had a lovely visit—everyone doing well, the tackers blooming. And the day before, Mick Doyle and a young priest/editor from the Camden Cath. paper. So we're being indulged. Best love to you, brother—you load the adventure with meaning and with truth.

> From all of us—in Christ—
> Phil

Dec. 4th [1980]

Brother Mine—

Two letters from you yestiddy—many good items. Thank you! You take such good care of us.

As for us, we're trying hard, opening the discussion again last night, and trying to deal with your questions. There's recognition of the love and sincerity of our friends; recognition too of their interference, and ignorance of conscience, and it seems to us, the course of faith which has in some great measure, dominated Sept. 9th from the start. Of course, that can't be said to them.

Well, we've seen some of this before during the Vietnam era, in a different face of course. But it's potentially explosive and divisive, not only with the "movement," but among ourselves. You said that very well.

Maybe this will help. As I see it, there are 3 factors leading to decision on the matter: personal (like family with Molly), health reasons and the third, wider community feedback and disagreement. The 1st 2 internal; the 3rd external to the eight. My, or as I suspect, our (the 4 here) would plea bargain if any one of the 8—for any reason—wanted to go that direction. There, the decision is kept internal—it's our decision. And a far different thing than the 8, or elements of the 8, bowing to the pressures of friends and lawyers.

One of the astonishing aspects of all of this is the trust given to those offering the [plea bargain] "deal." As it stands, it's only informal. We've seen numerous cases here where a formal deal has been betrayed. Moreover, once we're committed to the "deal," you're helpless—they can give you whatever time they wish. What's the source of trust in the deal—because Charlie Glackin believes them? These bahstids are masters at the "deal"—they handle hundreds of them every year, and they are treacherous as rattlers, yesterday, we saw an 18 yr. old kid with a wife and child (first offense) given 1½–3 yrs. after having bargained and after having been promised a drug program. A fortiori with us—they hate us with total relish.

I'm sorry you have to bear the brunt of controversy. Peace to you, and much love. We'll continue trying here.

In Our Lord—
Phil

[On December 2, three American women religious and a lay worker—Maura Clarke, Jean Donovan, Ita Ford, and Dorothy Kazel—were raped and killed in El Salvador on military orders. Phil here hopes it may mean the end of US aid to the Salvadoran government.]

Sat. Dec. 6th [1980]

Dearest Brother—

Called up Maywood this morning and had a lovely conversation with Carol (missed Jerry, out to the Post Office). Our brother is now off and running with 6 mos. sabbatical. The kids (students) gave him a fine sendoff last night. They are all wool and a yard wide, to put it minimally.

We're praying for the 3 nuns and 1 social worker in El Salvador, what a tragedy! But hopefully, it will spell the end of our imperializing there—how can we give "aid" to the very forces that murdered and raped 4 American women? And for the Irish prisoners. Did I tell you the BBC called here wanting to know if we were on hunger strike? I refused to call them back, for reasons you'd well understand. We love you—the brothers and I. Stay well. Every grace and peace.

In the Lord—Phil

"I will make right the measure and justice the plumb line." Is. 28

Mon. Dec. 8th [1980]

Dearest Brother—

The ironies in El Salvador imperial ones—the empire sends out its missionaries (who usually don't comprehend the politics of the thing—to put it mildly) and they get killed by the empire's hired guns. If the M.M.'s [Maryknollers] had any smarts, they'd pull them all out—but that's asking too much. But the Lord's rest to those 4 good women.

The Lord's firm hand—always,
In Him—Phil et fratres

Dec. 17 [1980]

Dear Brother,

I thank God every day that my pusillanimous bones were impelled into the Fakkktory, there being restrung with hammers and given new soul and blood.

What has been humiliating has been the 'dark woods' of the past weeks. One would have thought ho hum, I'm past all that. I wasn't. And I think the clacking jaws and furrowed brows of friends were also saying something; seeing something in me as well, some soft spot untouched by grace and life. Some part that yearned for them to prevail. And this after all we had gone through together, this time and former ones.

I guess this was a needful chastisement, for a degree of stand up pride. Now I know my size better, it seems as though that phase also is buried, among small beasties departed. That last visit seemed to set it right.

Having you in there, and the other brothers, is not easy. But it so to speak articulates the spine. And opens a third eye, on a reality dangerous, death ridden, jagged, and yet able, for healing and hope. What I long to send you at Christmas you already have; and you have it because you give it.

Love from here, in the great circle,
Dan

Sat. Dec. 20th [1980]

Dearest Bruv—

Your gorgeous Christmas card came—with customary Good News.

If I had health like yours—dare say this is true of all of us—we'd be nursing our health, not only not working our asses off as you do, but not even giving remote consideration to ample "time" and the possibility of cashiering in prison. I for one would say, most likely, "leave it to the healthy."

If this reaches you in time, then our most abundant love for Christmas, and everlasting thanks for who you are, and what you do for other hapless ones, including us.

In Christ, the Lord—
Phil, Elmer, Carl, John

Wed. Dec. 24th [1980]

Dearest Brother—

Another tip-top one from you today, many fine enclosures, esp. the piece on Dorothy. Well, dear brother, you not only knew her, but took her seriously. And that's all the difference. A superb piece.

A fine letter from Dean before he left town. He sez that Walter Sullivan and Peter Rosazza will be here on Monday, while Tom Gumbleton goes to the Pentagon. We'll try to offer them a little more than a "support" role—perhaps speak a bit as to their ministry + resp. a la Gospel.

That's it, dear brother. We'll try to call Maywood on Fri. morning. I figger we're gonna create a minor, or major, shitstorm. And as you say, it comes of keeping modest, and working together. We pray your

Christmas is the best ever—our love with you—the bestest and the mostest Peace of Christ—every grace.

Phil and brothers

Mon. Dec. 29th [1980]

Dearest Brother—

Your last 2, written just before Christmas, came today. Thanks for the articles on Dorothy [Day]—generally quite well done. Well, both [William] Miller + [David] O'Brien deeply admired her, and knew her. That helps.

Strange—your comments on the Bishops came—at least the letters came—just as we visited with them. Anyway, at the beginning, talk was evaporating into chit-chat, so John and I took holt of the bovine horns and went at it. They asked us "how much time did we have?" and we answered, "mebbe none." It could happen any time—the weapons more + more possess the madmen in decision making. Then went into same Act of God speculation—"we are the act of God. We are those who lean against the darkness,"—we being those who resist. Then Walter asked, "What's the point of entry? What's the breakthrough?" And we told them a public act of truth, civil disobedience, explaining how the law legalizes the Terror, as the church sacralizes it. The questions were generally not that good, but it appears they understood that we were asking, "What about you?" "When will you teach your people with your life?"

They're very nice guys—that can be disarming, can reduce any dialog to pap. The fact is, it's the old story of ministering to them. We parted warmly. And all of us will keep hoping. A Syracuse letter from Liz—she wrote of rather a harrowing trip up—the exhaust leaking etc. I hope to the Lord that she didn't have to start back in that fashion.

Peace and gratitude—
Phil et bros.

"Defeat does not come to those who trust in you, Lord." Ps 25

Dec. 30th (Tues.) [1980]

Dearest Brother—

Thinkin' of youse. Though we had gotten no mention that I can remember, presume that you'll be with the folks in DC for witness at the Hellhole. God bless you, Liz and all there.

We will fast and pray tomorrow for all the sisters/bros. at the meat factory, or as you identified it, the #1 abortion mill. Incidentally, the bro. bishops yesterday asked about the connection—"how come so many Christians take a stand on abortion but not the BOMB?" We waxed eloquent on that one.

Decided last evening that we'd follow up on Sullivan, Rosazza and Gumbleton—if Tom shows any disposition by his presence/action at the Pentagon—and write them a little analysis of the dialog yesterday. Then go concrete w/ them, and suggest a retreat with people like you and Liz and some likely truthsayers with an eye to resistance at the W. Dept. The above sounds very easy—and it won't be easy for their Lordships. But one lives in hope, huh?

Beautiful weather today—we all were so grateful for the yard. You're in heart, head, spirit. And we love you dearly—us 4 cabbages here, esp. me. Every grace + peace.

> In Our Lord—
> Phil

1981

Dear Bro,

> They brought us on death's own outing   jump suits
> pied like Mardi Gras & curses & groans
> & ten pound shoes   just like dray horses
> & starts & stops at every
> station of the cross   across Wm Penn's
> Sylvania
> 'Here's where that first trouble
> shooter set out on his last mile'   the guard yelled
> through his bull horn mouth
> '& here he did a certified phony fall & gaining time
>   was all
> But we hoisted him up   & here it was
> he rained like a red cloud   & precisely here
> we built him an everlasting memorial
> this mile square Christian tomb & closed the book
> You may all
> come down out
> take a 3 to 10 yr
> close look'

Here's a lil poem about our guided tour a coupla weeks ago. . . .
I have a call into the Protestant chaplain there to ast about visiting.
He's away, I'll try to get down there early next week. I hear Liz will
go with the chilluns on Satiddy. Great.

Dan'l

Sun Jan 11th [1981]

Dearest Brother—

Just finished at great length, letters to Sullivan, Rosazza and Murphy—the latter a Balto. Bishop that I knew when he was Sec. to Cardinal Sheehan. Laid it on them, as nicely as I could, and suggested the
utter urgency of pursuing Christian witness against the State—BOMB
demonology, via a retreat with you, Liz, and possibly others participat-
ing. Well—it's a way of thanking them for coming far enough to visit
us. I think they know that they must carry it further, but don't know
what that means. Another shot in the dark, huh bruv?

John has spearheaded a fast for Martin King's birthday—it
appears that at least half the jail has signed up—meanwhile circulat-
ing an excellent resume of the criminal injustice system across the
street. We don't expect waves in the jail—the honchos are already
well notified—but there will be waves in the establishment den over
yonder.

In the Lord—
Phil et fratres

Fri. Jan 16th [1981]

Dearest Brother—

Guess you'll (or we'll) have a big one in Philly on Sunday. I hope
Anne can get some clarification from Ramsey. To me, (of course
I've not been closely in touch) he's a big question mark, which has,
among other things, lengthened the vacuum for us all. By that I mean,
negotiating trial dates for us—always at later + later dates—merely
lengthens the time in which you have no sentence, no dim view of
the future. And all things equal, I wonder if it's worth it to have us
accomodating so readily to his schedule, + know he's busy, but I also
know Sept. 9th, and its significance.

The piece on Dorothy extremely good—like you say, it's tough to
write a short one when you have a long memory. Did you check out

[President] Carter's Farewell? Of course, the $184 billion he approved for defense a few hours earlier was fully consistent.

Peace of Christ—
Phil

Jan 21 [1981]

Dear Brothers—

Last night in Philly was 1 of the loveliest sustained paeans to life + hope since Beethoven's Fifth. For me the great joy was Liz + the chilluns + being able 2 hold them 4 a while.

I was 2 teach at Chestnut Hill Catholic school today, arranged by Glackin, but canceled by Mother Someone who "feared for parents' reaction." RIP Mother.

Much love—
Daniel

Mon. Jan 26th [1981]

Dearest Brother—

Jes wanna say briefly, that was one helluva job on the preface or introd. for The Long Loneliness. She practically lives in it. Personally, I think that you alone could have done it.

Well, you, Anne, Molly + Dean are meeting today—we'll be praying for that. When we get some feedback, we'll lend our minds to it. I think our position is getting stronger all the time. Faith + n. violence and lottsa rope for the sandlot (+ major league) barons.

Love ya. Everything okay here. Thanks for that splendid piece.

In Our Lord—
Phil

27 March [1981]

Dears,

As to the article on mom and dado, it's been fenagling around in my skull probly ever since I wuz conceived. The subject is still so sensitive I'd want both of you, and Jerry and Carol, to see it before it hits the light. I hope you like it; of course, any suggestions as to crossings out or additions gratefully received.

Everything else hunky dorey. Duzzent [Secretary of State Alexander] Haig make youse long for the good ol Kissinger days?

Luv,

Dan

[Phil responds here to Dan's article about their parents. Their father had favored Phil for his masculine traits but deemed Dan frail, unathletic, and more fit to help his mother than do farmwork with his brothers. Surprisingly, Phil defends their father by proposing that the reason he and Dan have so persistently struggled for justice is because their father was so constantly unjust; their fear that he might one day kill their mother may account for their concern for victims.]

Apr. 3, 1981

Dear Brother—

Thank you for the packet—and for the piece "Two Lives." Another evidence of your constant care of us. I've scrupulously saved most of the recent press stuff on the 8—it's come in from far and near. As Ridgeway sez—mebbe the trial is a turning point for the yellow press. Did a press conf. for May 3rd here in Balto.—the yellow press listened, seemed to imagine that their own cowardly hides were being hung out to dry, and reported fairly. The Blacks + Hispanics were all there—have made some essential connections, and are sore as hell at the heist. It's a new thing!

As for "Two Lives"—frankly, it devastated me. Two reasons for that—first, your memory is so true and your touch so deft, though uncompromising. Secondly, it faced me abruptly with my own emphatic liabilities thru the years vis a vis Freda—while Carol, Jerry and you maintained a loving presence and care. As for me, I was about cosmic matters, or at least, such was my attitude.

I view it totally to your credit that you've "fenagled in your skull," as you put it, with the matter of Freda + Pop, and the dreary years of upbringing. No wonder, since for Pop, it was John and you as betes noires (and worse) and a veritable campaign of terror and harassment. Freda fought for all of us—but especially for those that Pop most terrorized. You're right in asserting that she saved us all.

As for me however—and in contrast to you, I took it in sort of a myopic stride, and never expended myself overmuch in either understanding it deeply, or in struggling to help them both, especially Freda.

I wasn't under his ridicule that much—I was "my ole partner"—I learned to live with him in the most superficial fashion. And your recollection brings this home—as an expose of my dimwit and self-centeredness.

You write of the piece "hitting the light." What do you mean by that? Without knowing better, I can only assume you intend to publish it—either in itself, or later, in a book. If so, I question it mainly for the following reason—compassion for our poor Father (compassion that I was never prone to offer him). (Indifference was closer to my attitude, that and a thinly veiled contempt.)

I wonder if you're not seeing him too heavily from the standpoint of the terror he was to Freda, and secondly, the terror he was to you. True, from both aspects, his influence was tyrannical, was terrible. Nonetheless, what he did to Freda, and what he did to you, does not sum him up. The Two Lives is, as I read it, one life—Freda's life. A life that came to greatness (she was a great woman) because of grace and the awful reality of having to survive around him. And of seeing that we survived. But not his life nonetheless, in totality. In fact, I would venture to say that it would be impossible to encompass his life fairly—mostly from Freda's and your own.

I have mentioned my own indifference and contempt. But there has been another attitude—of gratitude, strangely enough. Gratitude that I have come to only since we got in trouble with the imperialists. Since that time, I've often asked—"why only you and me" (in any sustained fashion) to face them in their bloody dens, why only you and me to give a Gospel turn to c.d., to go to them with the truth? Others have said No! when the bahstids came for them, or have resisted secretly. But why only you and me—of all the Western clergy (in any sustained fashion), to enter their lairs and to shake them with the symbols of faith and justice?

Why? Maybe it comes from sweating on the clayhump with that poor wreck, living with fear so palpable we could taste it—day in and out, stunted year after year. When will he erupt again? When will the next battle royal happen? When will he hit her and possibly kill her? Well, with fear like that to be taken meal time with your grits, it makes of one a creature of fear, or it places justice and decency and human concerns in the concrete—just from the sheer horror and injustice of it. Places compassion and justice in stark relief. I suspect that we first learned justice under his boot, for the sheer lack of it. And learned it there most tellingly. For this I am grateful.

Liz has her own points to make, and will write them to you. As usual, you have done a great service, and we thank you for it. But, with my present understanding—or lack of it—I cannot see a wider circulation.

Frida had a joyous birthday. The little ones stretch and thrive. And everyone sends you love.

An Institute for Pol. Studies Day on ML King tomorrow (Sat). On Sun., an AHSC Conf. on the BOMB, and then Philly for the evening. Peace + plenty.

In Our Lord—
Phil

[ca. mid-May 1981]

Dear Bruv—

We're thinking of you in Europe—the Pope shot while you're there. God help us! We are patrons of the violence and the plague marches on. Be lookin' for you on return.

Love, peace, every Easter grace,
Liz, Phil, et al.

(June 25) (1981)

Dears—

Well. As to the local Eyerish & the fast, which continues in most serious fashion. I've been trying for some time to sell the idea that we'd better get some c.d. underway if we are to get anywhere near to saving some lives. At last. We now have 8 or 10 good folk who are ready to occupy the Brit consulate here on the 3rd. Including Ned, mesself, George, presumably MacDoyle, Sr. Rosaleen, & others. Send us a prayer, this is new ground here.

I was up to spend an evening with Jim, Rosalie, Ann, David, their daughter. We talked much of [their brother] John, whose silence and non-whereabouts are a prime worry. I've sent a check & book twice, both returned from different addresses. I can't remember when he's passed so long a time without letting us know where he was. Please say a prayer, and if you have anything to add to efforts—. Jim reported someone of Tom's family had seen John on the streets of Ely; but more than that we've not heard.

♥ Dan'

Wed. Aug 19th

Dearest Brother—

[W]anted to say—thanks for coming—that's huge understatement. I thank God that you and I run into no hurdles when pursuing a better mutual light. That's mostly to your credit—you love the truth and work at it—to the benefit of countless.

Your letter awaited me on return to my dog hutch—that and two others. Want you to know that I took it seriously, very seriously. And will pray over it, and as the jargon goes, try to remain "open." I sent it on to Liz and asked for her good judgement, and response, if she desires to give one. One from Jerry as well—he spoke of "bitterness" and "vengefulness" toward Salus. Sorry if my language extended that impression. I'd consider both attitudes crippling—indulgences I couldn't afford.

But I wrote Carol + him at length. And asked them if they'd please continue their observations and advice, if the inclination holds. The same applies to you, please. My somewhat perplexity rests upon the fact that most of the Pl. 8 [Plowshares Eight] appear to go along with the decision on bail, as well as Liz and the Jonah House people, as far as I understand. Carol, Jerry and you question it. I would consider the aggregate above as community (thank God for such a community) and if it ever appeared that this community thought unwise our decision, I would respond gratefully + immediately. Or if Liz, as I told you, said that I was needed for the birth of our little one.

I'll let this go, with my love. I pray you get the antibiotics and that they help with the bad sinuses. Thank you again for that damnably long trip.

> Peace of Christ, every light from the
> Spirit.
> Phil

"This is not a time for believing everyone. Believe only those you see modeling their lives on the life of Christ." —Teresa of Avila

Mon. Sept. 28th. [1981]

Dearest Brother—

Everything A ok. Liz came last Thurs.—one of my days off. She looked stunningly well and vital—her great constitution and peace makes the pregnancy attractive. After 4 hrs. drive from B'more, she had to wait nearly 2 hrs. while they checked the slave pens. But we had nonetheless, a solid 2 hrs. There is this advantage—the drive is a gorgeous one at this time of year especially.

Anyway, she ran down the signs of hope "emerging"—the women have a larger action planned for the Hall of Mirrors in Nov.; ourselves another large resistance Dec. 28th; 51 arrested at Anne Bazaar (only slowest of progress w/ Sojourners) etc etc.

Flash! Just over to see a counselor, and he tells me writing Carl, Elmer, John has been disapproved, and that any future visits from you will not be allowed. I ranted at the poor lame, but it's clear he's not resp.—[Superintendent] Mazurkiewicz is. I think we should move on both items. They have also discovered that Liz is an offender, and they might disapprove her. So mebbe Michael can handle it—if he does, then the appeal to the Superior Court should not be for 1 visit, but for visiting rights, and for correspondence rights.

Every light from the Spirit—
Phil

Tues. Oct. 6th [1981]

Dear Dan—

Yours of Fri. came yesterday—with its proper note of urgency. Liz wrote in similar tone—reminding me that we had agreed on acceptance of bail when the finest suspicions arose about twins. In a word, if the suspicions were confirmed, I would come out. That I agree to do, with gratitude.

Hope we may soon discuss the preliminaries to this decision. Liz and I, from my view, had fairly worked out conditions under which I would accept bail. And in a phone conversation last Fri., after she had had an M.D. examine her—I made it clear that twins would be tantamount to a green light, and I'd gladly come home. Now—even before her final exam on Oct. 8th—after which she planned to get word to me, I have agreed bail. So for the record, I don't think that it's one of intransigence, or insistence on purity of conscience. I think you should know that. In this last brief period in jail, I've had the temptation—once or twice—that our history together argues for a little more trust in my judgement. Perhaps I'm wrong in that—if so, chalk it up to my recurrent sensitivity. I know you make your recommendations out of love for me—and I profoundly appreciate that. But sometimes they get a bit galling, and I wonder if you trust me as I trust you.

Peace and much love. We'll make it.

In Our Lord—
Phil

[Liz gave birth to Kathleen Berrigan, their third and final child, on November 5.]

Sun. Nov. 29th

Dearest Bro—

   It strikes me, in the press of things, that neither Liz nor myself have thanked you for the marvelous + fulfilling afternoon after Kathleen's birth. It was truly marvelous!

   Thanks deeply for that RRI [Riverside Research Institute] action—sounds like a good 'un. Hope your Thanksgiving with the SJ's a splendid one. Love you mucho, all of us. Peace and blessing.

                    In the Lord—
                    Liz, Phil, et al.

Friday (March 12 1982)

Dears—

   Stringfellow has been ill with pneumonia, much to worry, but thank God, the worst is over & he's to leave the hospital on Saturday. He was brought to the mainland on Mon. during a terrible storm, by Coast Guard cutter. Remember the last time that transport was used??? The little guy is like a sack of dominos on end, one falls, everything goes; he's out of whack on sugar balance because he couldn't eat for days. But that's gradually restoring itself.

   I had a good evening in Richmond, some palaver with Sullivan. He avers he's thinking what to do after the letter is finished. I suggested (yet once more) c.d. He sed, Phil's saying that too!

                    ♥ Daniel

July 11 PM (1982)

Dears—

   Academe shows its incisors. The woman who hired me, she computerized + cauterized, invaded the class with a campus cop, to evict the unpaid + unwashed. Her prey were 2 friends, a USC professor + a campus chaplain. I tried 2 talk 2 her next day, she averred she wd. appear, combat ready, next day. So I recoursed me 2 a Dean who pulled her + minions off my back. There are all indications people go nuts in these festering foci; cross in right-hand, ROTC lore in left. Certainly, this Marianne is a different species than a year ago, from theologian 2 Amazon of order. Gawd help us!

Prayers for chilluns. As for yez.

Missing you,
♥ Daniel

[The Groton incident Phil refers to here is the Trident Nein Plow-shares action on July 4, in which two nuns and seven others entered the General Dynamics Electric Boat shipyard in Groton, Connecticut, and reached a Trident submarine by paddling in a canoe. They poured blood on it, hammered its missile hatches, and spray painted "USS Auschwitz" on it.]

Wd. August 4 (1982)

Dears,

I'm starting this before supper, with a meeting to follow at Kairos tonight, and finals on the 6th and 9th. This is a preliminary report, as some of us will have a later go at the retreat-action things after the reg'lar meeting. . . . Let me start by saying there's much interest & hope about sequel to Groton. I'll put thoughts down as they occur, in no particular order. . . .

–There is some feeling here that the next significant thing shd. be a NY action at RRI. They are now in the quarters on 42 street. I've advised cooling anything 'big' on the 6 or 9 there. Some wanted to go into the lobby (private to RRI) and do a blood thing. I argue for more time & casing etc. I've prevailed so far, I think. There will be upwards of—hundred or more at a general blockade, main entrance.

–Several from here want to go for the retreat. I think you'll have more than the baker's dozen. My thinking (if one can so dignify it) moves in direction of 2 actions, not one. The first by NYers here; the second to be decided over the weeks, elsewhere.

[The reference to Isaiah here is one that recurs in their letters. Know-ing their mail was often tampered with, they spoke of Plowshares ac-tions under the language of Isaiah, sometimes as "Is. 2," since Isaiah 2:14 inspired the name for their movement. It reads, "They shall beat their swords into plowshares, and their spears into pruning hooks; nation shall not lift up sword against nation, neither shall they learn war any more."]

Tues. Sept. 8 (1982)

Dear Bro. Dan—

Germany was good—many, many friends asking for you and conveying their love. It had aspects of the ludicrous about it—[Bishop Leroy] Matthiesen coming under Pax Christi and the official church blanket, and then choosing not to speak for the base Communities, even though he was free. I told him a few items about faith and the necessity of Germans hearing a Bishop preaching the gospel. But the Pax Christi honchos prevailed, refusing to release them.

Also met with Ernesto Cardenal and he is his typical sweet self—sends you much love. But he tends to unpack the qua when he speaks publicly. Less and less Chermans buying it however. Met [Dorothee] Solle and the German Theol. ([Johannes Baptist] Metz) inviting you in Oct. Both lovely people. He sez plans are going ahead and that you'll be hearing from them.

The next Is. 2 [Plowshares] thing in late Sept. Peter will run it if I am not available. Love you, dear brother. Liz + the kids + all say the same.

In xto,
Phil

Thanksgiving Nov. 25 (1982)

Dear Brother—

Among other great gifts—we give thanks for you. And what you've offered us thru the years. That comes under the genus of life.

Peace of Christ, love from every quarter, and vital thanks to youse,
Liz, Phil, Karl, et al. at Jonah

Jan 5. (1983)

Dears,

Well we have meetins meetins meetins, is that anything new? The other night was Pacific & productive. We've been able to shuck off the Himalayan dreams, and git downter bizness.

It appears it will be on Friday a week, Martin King's b'day. Prospects of good participation. We'll probly start with prayer at the Dwelling Place for homeless women, with some prayer, led by a black minister. Then proceed to RRI. Blocking, blood, ashes, the nosecone in the street outside.

I must admit to being quite consoled that the thing, after so many starts, has gotten started. This will also be a good intro to such realities, for Steve.

We've started the night shelter thing in the parish here, the pastor is a Goodfellow & it looks as tho a few of the Jebs will fall in.

All else switches and lurches along here. We resume the Revelation course Fri. night. Sun. I go to Providence for liturgy & small & big talk. The 3 ringer is on the road once more.

♥ + kisses

Daniel

[The movie proposal Dan refers to here would become In the King of Prussia, *directed by Emile de Antonio and starring Martin Sheen, which tells the story of the Plowshares Eight and stars the eight as themselves, including Phil and Dan.]*

Sunday (1983)

Dears,

It appears that we're cursed with spasms of fame—one more in the offing. The movie scenario we signed up for some time ago with the two young friends, is proceeding apace. The writing is in the hands of a young hot shot who was once a Jesuit novice in Canada, Yale grad, former CBS editor or something. Also there's much talk of a D.B. [Dan Berrigan] Reader, and Michael True is working with an editor in NY on this. (This I'll believe when the glossy jacket is in hand.) But I want to concentrate on the movie.

My philosophy in all this is that it's bound to happen; the only question being, can we minimize the damage n get something positive into the public. This is what I kidded Deedy about when he proposed that so called life. . . . But I meant it. If we can make friends with those who in any case, are going ahead now with the flick, I think we stand a better chance than if we leave it to them for whatever motive. (I think the Sheen-DeAntonio developments bear this out.) So. I've been meeting, I think twice, with this young writer of the scenario, had him for dinner here and Eucharist.

That abt. does it for now. I am working currently on Acts, in view of Pentecost the season. Dynamite rendered damp by time & neglect. But we try. In any case, and a long and hungry trek I've never seen such hunger for the Word.

Sat. Jan. 29th (1983)

Dear Brother—

You might have heard of the State of the Union demo in D.C.—
172 of us arrested in the Capital [*sic*] Bldg. incl. ole Fred Shuttles-
worth and your friend Rev. Mitchell from NYC. Also Paul Meyer,
Mitch, John Bach etc. And a good crowd from Baltimore. Frida was
arrested + detained—Katy had to be passed out to Peter De Mott—
Liz took it all from the vantage pt. of many years of "involvement."
A very good day.

Peace of Christ—
Liz, Phil, all at Jonah

Friday 24 June (1983)

Dear Ones,

The class (35 present + one dog) is quite responsive—surprisingly
so, since I had been led 2 think of a crowd of sanctified sleepers. We
have in attendance a lawyer, a dentist, an ex-Jesuit now teaching,
cousin Tony Fromhart who by now also qualifies as an ex-Jesuit also,
a young mover who makes fine comments and evidently lives by
them—then a number of sisters, teachers of religion, campus ministers, students, etc. Hardly anyone objects to my outrageous version of
Revelation. Even though the book is by now around, I find not reading
it's a great advantage,—as the book keeps offering boundless insights
that would never have occurred to me 3 or 4 years ago.

Sunday I lecture publicly in the PM, introduction by Prexy Carter,
S.J. Shortly the anomaly of theology-ROTC will come up. Even though
ROTC is sort of ghostly and lost here, its presence is the usual scandal.

In Tucson, two friends presented me with a splendid book, 'A Noble
Treason,' the story of the 6 White Rose, the students + professor [Kurt
Huber] executed under Hitler. I've been devouring some; will surely
see it gets in your hands. Question rises; WHY were not these heroes
+ martyrs, along with F. Jaegerstatter, considered for sainthood; why
has it taken 40 years for their lives to get around—and even now, not
through the church, though they were without exaggeration, fervent
Catholics? I connect after discussion with 2 developments: 1) fear
of "political" resistance and 2) shame of official church pro-Hitler
activity at the same period. In startling contrast by the way, to the

quickie canonization of Kolbe, whose life + death suffers no aura like the above embarrassment.

So it goes. But the book is splendid.

> Well, much love to all,
> ♥ Daniel

July 2 (1983)

Dears,

Work here goes well, I love the class, mainly women who come with something to offer. Tuesday I have a phone hook up with Loyola Chicago, who are showing a videotape of a public talk I gave here last Sunday: they want an hour of qq. + answers. Wednesday the U. shows our movie here, followed by same. Thursday I wind things up + depart. Next week I'll lie me out to B. Island to spend time with Bill + see what portends. I hear Kairos + others are working well with plans for August 6–9. Sure hope things are better with community folk in slump there!

I proposed to a few faculty here that they get to work on tax refusal. One has to stand somewhere.

> Mucho
> ♥ Dan

20 Sept. (1983)

Dears—

You shudda seen me phoning Jonah from a crossroads somewhere in rural Maine, after trying at every intermediate Hamlet on the ghostly coast. Was relieved to a degree to know things were at least delayed; one can set the jaw later when the hammer comes down. I also hope things went well at the Worker. My impression over the years that a big audience there means very little with regard to any marching. At least one can rejoice that Phil is once more welcome there—which wasn't true for years.

Did I tell yez our building is sold & they're warehousing apartments as they come empty? We're in for it. I wuz reading in the *Times*, a one bedroomer like this one is going for 1 thou to 1200. Stringfellow gave me a painting. That in itself is near miraculous. Wot he'll do with his consecrated junk, come the big move, I dunno for life of me. I've suggested a book called, 'The Theological Pack Rat.' Ha.

♥ Daniel

We don't know much about the new [superior] general [of the Jesuits, Peter Hans Kolvenbach]. He wasn't even at the convention, a dark horse—at least it means the end of John Paul's mafia.

Oct. 4 (1983)

Dear Brother Dan—

Well—60 yrs. tomorrow. I haven't thought of it at length, except in gratitude of being still, of some small service. Or at least, I hope I am. The health, thank God, holds firm, and it appears the convictions also. I sensed this impending jail thing has some significance. It's a way of opening another decade in some consistency with the last 18–20 years. So—Deo gratias.

With much love and undying gratitude for yourself. That comes from all of us.

Peace of Christ—
Phil

Sunday 29 Jan (1984)

Very dears,

We have a new provincial come June, an oversized shadow from Fordham. The last one I saw once in 6 yrs. His monument is that he put the retirement funds in order. But there was Joe Towle & now Tim Curtin, with whom was good first exchange. I've asked him to find out from the Jebs in El Salvador if it wd. be helpful for me to go down for two weeks or so. They're in hellish trouble, bombings, death threats etc., wrote us a painful letter saying they expect Reagan's bullies anytime. So we'll see.

I sure hope all are in good fettle, esp. the chilluns . . .

Much ♥
Dan'l

Sat PM (March 31 1984)

Dear Bruv + Sister—

I missed Liz by 1 day in Wooster. Curses! I spent an uneasy night in Jesuit gilded turf. Some Fathers wanted 2 be remembered 2 Phil, some wanted me dis-membered. It's like a dinosaur burial ground, with a few good gravediggers, just like in Hamlet.

Well we live as you do on the high wire strumming trepidation + Hope. But above all say thank you!

♥ Daniel

[Dan here considers going underground once more with their ongoing case for the King of Prussia Plowshares.]

May 2 [1984?]

Dears,

We had near 1000 at the talk, and even more at the demo. Several hundred were in process of getting busted when I left. If I have second thoughts, it's around the fine tuning of it all, quite a ballet.

As to Phil's reflection on the appeal, I'm inclined to give them as hard a time as we can, evasive or sanctuaried or legal mumbling & bumbling. All this a la St. Thomas More. I'd even go the underground trail once more, if that made sense to others, something about which I'm more than ordinarily bewildered.

Love,
Daniel

[Dan left in June for El Salvador, in the midst of a civil war, to see how the Jesuits there cope with death. The following letter was sent during his stay there.]

Sunday (June 3 1984)

Dear Brother,

Well we're leaving on Tuesday instead of Monday. This trip has been so assailed w- conundrums, delays, changes, one can only conclude 1) it's meant to happen, and 2) the demons are hanging from the ceiling. So be it. . . . I'm hoping one way or another, to get news of the trial outcome.

Jerry was very affected by my going, which shook me. I told Keck and Freddy I don't have any sense of fear, only of danger, a different thing. But I wanna see if there are Jesuits who are living differently than our crop, I mean with death, and coping for years now with harassment & squads & dogs & the whole shmear. How to live with death & flourish. I gotta lot to learn.

If the back sityashun proves too much, I'll just come on home. Seems sensible. I have a sense how painful these days are for you, and of course for Liz. She seemed exhausted Saturday, the long ride to and from N.Y. I was trying to urge People's Express, but she only assured me that Monday was a holiday & that'd be enough . . . I sure hope so. As you know she's the heart and soul, not only of us, but of the defendants as well.

A big ♥
Dan'l

June 9th [1984]

Dearest Brother—

Thanks for the remarks on Bob Bervard's reply to our observations. I agree that we have a rather formidable person on our hands, one who has done his homework, and one convinced that his approach will make for drama. I get the impression that he insists on posing as the dramatic expert, and that entails our tolerating his interpretation of our lives.

Liz has written a strong, and to me, valid appraisal of the work. I'll once more voice my reservations, first of his script and secondly, of his defense of it.

Our questioning largely centers on his projection of you and your "drinking", on my dabbling with violence, and lastly, on his portrayal of Liz and myself. These strike us as quite essential to any final rendition—to go ahead on the present basis makes us a play thing of his artistic sense.

Bless youse. We're all well and working on another exegesis of Is.—Micah. Love from all of usns, and the Lord's peace.

Phil, Liz, et al. at Jonah

[The Griffiss Dan refers to here is the Griffiss Plowshares action, for which Liz received a three-year sentence in May.]

Monday July 9 (1984)

Dears—

You + all Griffiss are in my heart. I try not to fear because you don't, or not greatly. It's a hellova world but not a bad Christ after all.

♥ Daniel

Aug. 14 (1984)

Dear bruv,

The nonsense in the housing continues. The landlord is a buck chaser aided + abetted by the ineffable Koch. I've held Christians don't go 2 court, except dragged in as defendants, but I guess we are going 2 go anyway.

Just talked to Stringfellow who is out of hospital; + has a respite from pain. I'll go out there Sunday. Jake will drive me to N. London for the ferry [to Block Island]. I'll spend one day there with Carol + Jerry + stay on a week.

I pray you + Kidlings + everyone is thriving. I keep green the time I was there last, before Liz was alas! snatched.

I'm workin' like a Trojan draghorse on the ms of my C. American diary. Orbis has bin encouraging. I'm feeling very Protestant work-ethical; as poppa wd. say. I can hardly stand it.

Much ♥ Dan'l

45 yrs. in the Society. God help us.

October 2 (1984)

Dear Brother,

I'm hoping in spite of all, this reaches you in the vicinity of your birthday. It never gets trite in my heart to say thank you for another year of the quality of service your life offers. How could it be trite to say thank you or the Lord who gives you verve, imagination, courage, cheerfulness—all the good things that add up to a wondrous life? Anyway, thank you with all my heart, and many more years to speak the truth to the powers excavation point and many fond thoughts and prayers in your and Liz's direction, and that of the chilluns on the good and great day . . .

Dan

(4 October 1984)

Dear Bruv—

We had the new provincial here last night. Remarkably two-fisted, upfront, a little like circus bear with its claws clipped. Not much power (as much as is granted, just like the justice dept.) much ego. It makes for endurance.

I hope the children are thriving, I'm sure they are!

Im off to B[erea] College this evening, from there to B. Island. I'll stay a few days with Bill, and try to size things up for the winter. I young friend is supposed to arrive, to stay with him. We sure all hope that works out.

Nice cheerful notes and drawings from Liz always a joy. I guess that's all. I'll write from the island.

Bruv Dan

All Saints (Nov. 1 1984)

There must be some sort of perverse fate or something at work, that we pass once more like those ships in that night. Well, we'll just hafta wait until Thanksgiving now & of the trip to Liz and the others . . .

I sent news to Liz that Fox called to say how much he liked her wonderful piece on the 'seamless robe', no abortion and no nukes, which she wrote & passed to me for some (very slight) editing. I was all set to pay for an ad if he'd not do it, and do it with italics; he now sez he'll give it a center spread. Also that a woman from Texas has been assigned to do a special on the Plowshares actions; some 5000 words. He reiterated his conviction that we are onto something he's coming to understand. Let's hope so.

♥ Dan'l

[Dan speaks here of what would become his autobiography, To Dwell in Peace. *While his idea here would not come to fruition, his decision to ask his siblings to write their perspectives in his book underscores the centrality he placed on family.]*

Sunday, November 18 (1984)

Dear Tom, John, Jerry, Jim, Phil,

A Thanksgiving greeting to one and all, and a fervent hope that (given the world) all are thriving in measure.

I'm seizing the moment not only for a greeting, but to solicit a 'sense of the family'. Something has come up that seems of interest. Winston Press of Minneapolis, has approached me to write something they're pleased to call an autobiography. I think the offer comes because a sense is in the air here and there, that our family has made a contribution to the church (and possibly even to the state). More to the point, I have a sense that setting the record straight would be of use.

I cringe from the idea of a merely personal account of my (or our) last fifty or so years. The project makes some sense as a family affair. All six should be heard from, in justice; because each of us has in his own way, suffered the times and contributed to them.

So I write to enlist your help. I'd be grateful if you'd each consider contributing—memories, impressions, changes. Publishing being a weirdly unpredictable game, I can't say what will eventually get printed. But I will do my best to work with whatever you write. Especially helpful would be reflections on work and war. Each of you has held interesting and demanding jobs. I suppose we still qualify as a working class family at least in background. Also how World War 2 affected you at the time, how wars and alarms since have brought further (or other) thoughts. This will be the main drift of the account, as I envision it; how a fairly typical Catholic working-class family took a close look at war in our lifetime, after undergoing war. And how such a family came to register its 'no', in ways that continue.

> Many fine thoughts to you and all,
> especially the chilluns—
> Dan'l

Sun. Jan. 13th [1985?]

Dear Bruv—

Forgive the silence—damn callus of me. Been workin', and picking away at a piece on Vietnam for some ex-students of Howard Zinn. And the correspondence—mountainous. Ugh!

See that deAntonio has nominated us again for the Nobel. Haw! Haw! What'll we do if we get it? On the infinitesimal chance, I'd have severe reservations about accepting it. I like Gandhi's approach to honors—we are only doing what we are commanded to do. Luke as well.

Our best gratitude for all the greeeeat thought + fulness and kindness—to us all, esp. to the chillun. Love you muchly.

> Peace of Christ,
> Phil

[The "project" Dan refers to here is what would become the movie The Mission, *featuring Robert DeNiro, directed by Roland Joffe, and written by Robert Bolt, all mentioned in this letter. Dan would be an adviser and also have a guest appearance in the film.]*

Tuesday 5 Feb. (1985)

Dear brother—

The typed letter (over) is to Tim Curtain and Don Moore, the superior here. I guess it speaks for itself. There's been a dummkopf from Life Mag snooping around here; I don't know if he got to you at Jonah. He ast real bright things on the phone like, I hear you and your brother are keeping the Plowshares incidents going, and what towns or what installations do you think will be hit next??? Beware. . . . As to the thing with DeNiro and Joffe, they came here one night with this project which I liked. They put me through my traces here, and I like them, and I think it's coming through. I'd like to show the world what a Jesuit like the one Bolt portrays might look like—since at least in this rare land, there doesn't seem to be a plethora of same . . . . . . Anyway, I'll keep you posted, as well as Liz and everyone else in the family.

> ♥ 2 Kidlings + all
> Daniel

(15 Feb. 1985)

Dearest bruv.

One thing about Seattle they're great huggers. Not being so in-clined, even with bearish strangers, I recoiled when one lady averred, "I'm gunna tell my chilluns I hugged D.B." But no one bothers 2 consult the embattled hugee!

Chilluns thriving?

♥ to all,
Daniel

[Though Jerry Berrigan has not garnered the attention or fame of his brothers, he often risked jail for nonviolent resistance. He and his wife, Carol, are always mentioned by Phil and Dan as, along with Liz, those with whom they felt closest.]

19 March (1985)

Dear Brother—

Well I've decided that I shd. be in Sarycuse for Jerry's sentencing, and was wondering if you could cut loose for same, April 3. It looks like the best chance I'd have for seeing you once more, as I leave our fair land on Easter Sunday. I know it's quite a haul, but it wd. surely be wunnerful if you could. . . .

I think the expectations are that he'll get 30 or 60 days, but not immediately, hizzoner be inclined to a rotarian jollity & bending the book. . . .

Please kiss all chilluns for me & in hopes of soon.

I hear Martin Sheen was smashing + suggested the $ go directly 2 Jonah, for your disposition there. Evidently (mebbe you heard) someone in Tom's family tract brother John down: he's alive + well in Montana. Jerry + Carol reports Tom much improved.

♥ Bruv

[The following letter was attached to a memo, part of which reads: "Dan Berrigan will spend the next few months in Colombia, South America, acting in a film which deals with the Jesuit reductions (mis-sions) during the colonial period."]

Mar. 23rd (Sat.) [1985]

Dear Dan—

About Jerry's sentencing—I can't make it, another sign for the times. It has to do w/ unmentionables connected w/ the Lord's Rising. Please let me know when you leave on Easter—might be floating around the general geography. And can see youse then. If not, we'll work out something else.

We're all okay, and better. The kids have finished a week off and are bloomingly well. Much gratitude to the Lord on that score alone. Hope you've got a few vacant spots prior to leaving. Best love from all—and every grace from the Throne.

Much thanks—
Phil

(April 10, 1985)

Such vivid thoughts of you + all friends govern my mind + prayer!

Easter has many gifts, sometimes in ways that made understanding, the tomb was already empty—the wonder being worked by better hands than ours. And ours in any case having only to ratify in blood a great work already done for us without us! So in spite of all, alleluia!

All well here after a hectic trip down. Now it's getting acquainted + getting 2 work.

♥ 2 Everyone
Daniel

Apr. 21st Sun. [1985?]

Dear Dan—

Mother McAlister died—God rest her. Funeral on the 23rd. Apparently, Liz has a 5 day furlough from the Powers. Wonders still abound!

We now have 8 stalwarts in prison from the house; 4 of us left. The scrubbed witness came off on the 18th, despite hopped up security. God bless them!

I go up to the funeral tomorrow—w/ the children. Carol—God bless her—will come down. It appears that Liz can't come here in the course of the 5 days.

Thinkin' of you, brother—prayers and love. Send us a good address when you have a moment.

> Peace of Christ—
> Phil et al. at Jonah

[ca. May 27, 1985]

Dear Bro. Dan—

Was down at the Sojourners hoedown on Peace Pentecost today. Looks like our friends have found their niche. Wallis gave a fine opening talk (I didn't hear it) cited you and me as examples of a fairer weather, foul weather fidelity and the some 1,200 rose to a standing ovation. It's at Cath. Univ.—Wallis sez 5–600 will go for c.d. on Tuesday. Scores asking for you and Liz—and some noble regulars there. Good spirit, lots of hope and real talk. Go back tomorrow for 2 sessions on jail witness.

The chillun are pissers—the little one more astonishing day by day—and all send their Uncle Dan massive hugs and big kisses.

> Love you much—
> Phil—Peace of Christ

Mon. June 10th (1985)

Dear Dan—

And our unpopularity grows. Less and less will work with us—they would rather do nothing. And so the Pentagon presences recently have been sparse, understandable if folks stay home and do something worthy. But such is often not the case.

Don't mean to burden you w/ inconsequentials—I often read your Peguy piece on the front wall—he's right as rain. Less and less takers on the road to Jerusalem.

The children are full of pizzazz, pray for you, ask for you. We'll have a big party when you return. Love you much. Every Pentecost gift.

> Peace + hugs—
> Phil

Sun. June 16 (1985)

Dear Bruv—

We're short here (4 adults) but scraping along—lottsa work, tryin' to keep faithful. Fox has just sprung a big story on pedophile priests (child molesters). Very pitiful, very shocking, esp. how church authorities went into their cocoons after repeated evidence. One guy in La. had the kids staying overnight with him in the rectory.

Carol + Jerry okay—we all miss youse. Martin Sheen's agent (gigs in Mn.) went bankrupt, or nearly so. So the $ is kaput. And I suspect Martin will try to reimburse from his own pocket. Poor Martin! Much love from us all.

Peace of Christ—
Phil

(2 October 1985)

Dearest brother—

Many fond and grateful thoughts wing your way, as we celebrate—with what gratitude, another year in your company. When I count the graces of my life—the gifts never deserved and hardly ever welcomed + emulated as should be—you come to me, at Thanksgiving.

Thank you from my heart for another year, for all of us. For holding fast to the Promise + the faith + Hope of the Saints. For surpassing the clichés—'needs' + 'moods' and 'comfortableness' and all such shit.

Before being sweet and strong and outside of so many, by locating and overflowing and multiplying hope—everywhere!

For being my brother,
♥ Daniel

[Dan volunteered for years at a hospital tending to AIDS and cancer patients, scrubbing bed pans, and doing other odd jobs. He would often lament the young who died during his time there.]

Satiddy (12 October, 1985)

Dear Brother—

The work at the hospice is emotionally tough! More so than it was at St. Rose, where older people dying seemed more in the course of nature and easier to take.

I failed to say that the book of our young friend on Mark's Gospel arrived here, thanks to you, and I'm starting to give it time. Seems very helpful and learned, but not in the deadly old way that sets my teeth on edge. Someone also sent me a new book of [John Howard] Yoder, *The Priestly Kingdom*, which makes hard going, harder by far than need be, at least in my range. So I look to Chet for some light, and more.

[leading up to Ash Wednesday, 1986]

Dear Bruv,
Just talked to bro Tommy and Virginia on the horn, they sound muted by midwinter but making it pretty well. Seems Tommy is able to do short walks, his speech seems pretty good, but probably we shouldn't expect too much by way of complete comeback. . . .

Talked to Carol & Jerry last night; seems he's to be tried next Thurs. by a Judge Scanlon whom they've corralled from somewhere to replace Conan. . . . Jerry's diagnosis continues puzzling but still encouraging, they've got him on something called dialantin and he sez he's not had a seizure since. ALSO MANY TESTS CONTINUE, I dunno, he so calm and contained through it all, a temperamental thing that I guess makes for his favor. I hope Carla & all in the house are thriving?

There's 2 be Ash Wed. action here at Riverside. I hope Pentagon lent is shaping up!

Much ♥ 2 all in the house!
Daniel

Feb. 25th Tues (1986)

Dear Brother—
Lemme tell you about yestiddy. Mitch showed up w/ the *60 Min.* crew—4 of them. The producer is Holly Fine. The cameraman, and I guess head honcho is Paul Fine, her husband—and two women writers, who have already begun their homework. We talked about 2½ hrs. They—inter nos—went to do the whole schmeer, incl. the testimony at a hellhole. Mitch has told them about the retreat regimen—they wanna get in on the last one, and then the climax, they swear to trustworthiness, say that nothing will go on the tube that we don't want

there, assent that they will take any risks with the participants. They are in short, sniffing the spoon of a big, big story.

Against the obvious shortcomings of this, there is the integrity of their show, a huge audience, and the possibility that they might peel away some of the protective coloring of the summit Mafiosa. I don't see how the gangsters could ignore it—the shit storm would strike in all directions. So that is seductive and enticing.

They want clips of you in NYC; of we here, of the prayer gatherings, of the hammers raised. We will have to do some tall pondering and prayer before committing ourselves—as for the minuses, there's probably a hundred. And the pluses, how many can you line up from the media? If we say no to the climax, I don't know if they're interested.

We're praying for Lew Cox. Sorry he's going the chemo route—he'd be immeasurably better off with Rad. God help us—it's a real epidemic. They're poisoning us.

> Peace of Christ,
> Phil

4 March [1986]—

Dear brother—

I got yrs finally tonight about *60 minutes*. Very interesting. These are a few preliminary thoughts you might find helpful.

- When I was underground in '70 we made a program with Ed Newman. CBS (NBC?) hassled for a long time before they would even agree 2 show the interview. They finally did but only when Newman stood up to them. What would this team of *60 Minutes* offer by way of putting jobs or careers on the line?
- Of course the people most closely concerned must have final say. Is this agreed to?
- Short of the access being urged, there is still a great story. There have been all these actions, there are clips from *King of Prussia* movie. There are people to be interviewed who have taken part. Why must media be on the scene?
- Even if all goes + *60 min.* shows what it wants, so what serious effect on the arms race? I dunno. I don't think we should get out of joint with expectations. The great + good work continues, thanks to those in prison, on trial, and encouraging retreats. Such things must go on. Media appetite is voracious. (Which is 2 say, I don't understand you when you write "the s-storm wd strike

in all directions." From a tv show? presuming it's even shown?)

- How come *60 minutes* was sniffing around us in '81, around Montgomery jail, at my place in NY, and nothing came of it? Who killed the story then (along with *Life* Mag, who had an old trusted writer at our trial, and killed the story he wrote? along w- *NY Times,* ignoring us for years?)
- The show (presuming its showing) might also blow a lot of cover for the future, increase surveillance everywhere, including on Jonah + everyone, determine worse conditions against resistance.
- I think we're being asked 2 give a lot with prospects of not much. The offer is a quick fix. Mebbe if we want media present, we should call de Antonio back. He always regretted not being inside G.E. guts in '81. Then he could dicker with the biggies. Meantime inviting Martin Sheen to come along—old home week.

I talk to Keck and Lew every few days. Lew continues wondrously cheerful & up. We're all praying to Jagerstatter for him, Don Moore has contacted J's widow for prayer in Germany, as Lew is offering his illness for peace, he tol' me this right after the horrid operation.

Sunday night I was called to the bedside of a young man some 5 miles from here, dying of AIDS. His friends wanted some prayer. One never gets away from it.

Well, love 2 everyone. I shd. be home by 18 or so March. Meantime academe has me on skateboard.

♥ Daniel

June 13 [1986?]

Dear Bro,

I jes finished with the CBSers & Mike [Wallace]. They all but tore the place up, there were eight of them & enuf tech, high and low, to electrify the moon. But we got through it. Mike insisted on quoting yer embarrassing approval of my life & pomps, which all but made me wanna join the Trappists. But at long last he saw how mute I wuz made to be, and went on to other things. I can only say thank you and I wish it were true, or could come true.

We're getting ready for some RRI arrests on 20 June. Martin Sheen has come in for the first time. We're going to have a huge poster with the crimes of RRI on it, glue it to the doors, and sit down. It's the start of what we hope will be a summer campaign. We'll see. I go to church (!) every Sunday with Martin, he loves the Spanish mass at

Holy Name, then we go out to brunch together. He keeps bringing folks along. Wotta good man.

I'm enclosing some recent gum-wagging. I couldn't let [Cardinal Joseph] Bernardin get away with his asinine 'proportionality' gobbledegook.

Lew Cox continues to amaze and gratify us all.

More & more AIDS tragedy. One young black fellow, 26, kicked out by his family, beat up by his brothers. I spent an hour with him, holding him as he droned on about his terrible life. He had been diagnosed only weeks before. He died two days after I first met him. Surely there's a clue here as to the bottoming out of the Amer. dream; whether it's middle class whites or drug takers. The prognosis, as they say, is not good—for anyone.

Waal I guess we keeps at it. I'll report on the Riverside Research thing.

Sure lovs yez & all there,
[Daniel]

July 2nd Wed. (1986)

Dear Brother—

A midnight note to welcome yew back to Liberty-land. Figger you'll land in the midst of the burlesque. Pretty much booby-hatched stuff.

Martin was in L.A. burying an old actor friend. I went to the funeral parlor (minor-league Loved One stuff) and saw him, met Janet and many movie friends. He was still high from his arrest in NYC with you. Like lifting an albatross from the neck. And told me of 250 arrested in San Diego or Long Beach blocking the *USS Missouri*. Wouldn't let the sailors off. So—more hope'n we can stand.

Thass it for now. Much love from us all. Peace of Christ, and hugs.
Phil et al. at Jonah

Tues. 5 August [1986]

Dears,

The AIDS work goes on. And yesterday I flew to Bawstin to see Corita [Kent], in hospital with very serious recurrence of cancer.

Lew's situation is so grave and uncertain and I'm no. 1 here, for a variety of reasons. One way or another, I've gotta see him through this before I can hope to get a bit of clarity as to the next move on Isaiah. It reminds me of the way (and I take hope from the thought)

Jerry and Carol saw our parents through the gate. I'm gonna tool up to Sarycuse this Thurs, if we're not in the slammer here; stay until Satiddy, as Keck is now at home & can cover things. . . . I doubt I'll be able to repeat the trip later in the month, but we'll get our chance to talk yet. I love yr. idea of sounding out the family.

♥ 2 all!

Daniel

[*Phil's letter indicates the level of interdependence and trust in place among himself, Dan, and Liz, as well as the fluid circumstances that affected the planning of their actions. It gives a sense of the balance he and Liz struck among their commitments to their children, their nonviolent convictions, and the faith he placed in Dan to help decide his level of participation.*]

Wed. Sept. 24th (1986)

Dear Dan—

Shure was a blessing being with youse, and Carol + Jerry + them good folks. I got some intuition that with many, there was a good measure of faith and hope, to the expense of belly-up.

Re our early-morning conversation on Sunday. On the return trip, I shared Carol's concerns and yours with the scholars and later, did the same with Liz, Ellen, Peter etc. The scholars agreed that my participation was not necessary—the group was clear, experienced (somewhat) and devoted to one another. Even after but 2 meetings. So they can make it, with a suggestion or two from Elmer and my-self.

As for Liz, we discussed your observations at length and she maintains that my presence here is desirable but not essential. Given the time and the Gospel of Mk.—we consider one of us with the children needful—not both of us. She remembers, as I do, the many years of separation since our marriage, and agrees that another fumbling act of fidelity will honor God's Will more than our hearkening to personal/interpersonal requirements. We do think of the children constantly, including our own.

All of which leads to your last point, and your devotion to Lewis. We all respect your loyalty to him, and love you all the more for it. Furthermore, I agree with all my heart that a community of action which includes you is a gift in more ways than I can count. What you offered Catonsville and the Pl. 8 was immeasurably more than from any of us—your faith, imagination, ability to explain and translate, etc. The same would hold true again, perhaps even more so. Finally, we would be together again—the main leaps into the unknown we have made together. And your leaps have been immeasurably more faithful and costly than anyone's, incl. my own.

So I understand all that—to some degree. And I am willing to wait for the next community. Nonetheless, questions arise which I must resolve with you, in so far as we can. If Lewis lives beyond the present, projected witness, what is my course? Would you support my going ahead with others, if you cannot because of Lewis? In other words, I'll help with present study and not participate if you—in the event that Lewis still lives—give me your blessing for the next one.

I hope these questions are fair, if somewhat hypothetical. A great deal unforeseen can happen in the next few months. But I will gladly put brakes on participation if you judge that my proposal is a non-violent one. In any case, you can ponder this and pray over it as I will, and then, let me know your mind.

I'm gonna share your two presentations, or my notes of them, with the others. They deserve some exposure to a better mind, and a better life.

We're all well and pray you're as good or better. Bless you, and much love from all.

Peace of Christ,
Phil, Liz, et al. at Jonah

Sept. 29 [1986]

Dear Liz and Phil,

I was also so happy to be with my dear ones for the retreat. Missed Liz,—but that was at least known beforehand, so bearable. I never know what becomes of all this biblical study & prayer, year after year U venture to that oasis, get much myself, and hope for the best. I guess it's my middle ground, certainly less intense and immediately fruitful than the P'shares retreats, but I think a good seed anyway.

Well, as to Phil's questions. As to the goings on here, I hope I've conveyed that there really isn't anyone else around for Lew, at least in the sense of morale & certain pressures & care of meals & plain being there. I guess that's worthwhile saying once more. I'm not his luxury. We could go into the question of why there aren't many cohorts or guardian spirits in the community, but that wouldn't be very fruitful, I think. I'm his closest friend.

I think it's a little like a marriage—at least the closest I'm likely to get. For good health and ill.

He's making it very much day to day. Some nights he has terrible vomiting, cramps, etc. This week it comes up that he may have to make another return to the hospital, anemic again, and very weak. That means, if it comes about, someone making sure he survives the inevitable shitty pseudo food, which he can't stomach, and no wonder; trying to maintain his weight (he always loses weight there) by getting food to him, prodding his flagging spirit,—again, who wouldn't exist at half mast in those places. So it goes.

If he doesn't have to go, I'm going to try & steal away to B. Island; the last time was mainly occupied in cooking & entertaining the dist-ing. guests for Bill's burial, getting Bill's books in, etc. We'll see. It may be that someone will fill in here so I can disappear.

Sometimes I swear, I feel like an indentured servant, with no options except those on the calendar.

Like, I agreed (long before Lew's illness) to teach at Berea College for a semester. The only contingency at that point, some two years ago, was the immanence of our roundup for the K. of Prussia tour. They understood that at the college, and agreed they would take the chance. I'm to go Feb—May. I will go, if Lew is fairly in shape and others here will take up the slack and be attentive to him.

Among other furrows to the brow, I reflect that this commitment removes me from the Plows. retreats & consequences for that length of time, some 3 months. How that affects yr. sense of my part in things, I leave to all of us for further palaver.

What Phil refers to as 'my blessing,' I can only think of (cringing meantime), as a sense of you, my heart's dearest, a sense that lies on all my life like Christ's own hand blessing me every day and hour. Sometimes I think of all of us in the 'great ring of pure and endless light.' This is as far from b.s. as I can get, whether at prayer or in this letter. We bless one another, in trying to live the way we do.

Phil's last talk on the child and the demon war will not easily be forgotten. How does one say thank you—except to say it!

Love you, and to the chilluns!

Daniel

[Early October, 1986]

An all too brief birthday greeting to my dear brother.

Thank you for such a life as you place now in the frying pan, now in the fire—and always in a good spirit.

Thank you for showing me how and when and where, year after year. And for Liz, and the children, and all who foregather at Jonah, and find the right way.

And for not giving in or giving up. We love you, we thank God for you.

Happy birthday—every day!
♥ Daniel

[Oct. 16, 1986]

Dears,

So many thanks for Phil's cheery call the other night. It helped my reentry on this loony scene here.

News is that Michael Roccosalvo, brother of Joe, died last night of AIDS. We'd been keeping the watch for some days, the family has had two nightmarish years of this. He made as the Irish say, a good end. I had had liturgy in his hospice room some weeks ago. He was blind and deaf and brain damaged at the end. His partner is also terminal. I spose someday we'll understand all this, the wipeout of hundreds of young who've by and large bought America & been had.

I'm to give the homily at the funeral on Satiddy.

At Yale, where the N. Haven folk showed *K. of Prussia* film, I met John Hogan; he's recently returned from Nicaragua where he did carpentry with a team of friends, housing. It's been strictly memory lane of late.

I sure hope all is well there & everyone thriving. Our friend Lewis is very much up & down. He's back from hospital, blood transfusion and chimo. Nip & tuck. Mostly as I know so well, matter of morale.

Much ♥
Daniel

Oct. 30th Thurs.

Dear Brother—

I came home sorely perplexed and torn. Liz and I discussed my dilemma at length—and getting it on the table was some help. The community of action is pretty well advanced, and deserves a definite word from me at the next campfire, in a few days. So—I'll tell them I'm out, and painting for the next one.

That's a clear decision and I'll go thru with it. The reasons however, are unclear and hence, the conflict emerges. Mebbe, I dunno, my ego needs some bruising. And I'd welcome that if it does. But as I wrote you before—Carol, Jerry and yourself too see things differently than Liz and the community here—and I stand in the middle, loving and respecting both sources. But still in the middle.

Secondly, "timing" seems to me interpretable only from a non-violent context. Which is to say, neither Liz nor the Jonahs here give evidence of irresponsibility toward the children or the house. Hence—so goes my reasoning (or my ego)—and given the Gospel and the Terror—how can "timing" be off my going ahead?

I'm not referring to the group not needing me—most likely they can make it on their own. I'm referring to myself, and being out of jail since Fall '81, and having excuses beyond Liz's imprisonment. Like now. Who wants another rhubarb with the bahstids? I don't! Who wants more time in the dumpster? I don't! Or for that matter, struggling with the judicial booby hatch? I sure as hell don't.

I don't have much more time to be useful—that's true of all the Berums. And in my epic view, getting caught by the Pa. courts short of another disarmament would be a commentary on my un faith. So I had to throw that into the hopper also.

None of this will have the slightest influence on waiting—I'm just being confessional. I ought to level with you—you deserve that, God knows. In the Lord's Providence—I'm sure things will eventuate for the best. And to repeat—mebbe I need the discipline of this.

Peace of Christ—
Phil

Oct. 30 [1986]

Dears,

It's bin quite a few days. On Satiddy we buried Mike Roccasalvo who died of AIDS. He'd been a Jesuit for some ten years, then as they say, took up with something different. I dunno. I was asked to give the homily, which I allus find emotionally wipes me out.

The real 'thing' in all this mess is not sexual at all, the Pope, bishops etc. etc. to the contrary. In most drug cases & gays, it's buying into America to the point that one self destructs. Munny munny munny. Simple as that; and on the basis now of years of dragging through the mess, I guess I don't need a helluva lot of instruction from aforesaid Poppa or shepherds in the mist. . . .

Last week, a call from Martin Sheen. He was on his way to Pa., the usual midnight junket, on behalf of a woman down there who's running for some national office. Martin wanted yez & I to know that he's assigned profits from some tv taping recently, to Jonah house & me equally, for our works & pomps. 2500 each. I seem to remember he phoned you also as to this. Ain't he something?

By the bye, I wrote a letter to the General which everyone in the community signed, protesting the imminent dismissal from the order, of John McNeill. He refuses to give up the gay work he's been doing in so many valuable ways. John and sed Gen. met in NY over the weekend, and said G. refused to change HIS orders, which were, Git Im Out! So the cold breath touches us up close, and then some.

John is quite smart, in some ways, dumb in others. He would never be in such a fix if he weren't a loner whom we never see. He could have had terrific support here—and then what wd. the brahmins have done? Kicked us all out? I guess we'll never learn from the nuns that you've gotta have chins up.

♥ Daniel

Nov. 7 [1986]

Dears,

What I hope for is that Phil & everyone will be free to follow the lead of the spirit. We've all done a good deal of trying our best for one another & it appears to me now that whatever is decided will have its blessing.

Lew continues so so. Keck and I drove with him to Bear Mt. last week for his birthday. We did some walking though he seemed very feeble. There isn't anything to do except keep shoring him up; we pray together, and of course there's liturgy here. His faith and hope are really remarkable in midst of it all.

I'll be amazed if the *60 minutes* comes off.

The AIDS terror goes on unchecked. Two young men died past week. I hear by the grapevine 2 Jesuits have died of AIDS so far. The NCR is on the tail of a story; priests & aids.

John McNeill is advised he's Out. NCR is covering this latest Roman turkey. Did I write I composed a letter to the General, protesting the move. Everyone in the community signed it. But of course we got nowhere.

Much love,
Daniel

Dec. 11th Thurs [1986]

Dear Dan—

Thank God for Lew's passing—the Lord is gracing us w/ easy deaths in a time when most deaths are despairing.

Hadda write you about your sermon which it seems to me, sez it all about Is. 2. Yes! Isaiah calls for the impossible. May God raise up more for that task. But—the piece was marvelous—a great song of hope. We'll have to get it around.

I'm praying daily, in what I hope is the spirit of the Psalms, that the Lord brings down Ronnie [Reagan] and his Thugs. Not for retribution, but to save lives, and to instruct the amoebas. It seems to me that if the terrorists are hauled down from their high + mighty places, and even face prosecution—they'll do far less terrorism.

> Much love—peace of Christ—
> Phil

[*On January 6, four people, including Greg Boertje, who Phil speaks of in his reply to this letter, entered the Willow Grove Naval Air Station in Horsham, Pennsylvania, and hammered and poured blood on two planes. The action became known as the Epiphany Plowshares. Dan here expresses his hesitations about this particular action and the general direction of the Plowshares movement.*]

20 Jan [1987]

Dears,

I am writing for some light; especially re the Philly action, and the reaction I've gotten in some quarters, when I bring up Plowshares, especially this mounting cost, and sentences; equivalent, I would judge, to the mounting damage sustained by Mars & cohorts. In other words, yer thoughts on what I take to be a loss in the symbolic, as there's a larger measure of damage.

Are we losing something? I suspect we are. That something has entered the minds and hearts, about 'matching the growing fury, expense, waste, of the weaponry', with our own efforts to 'up the ante.'

This seems to me to enter into the purely material cost equation, and to open us in ordinary eyes, to largely wasteful discussion on sabotage, violence, etc.

I sense a loss of the modesty of the first enterprise, where the hammers were small, as was the damage in $$ terms, the whole thing quite manageable in the explaining, and public understanding easier come by.

I felt more peaceableness and equanimity of spirit in discussing those early acts, than I do now. I wish we could get things back to base, so to speak. To announce a quarter million in damage is to set the head spinning, and (I think) obscure the intent, which I take it was first of all to induce public awakening through the symbols themselves, rather than to attempt a direct impeding of the machine (impossible in any case).

Well any thoughts on this will help me, as well as those I talked to here & there.

Love,
Daniel

Jan. 22nd [1987]

Dear Dan—

You say "Are we losing something? I suspect we are." That may be part of the difficulty—you suspect we are. Your suspicions feed mine. I suspect you trusted the reactions of friends more than you trust me or ole Elmer, or the Epiph. Plowshares. Or so it appears.

Where does such language as "upping the ante" come from? I haven't heard that since the 60's. It certainly is not my language, nor do I subscribe to the thinking behind it.

The fact is we spend considerable time on "preserving the symbol" as it's called. The fact is the Epiphany Plowshares worked, paused, prayed, waited, and went thru that cycle again. The fact is Greg Boertje called assuring us that they didn't go berserk, that they didn't go for maximum damage. The fact is the size of the hammers haven't changed—they're the same size as at K of P. The fact is they used sledgehammers in the last one in Mo. because of the track and only for that. The fact is the press reported sledgehammers and light. The fact is the dollar total is so high because the plane was stuffed with computer technology.

I probably would have gone lighter myself, but I know the people and trust them. I think you ought to also. As far as I'm concerned, none of these groups that we had anything to do with have gotten off base. They went thru long, prayerful, exhausting preparation, and following that, knew pretty well what they were doing.

Frankly, I'm riding with your letter. I don't think it's worthy of you. And if I'm wrong in this—then you ride with me. As I've ridden with you and your letter.

One last point—the mounting costs in sentences is not equivalent to mounting damage. Martin Halloday did a couple of hundred dollars worth, and got 8 yrs. And I could cite other examples. It seems to me that you know the courts better than such a remark indicates.

Well, enough of this.

Love from us all—
Phil

February 27 [1987]

Dear Phil and Liz, Jerry and Carol,

What follows qualifies as small potatoes, but since it concerns all of us, I wanted to catch you up, and ask some advice.

I've finished the autobiog at last, some 500 ms. pages, and Harper professes themselves in the main, satisfied with the thing. Some additions & subtractions, but in the main, in their hands. There does remain, though, one important matter; that of title. I wuz attached to 'Keep Yr. Eyes on the Prize'; but the savants remind me there is a tv series & book now on the shelves, on the civil rights movement. So that's that, dammit.

What they're talking about now, and bruting about among their workers, is 'Prisoner of Hope'.

Now that strikes me wrong. I haven't been in prison that much; and even though they obviously have a double meaning here, I guess something like, 'hope keeps one in bonds, in a certain sense, to itself,' it still strikes me too much as a claim rather than an illumination.

Anyway, I wonder what yr. thoughts are, and wd. be sooo grateful for either yr. approval, or an alternative.

They also want another chapter, or are there at least urging it, on something about 'living in the spirit and in the world.' We'll see.

Thass all for now. Things here copasetic. Say a prayer for the students, and all of us.

Much ♥
Daniel

[On May 5, public testimony was to begin in the joint House and Senate investigations of the Iran-Contra Affair, in which President Reagan had become embroiled. The rallies Phil refers to here are in preparation for the hearings.]

Sat. Apr. 25th [1987]

Dear Dan—

The house full for the big rally in D.C.—some 200 thou there. And a good spirit.

Tomorrow, an Impeachment Coalition rally on the Capitol steps. And on Mon.—the big c.d. At CIA headquarters in Langley. Hafta speak at the rally. Figger that impeaching Ronnie, Bush and Meese will save a lotta lives, creating a Reagangate Syndrome (after the Vietnam Syndrome).

Guess you'll be returning in a coupla weeks. It'll be so good to see youse. Jim [Berrigan] reports that he heard from John [Berrigan], from Anchorage, Alaska—no less. He still grinds out the old grievances. God be good to him. Jim is his own true self, anguished about low-profile peace people on the Eastern Shore. Waaal—that's all over!

Best love to you—Peace of Christ,
Liz, Phil, et al. at Jonah

May 3rd Sun. [1987]

Dear Brother Dan—

Liz and I wanted to write a line hailing your birthday. May always offers an occasion to count our blessings—and you're the chief one, outside of God's grace. In fact, you're a version of God's grace.

As Reagangate enfolds in D.C. and the crooks go down in disgrace, one by one—the contrast offered by you and Jim and Jerry stands in healing relief. What more can I say?

The scene at CIA very good for a mass effort, remarkable spirit. Greg, John and myself for the first of over 600 busted. Incidentally, Greg and John are in the dumpster for APL [Applied Physics Lab], mebbe for 12 days. It's liable to make Greg late for his trial in Philly (May 11).

In any case, dear brother—a blessed birthday, and all sorts of gifts from the Risen One.

Phil

June 5 [1987]

Dears,

What one can think of only as the BIG SUMMER FUN FESTIVAL is in full swing here. [Jack] St. George is in town, just fine in health;

also Nhat Hanh and Phuong and today I'm to lunch with Joe Mulligan. Sunday I have something known as a 'commissioning' of some 20 local folk who are departing for Rocky Flats. Steve Kroeger was here last night to say hello-goodbye as he's getting ordained in a week, and then off to altiplano of Peru for his last year; among Indians and seminarians. Whew!

I sure would love to tool down on Monday the 22 if that's OK, stay overnight. I have a trial date with some Jesuits arrested in March at Riverside, on the 25. Last week a judge dropped charges on Ned and me, 'in the interests of Justice', whatever that may mean.

[Robert] DeNiro had a smashing (small, thank God) return party for me this week. Six members of the family, including the wondrous grandmother, 86, and friend of Mary Rizzo. Also Bob's father, a renowned artist of the NY school. I enjoyed meself thoroughly.

Martin Sheen is in town, and I'm invited to his premiere on Monday. I cringe at the thought, and will surely get out of the paahty afterward, which is bound to be a mob scene. The film also, I read, wd. make the molars grind. . . . He's his usual lovely self, and asks tenderly for you all. I guess that about all but covers things.

Well this goes with much love to all, and fond thoughts & hopes for a good talky reunion.

♥ Daniel

June 17 [1987]

Dears,

You'll be glad to know that Harpers yielded, with a certain amt. of kicking & screaming, on the cover & book title. The new one (entirely acceptable); *TO DWELL IN PEACE*. Now & again we win one.

Also Orbis is asking for the ms. compiled by Mike True some yrs. ago, a B[errigan] Reader. Mike is in China until July, teaching. I sent some things along. It really is sumpin reviewing one's pecadillos over all the yrs. Mike, the kindest & best of peepul, tends slightly toward the archaic in lit. & theology. He apparently thinks I did my bit for literacy yrs. ago. And the selections favor that. Ego however suggests that one is still slightly short of senility on most counts. So the corrective.

Well I sure hope & pray this new honeymoon with [Orbis editor Robert] Ellsberg & company goes somewhere. You probably know that Harper was bought out recently by some tycoon or other. Which accounts at least in part, for the present near chaos of the operation.

So, as they say, it goes.

Life as usual here. Much AIDS tragedy to cope with. The community is pretty much away for the week, at Lemon [Le Moyne] college for a province hoedown. I figgered I paid my dues at the earlier congregation so I'm sittin tight.

♥ Daniel

[Jerryknoll is the name their father gave to their childhood home in Syracuse.]

17 August [1987]

Dears,

There was no flak from the Order when I ventured to give a ss. meditation to some 2500 Catholic & Protestant gays in Miami. I was expecting the worst; but I guess the s. is still intact & legal. We can't say Mass for them, they're exiled from our church, etc. etc. There was such grief and forgiveness and joy in Miami, I thought I was translated to a black church in the '60s. Something is happening to these achieving darlings of the kultcher; it's all the loss and dying and ghettoizing. I see it too in the dying here; they're dying better.

August 15th marked FORTY EIGHT yrs. since I left Jerryknoll to try sea legs in unsteady waters. Kin you believe it?

Mindful also of so many trials coming up. And so so grateful that swords are bending, thanks to yez.

Daniel

[On August 16, peace activist George Ostensen cut down three Extremely Low Frequency poles and ground wires at the ELF Communication System Transmitter Site in Clam Lake, Wisconsin. He was aided by Plowshares activist Helen Woodson. It became known as the Harmonic Disarmament for Life. Phil's letter reflects the growing discomfort he shared with Dan regarding the motives and tactics of the movement they had helped begin.]

Aug. 23rd Sun. (1987)

Dear Brother—

Our friend George Ostensen (who was in jail with us in the PSB in Syracuse), has done a solo Plowshares in Wisc. George went West intending to act with others. That got aborted for some unknown reason, so he goes it alone—with Helen Woodson, like our friends in Missouri. All this is grist for Helen's mill (she loves it) and idiotic from any other thoughtful view. Last we heard, he was doing a truth and openness thing with the FBI, and they be confoozin' George. I'm afraid his heart is light years ahead of his head. Some folks thought there was danger of George making a Md. connection, but that appears slight.

Let us know how you are.

Love youse—prayers and peace.
Phil, Liz et al. at Jonah

Aug. 27th Thurs. (1987)

Dear Dan—

Blessings on the 48 years. I guess we in the family know—and we alone—what that means. And has meant as singular grace to us first of all—and literally thousands of others. Liz and I and all of us send our love, and unquenchable gratitude.

We're sloggin along with work and sundries.

Thanks for the $ from the Fund for them Plowshares. We sent down the same amounts.

The kids start school next week. Where has the Summer gone?

Peace of Christ, much love again,
Phil, Liz, et al. at Jonah

[1987—early October]

Dear brother—

I couldn't think of a gift to send for your birthday—then I thought of this scrawl, it tries to say what can't be said—what you mean to me, a gift every year of your life presses down and overflows more and more wondrously.

Thank you for verve and good humor and a heart big as the world, and beautiful as we long to make the world. Thank you, not for 'not giving up', which says nothing of keeping at it; as you do with style and celebration and a single eye on the 'one thing necessary.'

Maybe 'friend' is after all the best I can come on. Thank you for being my friend.

Much ♥
Daniel

Sun Oct. 11th [1987]

Dear Brother—
  The piece on Friendship's terrific. I pondered it long and hard. I figger you can say something to the point about friendship because you've been a friend to thousands or tens of thousands, or the whole human family, more precisely. But esp. to me. Thank you most deeply.

Love you muchly. Peace of Christ—
Phil, Liz, all at Jonah

Nov. 16 [1987]

Dears,
  We've bin hit with a 30% (at least, may go to 40 or more) rent increase. The bloodsuckers made the elevator work, put a lock on the front door, a roof, windows, etc. and then stuck us with 'improvements'; when of course he was only being forced to correct violations. And the state housing board went with the bahstid, hook & line! . . . Even the new yuppies in the building are yelling; they were told their rents (3 times ours) would be stable for a long time. Ha!
  Well so it goes. I pray youse is all thriving.
  I'm off to the theologians at Cambridge Mass. on Thursday. Pray for me. Or better, for them.

Daniel

Thurs. Nov. 19th [1987]

Dear Dan—
  Thanks so much for the latest—as usual, a real joy to us.
  Jerry sent on John's latest. It appears—as our hopes go—that a rebirth has happened. Praise de Lawd! Now to get his address and write him. Think you're entirely on target—Freda's prayers making the difference.
  Am deep into the autobiography [*To Dwell in Peace*]. Can't say enough in praise of it—to get that much of life and perception and integrity between two covers is almost unendurable. Folks should study it, not just read it. But alas, you're publishing it in Amerika—and the capacity of our poor country friends is not that impressive.

Thank you for wisdom and wit and discipline and eloquence—it all comes out in this book. We'll have to get our hands on some copies, and get them around.

Three of us had our little jail bags packed for Tues. But the judge proved unusual, and listened—finally finding us guilty and telling us to pay $20 for court costs. We questioned that, and he backed off. Seems he offered to join the defense at H'burg but was turned down. I had a chat with him after the trial.

Much love, peace of Christ, lasting (and profound) gratitude for *To Dwell in Peace.*

> Phil

> The elements of our world view include
> healing, shalom, integrity of heart,
> the dignity of each + all,
> and a world that works—for everyone.
> We are resolved
> on disarming our lives, our church,
> and the nations.
> We want to help create
> an ever growing
> beloved community.
> > Jan 6 (1988)

> > > Fondest—
> > > Daniel

[Dan here reacts to the news that their oldest brother, Tom, had converted to the Jehovah's Witnesses, testing their commitment to ecumenism.]

Feb. 8 [1988?]

Dears,

We were driven to the train by a young woman, Janet, who is a Jehovah Witness full time minister. I had been hearing these hints & starts about Tummy [Tom] & the JW's for some time. It appears that Janet does bible study with him each week, and that he reads the bible each day. This all came out in the car, with a certain fear & trembling, from Virginia. It appears also that she takes no part in this new dispensation. But T. has in effect joined the JW's, short of the baptism by immersion, due to his condition.

I think both women were quite apprehensive about my reception of the news. I allowed he had his right to his own choices (not adding, however bizarre). Janet is a fine woman, very balanced, herself a former Catholic, and has by all accounts, rendered great service and attentiveness to them both since he's been incapacitated.

Was led to speculate that, presuming T., like the rest of us, is mortal (even though the idea comes hard), what form his funerary rite might be thought to take. We had best prepare ourselves for a new stage of ecumenism, as JW's & Catholics in tandem do their thing, however uneasily. Do the JW's immure the loved one, do they burn, do they embalm, do they view, do they hide, do they incense?

I hope all are well, it was a joy to see Liz & Frida, and many thanks for the exotic care pkg.

Daniel

Feb 23 [1988?]

Dears,

I was in Cleveland over the weekend, returned Sun. AM to go to Ned Murphy's opening of shelter in Bronx. We're to see Martin Sheen in *Julius Caesar* tomorrow, he scrounged some tickets for the local scruffs, though the show has been sold out the day the office opened.

Takin my lumps on the Book [*To Dwell in Peace*]. Latest in *Sunday Times,* where the religion editor of *Newsweek* [Ken Woodward] (a Jesuit grad) takes me to task for reviling the Church & the Society. O vell as grandma uster say. An equal blast in the *LA Times.* I must be doin sumthin right.

Many fond thoughts, you bring spring closer!

Dan'l

[On April 3, Phil and three others boarded the USS Iowa battle-ship at Norfolk Naval Station in Virginia, disarming two armored box launchers for the Tomahawk cruise missile, hammered, poured blood, and raised banners reading "Seek the Disarmed Christ" and "Tomahawk into Plowshares." It became known as the Nuclear Navy Plowshares. Phil writes the next several letters from jail.]

Wed. Apr. 6th [1988]

Dear Dan—

Guess you got some details from near or abroad. Only had about 2 min. before a young Marine pounced us—frightened at the blood and furious. But as they say, enuf for symbolic yet real disarmament. The Navy treated us well seein' that we had wounded their pride + joy. The FBI were their usual selves—cynical and taunting. Sometimes I think the political po'lees make more of a Faustian bargain than the politicians.

The jail lets the press in—Andrew and I did 2 long interviews yesterday. Press coverage locally has been very good. We'll do another today. We have a phone in our cell and can call collect. If Gallagher or others want to do an interview, we'd be happy to oblige. All we need is a phone no. and a time to call. The Lord provides. The jail itself is quiet, the food is very good, if heavy on the meat. The only rub is no reading material—the books (paperback) in our jail bags were turned back. But we compensate by talking w/ prisoners and having 2 Bible study periods per day. We even have a boob tube for the news. The Lord again, provides.

We're in excellent spirits and health (lots of yoga and exercise) so please have no concern. Every Easter gift to you—

Much love and gratitude,
Phil

[Earlier in the year their brother John had been hit by a car and Tom had suffered a stroke.]

Yorktown, Va. 23692

April 12th [1988]

Dear Brother—

A great Easter boon today hearing from you. I thought your Easter letter excellent—eloquent and covering all the stops. And I was so happy that you included John and Tom at the end. God knows they deserve every attention. Like you, I attribute John's recovery to prayer, above all, Freda's, I guess.

But mostly, we have it v. good—providentially so. The trustees (prisoners) serve us w/ the most embarrassing consideration. And the guards are decent folk—a couple of them excellent.

Incidentally, Bish Sullivan came and brought some books. Had a lovely visit. He sends love to you. So do we—much, much love. And thanks too, for the tireless witness on Good Friday. We're wearin' the bahstids down—not vice versa. Hah! Hah!

Peace of Christ—

Phil

Sun. May 1st (1988)

Dear Dan—

May begins—your month, and that of Jim and Tom.

I've been floundering around in trying to say something sensible about you, and your birthday—finally settling on this one from James' Letter. "For if any be a hearer of the word and not a doer, one is like a person beholding her natural face in a mirror. For s/he looks at herself, and goes away, and straightway forgets what manner of person s/he is."

Apparently, hearing the word and not doing it is like looking in the mirror, seeing appearance and not substance and even forgetting that.

Your life reminds me of the apprentice/artisan relationship in John. Christ heard what God was saying. He saw what God was doing and did it.

Somebody said recently that moderns have lost the meaning of obedience. You never have—but your obedience has been far less to the Church apparatus, and far more to God. You listen to what God said, and you hurt. You saw what God was doing and did it. Whether works of healing or resistance (reconciliation also—like healing.)

I've long considered you as one of God's foremost gifts to us. May you continue as that, with good health, in joy and in peace. We all love you.

Phil

May 10, 1988

Dear Tom, Virginia, Jim, Rosalie, Jerry, Carol, Phil, Liz,

I'm just home from Phoenix & Prescott and a delightful, all but miraculous day with John.

It seemed to me, as I knocked at his door and he rose to answer, as though the awful months have been rolled back. There he stood, very much himself. And, as I came to see, he walks & talks & eats & enjoys life in ways that were beyond the planets just weeks ago.

I told him about the newest Plowshares action. He responded to the effect that 'this was wonderful, what an example to the rest of us.'

I gave him medical news of Tom. I also told him of Tom's change of religious affiliation. He heard this out in quiet.

He wanted to talk at length about the next generation—and the third. I had a sense of great loneliness. Something of his love for children, which he averred, and his sense of being cut off from them.

Well, I flew home, much moved to gratitude and reflection.

I told him at parting that the next family visit was to be his voyage to us. He had no big objection.

I strongly sense he needs a life line. Ourselves. (As who doesn't?)— not only from his peers, but from the children.

I told him I would write a 'report' to everyone. He riposted (in true Berrigan fashion, a touch of gloom saves all)—"well don't make it too rose. I'm liable to cash it in anytime."

Which I took to be a good sign of recovery. Among other things.

Much ♥ to all—
Dan'l

Mon. May 16th (1988)

Dear Dan—

Bro. Jim wrote about Tom's condition—seems he couldn't get thru at Virginia's so talked with Liz mainly. It appears that things are pretty grave with Tom—it substantiated what you said. I've written several times since here, and pray hard for him. God did miracles with John— why not with Tom also? But in any case—that God's Will be done.

In so many respects, the time has been a grace to us. Much love from all three, and that comes w/ our gratitude.

Peace of Christ,
Phil

May 29th Sun. (1988)

Dear Dan—

Bish. [Walter] Sullivan visited yesterday—we had a nice chat. He, like his priest in this area, is a good pastoral man. He announced when he came in that he had just met w/ gays and lesbians from the area. When I asked him about this contact, he misunderstood me, and began on the question of deterrence, contact with Gumbleton etc. So we never got on the subject of the gays.

Jammed up this weekend and perhaps beyond with a couple of guys charged w/ drug pushing. One has no bail on him, so it appears serious. But Davis settled down after 2–3 days and it goes fairly well. New people disrupt our little programs and routine—like Christ knocking at the door.

Nothing else earthshaking. Thanks for being here. As usual, you create something true and vital. Much love from the 3 of us—May God's Spirit enrich you.

Peace of Christ—
Phil

[In July, Phil was sentenced to six months for the Nuclear Navy Plowshares action. He here writes of his first reading of the newly released book, Daniel Berrigan: Poetry, Drama, Prose, *edited by Michael True. True's introduction pairs Dan and George Orwell as critical writers in countries at the height of their empire who were censored by their superiors and used their role as artists to challenge the language used by powers, to which Phil responds.]*

Oct. 5th Wed [1988?]

Dear Dan—

Am into Mike True's work—I can see what you mean by his "objective" reporting. He seems to be striving to imitate comparable types writing for the *Times* or the *NY Review of Books,* i.e. seeking literary landmarks which mark a stage in growth. He ought to read *The Bow in the Clouds* again. And make a few remarks about your struggle with SJ censors. No word of that.

In any case, once I left *Time* and got into *Dan Berrigan,* the selections began to speak for themselves. And they will carry the book. I expect to be renewed and reinspired by them.

Michael did a good thing, however, in comparing yew with Orwell. But the comparison limps—Orwell might have taken some shots during the Spanish Civil War (I don't know) but beyond that, he didn't pursue risk as an ingredient of truth as you did. And so predictably, your mark will be deeper and more pervasive than Orwell's, because your integrity is far deeper.

Was reading the Bk. of Daniel this morning—"God loves you, Daniel!"—said the angel (Chapt. 10). I for one believe God loves you as he did the prophet Daniel. In fact, regards your prophecy as highly as that of the first Daniel. This book will once again display this—for "those who have ears to hear."

Went over the barren fig tree treatment in Lk this morning. Got to thinkin' that I have another year for fertilizing and care by the gardener (Christ). Certainly a time for accounting—one of these years I'll be required to bear some fruit.

Will sneak this off with profuse thanks and much love. Hope the winds blow warm and temperately on B.I. See youse on the 15th.

> Peace of Christ—
> Phil

Sat. Nov. 12th [1988]

Dear Dan—

Spoke at the CCNV rally in DC on Mon. The saving grace was the hundreds of Poors that Mitch + Co. can turn out. Nearly 400 arrested, only 7 refused the fine + went to jail. Cher was on hand, mobbed by the crowd and by the papparazzi. But she spoke well, marched, gave 10 grand and went off to selling her perfume ("Uninhibited"). To give her further credit, she spoke of the homeless to the feelthy rich buying her perfume.

Meanwhile, the Poors at our door multiply. And we must shy away from being drawn into work—however laudable—that we have always drawn the line upon. For the ex-poverty workers in the house, who instinctively get into a CCNV approach, this is hard going.

> Peace of Christ to you—and best love
> for each and all,
> Phil

[Phil writes here of some of the hardships of living in community. This letter represents one of the several times he and Liz proposed moving out "to start elsewhere" if the others would keep Jonah House running for two years, "as a means to reconcile differences." No one ultimately took up their offer.]

Thurs, Jan 12th [1989?]

Dear Bruv—

This is inter nos. We're going thru a particularly critical time with friends here. Liz and I finally invited four of five to move elsewhere in community (subsidized by Jonah like in 4 or 5 experiments in the past), or to take this place and keep it open for two years.

I figger a good, even sizeable, share of the fault lies with me. I have increasing trouble with the wheelspinning, nitpicking and reliance upon "talk" as a solution to differences which it seems to me stem from private agendas and ideological (not Biblical) priorities. It may be that I get more rigid as I get older, and less tactful, + gentle. Those are matters, if they intrude, that I must resolve.

In the meantime, we slog along, looking for whatever daylight might appear. Keep the prayer mat warm for us.

Please don't be overly concerned—community has been this—more or less—from the time of Our Lord. And we'll do our utmost to resolve it non-violently.

> Best love to you—and the Lord's
> peace and promise in '89,
> Phil, Liz, et al. at Jonah

20 Jan. [1989]

Dears,

Phil's came yesterday and I opened it with fear & trembling, feeling sure it would bring hard news. As it did indeed. And I'm trying in my feeble way, to 'keep the prayer mat warm. . . . ' At the same time, sensing that good decisions are in store, that painful learning is going on on all sides, that whether at Jonah or elsewhere, your unquenched light will shine; for all of us. And perhaps brightest of all, for those who have yet to grasp things. . . .

I was led to reflect also that the pains come about just because you aim so high, wide and biblically handsome! And further, in my mind's eye; what a storm would erupt among us here, if we were to make our marriage vows in the biblical sense, around prayer together and resistance!!! That would be a stormy arrival of the kingdom indeed. But for now, it's wishing on a wishbone.

When I drag the bones off to Riverside yet once more, it's allus alone. Practically no one knows what I'm up to, which amounts to, no one gives a damn. I'm generally thought of as an achiever & a loner;

and this amounts in the practical order, to hands off socially—except for Keck & Fred (to a degree).

I guess I wrote Martin was arrested with us, his usual luminous self. Bused in from Wilkes Barre, started at 2AM. Typical. Returned to NY Sunday for liturgy here & celebration at All Saints in Harlem. Martin sends much love. As do I.

Fondly.
Dan'l

Jan. 23rd [1989]

Dear Dan—

Thank you for words, prayers, everything. Leave it to you to understand. Not many can, or will.

It appears that the worst is over. Four of our friends met, and have pledged themselves to meeting weekly. It's clear they have 3 options—continue here for 2 yrs., start another community, or leave individually. Further, they understand that our decision rests on theirs.

Glad to hear of Tummy and Tony. Yes, the J. Witness are a drab lot indeed. I wonder if Tummy adopts their anti-war stance? At Allenwood in '68, after Catonsville, where they had mebbe 60 youngsters locked up for refusing conscription—they told me that any war related work would end in excommunication from any Witness community.

Much love to you, many thanks. Many blessings.

Peace of Christ—
Phil, Liz et al. at Jonah.

January 31, 1989

Dears,

News has mainly to do with last Sunday, the period before noon; a time I wouldn't want repeated in my life if I lived like Buck Rogers, well into the 21st century.

First came a phone call from Jim Rice in Washington state, announcing his father Everett's death the previous week. I know how close the Rice's have been to Jim, Rosalie, and family.

Then a call from a nun, Sr. Mary Lou Steele, announcing she had just found an AIDS patient and mutual friend, Alberto Arevalo, dead. I had known Alberto over two years, he had lived in this apartment for two weeks while I was teaching in New Orleans last summer, An ex-Trappist novice, very gently and good, desiring no more of life than to lead a monk's life. But was put to the door by the Trappists when illness was diagnosed as AIDS. He was assigned to me by the St. Vincent's team, we became good friends, he took meals here and met other Jesuits.

He had almost died in hospital two weeks previous, of the awful pneumonia peculiar to AIDS. He rallied against all expectation, and was released. They often go this way, catastrophically, suddenly. We are planning a service and getting past the worst grief.

One never gets used to such losses. My second patient Patrick died after a three year struggle, three weeks ago. My third, Richard, is being lovingly cared for and is slipping away. So it goes. I commend these good folk and those who see them through, to your prayers.

Third call, around noon, from Coventry, England, dean of the Cathedral, Paul Ostreicher. His adopted son and my young namesake, Daniel, 24, had committed suicide. I had visited the boy in mental hospital last summer in London; he had twice attempted suicide at that point. He and I walked for a couple of hours in a park, then his parents and I hosted his birthday celebration. I felt in my bones there would be further and deeper sorrow to come.

So went a few hours of one; I hasten to add, not typical. Only brutally symbolic of so much of 'the world, the way it goes.'

In midst of it all, I give thanks. We survive, even on occasion lift a glass to the holiness and goodness of life.

It goes without saying, you are all in my heart.

I'm off Thurs. overnight to N. Carolina. Then you, Phil, to Europe + I to Nevada next week.

Time in Richmond was good. [Bishop] Sullivan though seems depleted by Roman Emory wheels applied to sensitive parts. No party, no supper at his house—bed + no breakfast, so to speak. He was up at dawn and off somewhere. The choices are austere, as ML King would say.

Guess this does it. All well here, given everything!

♥ Daniel

6 Mar [1989]

Dears,

Phil's came today, that whirlwind into Minnesota, and all the friends & relatives gatherin! You're probly as grateful as I am when it's over & terra firma looms under the smoking wheels. I was in Chi for a weekend, retreat & workshop w- Monica Helwig. I wish the Chicagoans had been up to this lady; she's adopted 3 troubled children & raised them, single, keeping up the teaching & writing meantime. When one of the savants objected to the hammer symbolism I was expatiating on, (he averred, "you could beat my head in with a hammer', I riposted, 'I could beat your head in with a bible too.') she was quick to the defense of hammers & me. "What a relief to hear of something being done in the face of religious passivity & paralysis. . . . " Great good lady!

Thanks for kind words on 'Stations'. I'm reading 'Discipline' [*The Time's Discipline*] slowly, for meditation. What a fine para scripture + how proud I am!

Daniel

April 17, [1989]

Dears,

I need sometime soon some info from Phil about Berlin doings. (I presume I'm to take care of airline tickets here & bill the Chermans.) If we voyage the night of the 5th June, we'll have a day to get bearings. Torsten sez the program ends on the 11. Does Phil want to return that day? I'm half inclined to rip over to Ireland for a few days to see friends; I could thus order separate tickets for return.

Much love
Daniel

May 15, 1989

Dears—

It's bin a nice birthday week, people were stroking me from all over, pelting me with flowers & meals & cards. Then came the lovely card from Jonah, what a sunrise Frida painted me, nicer than the 'real' one here, we've been raining on the earth all week, & quite chilly. But I wonder too that mother earth keeps coming back at us with blessings for our insults. Then too, thanks for the [Wendell] Berry poem, I keep reading it over & wanting to become hook or crook, like that. Some distance to go, but wot the hell.

I was in Bawsten for anti death penalty conference on Satiddy a week. There were good folk there; as you know, the strap is thin here in NY, one vote short of overriding [New York Governor Mario] Cuomo.

I wanna move to Iceland if they start the killing. Tues. we had a press conference with every Xtian & Jewish group in town stating opposition, even O'Connor. Not a word in the (literally) unspeakable *Times*.

NEVER THE LESS!

♥ to each & all . . .

May 22 [1989]

Dears,

Well I enclose clippings on the Rochester caper. I thought I'd tried pretty much everything folly ridden in this life, always a temerarious idea as I wuz shortly to discover, being perched atop the ten foot fence, one leg over, the other unable to git itself over until some fine enterprisin' chap gave it a quick uppercut & the tumble was complete & the spine still somehow intact. Ground zero. Home free. Something like that.

The next AM up at 5:00 for some damn reason, it being as explained by the powers, sos we could get to the abortion mill before it opened. Which we did, in Rochester, having driven after release the 70 or so miles back from Seneca. Found the place guarded and locked, sat in for four hours, sang & prayed much like the scene at Riverside Research here. Finally the cops arrived, there was much conferring, finally (as they said to some of the folks) because Berrigan was part of it, the hsptl moguls decided no arrests & no bad news for them & no more children disposed of for the day. One young woman held briefly in converse with a few of us, decided to take up our offer of help & went home. So I guess it wasn't a bad thing, none of the mob scene I've read often accompanies these 'rescues', everyone calm & collected etc.

We had a nice liturgy at the parish, then lunch at a restaurant run by ex cons out of the same parish. By the way, they have 40 people on the payroll, part or full time, 400 volunteers, everything from the above to a home for the dying, one for battered women, one for the homeless, food pantry & soup kitchen, sister parish in Nicaragua, and now opening a home for single pregnant jobless women with AIDS; if you can feature that combo of human misery. One priest and one nun; parish council of 30. I was dumbfounded, realizing once more how powerful THE THING is when followed; also what a desert we normally trudge here & elsewhere. . . .

The pastor tol me he was denied ordination for a year; and a year afterward, was suspended 'for refusing to live in a deluxe rectory.' He lives with four other layfolk in the house I stayed in overnight; gave the rectory to the homeless. I sed how do you support all this in the inner city? No help from the state or feds, no help from the diocese; 'it comes.' How do you support yourselves? 'We take no $$$ from the parish, people know it & help.' He made Xtianity sound so plain & bonebuilding like good bread. Wotta great time!

Gawd willin' I'm off to Block Island in the morning. I'll write from there, wish me good weather & as you've heard before but one can never say it enuf, so much ♥ to all.

Sure hope the north country wasn't too frigid!

Daniel

[The next two letters represent several that display the frank, open, and vulnerable approach with which Phil and Dan worked out their issues, as well as how deeply rifts in their relationship affected each.]

June 20th [1989]

Dear Dan—

As for the experience in Berlin—it still has me marvelling. Got the impression—subjectively or no—that I was an appendage to you, your acolyte or something on that order. The simplest request—for a sweater in that nasty Berlin weather, was met with inaction; or an Engl. speaking newspaper, to remain aware of the Chinese scene—inaction, too. It reminded me of little German martinets sacralizing their schedule, and the whipping their muscles into step. As for the Plowshares scene—I worked on that more or less—many letters + phone calls for several months. Now, I must write—I already have—encouraging not to drop the European Pl., and to a degree start over again.

I don't want all this flysh_t to reflect on you, save that you apparently missed a great deal of it. That's understandable—you had to deal with the Cherman schedule (no great volume of work) and its naive and unilateral assumptions, just as I did. Nor do I want to claim that you reflected the attitudes and imperceptions of our two friends. But merely to achieve understanding for the future, and possible joint efforts.

I approach working with you in reverence. Need I spell that out? You are the best interpreter of God's Kin-dom and the life of Our Lord in the Engl. speaking world—mebbe in the world itself. And your life solidly backs your eloquence. As for me—and perhaps here my ego speaks—I would prefer being treated by you as equal. In my sight, perhaps not in God's, I have expended as much for peace as you have.

We—Liz included—listen to you with attention, relish, gratitude. You don't listen that well to us, creating a frequent impression condescending and patronizing. You weren't listening too well in Berlin. And that had me in a quandary, much more so than our Cherman friends.

Perhaps I'm off the wall in this, perhaps I'm stumbling over my own ego, allowing "feelings" to create false issues, even unjust ones. If that is so, tell me. Moreover, if certain purple patches of mine are offensive, crude, domineering, tell me. And I'll do my best with them.

Coming home on the plane, it seemed sane to conclude that we shouldn't work together again without a better understanding. That's apart from overloading a scene—too much experience, too much experiment, too much study—for folks to absorb. There's that factor, but another as well. Which I've attempted to spell out.

Enuf for now. Forgive me if I'm beating a dead horse. If that's the case, give me your view. And I'll ponder it, cost what may. Much love from all here—we're all well, and pray you're better than well.

> Peace of Christ—
> Phil

June 28, PM [1989]

Dear Brother,

Just in from the coast to receive your letter, and grateful to have the air cleared to some extent. I had sensed something was amiss when I hadn't heard from you.

I've been through some hard times lately, since Germany; as evidently you have too. It's kept me kneeling in prayer as hasn't happened in a long time. Such questions kept troubling, festering; What went wrong on that trek? In what had I offended my brother? I did a long review of conscience, and prayed with all my heart for you, for your family, for myself even, so deep I was in darkness since that evening in Berlin, when the thing broke open. Then your letter.

How could it be, I tormented myself, that two brothers, who so love and respect one another, could have such different views of the same events,—almost as though they were receiving and sending signals from two planets? I am still dumbfounded.

Let me start. I looked forward with all my heart to the prospect of being with you, whom I love so dearly and learn so much from, year after year. I was so happy on the plane, just to be with you, to eat and drink and talk the night through.

From then on, I must be faulted, thinking that given the usual bumps and bruises of the road, being at beck and call of everyone,— still things were going reasonably well. I knew nothing of your difficulties with the sparse food, or with the cold; for several days. You said nothing. Then came the explosion.

I entered our room that evening and found you angry (with me as well as the Germans). I was speechless. I had asked them not to call you to supper, to let you sleep. The fact that you were reading the bible, and would not speak to me, or explain what was wrong, hurt me beyond words.

But I was not devastated,—as I once was. I said to myself, I've done my best, I'll await my chance and try to keep something going. I made sure you had a sweater next morning. When you were ready to talk, I listened. On the street, I kept quiet while you blew your anger. Later I told our host about the money you'd spent Baltimore–New York, and was assured they'd recoup you. I condescending? Come off it, I was serving you with all my dumb heart.

Your words about you being my 'acolyte' are particularly unfair and leave me bewildered. As you offer no examples, I deny the nonsense. When a question arose as to who would speak in public I constantly deferred to you. In my mind and conduct, in Berlin you were my equal at every point (as you are in my heart) and my teacher as well.

Why this talk of competition,—as though you must declare that your contribution to peace work is equal to mine? For my part, I have no least doubt that your courage and steadfastness are unique; I have no interest in comparing your work with mine, as though we were in a game of winners and losers.

Over the years, I've seen myself perforce as a listener and learner in your regard. This has not always been easy for me, but I've taken that stance, since your opinions on people, politics, peacemaking, etc., are usually offered not as occasions for discussion but as incontrovertible. I seldom if ever feel invited to offer something about my work, my community, my troubles,—nor do I often gain the impression I have something to offer. So I clam up.

In Berlin it was astounding to me that your troubles with the Germans were laid at my door; in silence and rejection for hours on end. Why me? I've no clue except your remark about not being treated as my equal. Please enlighten me on this.

What in me offends you? Sometimes I think it's my silly humor, rep-artee, breeziness. I fail to take seriously what you take so deadly serious.

Believe or no, what goes badly with you is simply my way of coping with a heartbreak as deep as ever yours is.

I think the troubles arose in Berlin because you arrived exhausted from the past months and the long wearing upheavals at Jonah. And there I was, dumb, thinking all was going reasonably well! Uncon-scious most of all, of being an irritant. Just happy to be with you and work with you, so rare.

When I was trying to get to the question 'why me?' it occurred to me that for a long time, I've been a kind of lightning rod for your wrath, never understanding why, yet taking it, letting you shake my bones. But no more, not in Berlin or anywhere.

Dear brother, there's a certain violence that afflicts you. It reminds me of our father, and his way of 'taking it out' on his own. In the old days, I used to cringe from him; and later from you; but no more.

Maybe we're also talking about two ways of doing the job we've long ago set our lives to. I learn from your way, or try to, and swallow the differences. You have much greater trouble accepting mine. And there we are, in mid and late sixties.

You conclude that we can't work together without a better under-standing. I agree with all my heart.

We face the autumn, and the very real prospect of prison. A time, I judge, when we need to be closer than ever.

Please tell me how I treat you in a way that affronts you or Liz. She left me equally bewildered about alleged conduct in Norfolk some time ago.

My own conclusion, after days of prayer and trying to gain some light, is that your treatment of me, and your letter, does you small honor. There are difficulties in your life much deeper than myself. I am small potatoes; a symptom—and at times a victim.

But one who would be first and foremost and always, your brother.
                                    D.

[On September 4, seven people canoed and swam the Thames River to the Naval Underwater Systems Center in New London, Connecticut, to board the USS Pennsylvania *Trident submarine. They hammered, poured blood, prayed, sang, and read from John's Gospel before being fire-hosed. Phil reacts to the action, the Thames River Plowshares, and his first read of Gustavo Gutiérrez's* Theology of Liberation.*]*

Sept. 5th Tues [1989]

Dear Dan—

Liz, the kids and friends returned from Kirkbridge with the great news of the Thames River Pl. Some swam, the rest in a canoe. Can you imagine Anne [Montgomery] swimming? She's frail as a butterfly, but I hear, a fine swimmer. The USS Pa. [*USS Pennsylvania*] involved—disarmed I hear, symbolically yet really. This time, apparently, the feds will prosecute—they have a hearing in Hartford today, federal court.

God bless them. Their faith will reawaken some and awaken many. I get the impression that most will accept p.r. if offered. One question came up—what about Anne who is unlikely to get p.r.? What of solidarity with her?

Am stumbling thru Gutierrez—*Theol. of Liberation*. He's very good—but Lord! The language is the language of the club. And he's read all his confreres—the same for them. Without getting overawed— I figger we (esp. you) were sayin' the same things twenty years ago. And sayin' them more simply and comprehensively.

Much love to you—good health and cheer. You will speak with God's Spirit at Loyola.

Peace of Christ—
Phil

Nov. 7 [1989]

Dears,

I was down spending an afternoon with these fine nuns & the cards were presented. Not my favorites, but the poor women hardly make a living with such mementos. They're dying out as to vocations, just like everywhere.

The non-news policy from Pa. is a scream. Schwartz called yestiddy, it appears they're about to launch a habeas corpus from Ramsey and Philly. I don't entirely get it, but it all gives time for another series of guffaws from the gods. Ramsey surrendered our current addresses, accd. to S., obleeged to do so as our megaphone. I don't give a tinker's damn if they know where I'm rusticating, but helping them list a decade of crimes is another matter, no.

I'm assembling some notes on Acts. Taught it for years, but it took McNichols to prod me into getting things into semicoherent shape.

By the way, he and Keck are due down here for the long weekend. Bill is leaving soon for tertianship, so this'll be a swan song of sorts.

Well, love, warmth, light, hope—

Dan'l

[*On November 16, 1989, six Jesuits were assassinated along with their housekeeper and her daughter at the Universidad Centroamericana in El Salvador. The Jesuits had openly opposed the actions and policies of the Salvadoran government, whose military carried out the murders. The specific actors who carried out the operation had been trained at the US-run School of the Americas.*]

Dec. 2 [1989]

Dears,

Thursday we had eight trees planted, each with a marker and a name. There were 8 empty chairs on the podium, as the names were spoken, a student placed red roses and a placard and a name on the chair. Very moving. People spoke well and sang in Spanish.

Yestiddy we had ourselves a fracas almost, at the fed bldg. 24 of us blocked all elevators for two hours. Then the d.a. arrived in a black mood, leveled on me, called me various names and 'wished he had my provincial here to denounce my life.' I pointed to the provincial who came right over, there followed as they say, a passionate exchange, the d.a. averring he was a Kathlik & Jesuit trained & found it disgraceful that sed p. would countenance my ilk. Which sed p did vehemently & well & thoroughly. Then the d.a. blew his stack and ordered us, one and all, carted off forthwith. We were out in four hours.

It was all quite good, the students were outstanding.

Thanksgiving day the rector & prexy [of Loyola University, New Orleans] announced to me they were offering an honorary degree in May. Would I accept? Sed in view of the virtual vanishing of ROTC (there are still 3 students here in the program, but they take all military courses at Tulane) I'd ok it. If I'm in jail (we're in jail) Jerry or someone can come & pick it up. I thought all this somewhat touching, can you imagine Fordham or Lemon [Le Moyne] making such a gesture?

Much ♥

D.

1990–2002

[The final twelve years of the correspondence sees a shift in emphasis. Dan asserted early on that he would not participate in more Plowshares actions and questioned whether jail time was good for Phil, Liz, and those at Jonah House. The general pace of their lives began to slow as they moved into their seventies. The letters became shorter, sometimes becoming a space for reflection on their own relationship and its place before God. Speaking of what he owed Dan for his friendship and love, Phil wrote, "The debt is more than I can ever pay. It is like the one I owe God, and Christ and God's Spirit." "The Providence of God definitely enters here," Phil said again of Dan's role in his life, without which he would be "looking at death and muddling over what I missed."

The scene of action changes in the letters, as well. Where once strategizing, planning future actions, and working out nonviolent philosophy dominated their conversations, a slow transition takes place toward life updates, the activities of younger friends like Steve Kelly, details about Dan's retreats, or news regarding the health of their aging peers. The former conversations never disappear but cede center stage as they approach the millennium. One thing that did not change was Phil's drive to witness in jail. He participated in more Plowshares actions and remained in and out of prison to the last year of his life. His reaction to the 9/11 attacks, which occurred while he was in prison and spurred a trip to solitary confinement, speaks to his continual resistance against nationalism while America prepared for war. As the focus on health shifted from Dan to Phil, it was his body but never his will or faith that gave way. He reconciled himself to the possibility of death weeks before it came with the simple statement, "I pray for healing daily, but if not that, may God's Will be done!"

251

To the end, Phil and Dan exchanged professions of love. Phil, on the last of Dan's birthdays he would celebrate, wrote that Dan was always "brother, friend, counselor, bulwark of decency and integrity, shining example. And I love you for all this, but will never love you enough." They had long ago stopped signing off with "Devotedly, in our Lord," but through all their developments and conversions, from the first letter to the last, they still understood their relationships with God and each other as intimately connected. "A brother's love," Phil closed the same letter, "and Christ's peace."]

[Jan 15 1990]

Dears—

Herewith, over, the offending letter to the N. Orleans magistrate. I just learned from Ramsey that the eminent DA there has filed another charge; contempt. Tomorrow we'll learn where it all goes, hearing at ten thirty AM.

You'll note a NY province Jesuit killed violently in Africa. I didn't know Ray Adams but everyone speaks well of him. Wotta world.

Sorry I can't get to say thank you to Joe Mulligan for his yeoman's work around the demo. I sense he's undergone some second thoughts about sandinista discipleship, after our sharp exchange of a few years ago. So good to have him at our side again.

♥ Dan'l

Sunday, 25 Feb. [1990]

Dears,

Martin Sheen was here unexpectedly yestiddy. In town to record some music by a fellow at Emmaus House who's playing in M's new film. He (M) directed the film, a first for him. Thereby hangs a vignette.

Martin had been in touch with a wealthy Texan who'd read my autobiography, wrote me offering to do a screenplay, mucho dineros $$$ etc. etc. I wrote Texan back thank you but no, explained the Sandhaus connection. Of this latter Martin knew nothing, so at lunch I explicated things, as the lit'ry folk say. Martin was alert as a hound dog, ears went up. Do you have a director as yet? Not as far as I know.

How's about if I were the director? Well, I'll write Phil & Liz & we'll both write Sandhaus urging the same.

Therefore this note. Martin is off to Paris to make some godawful flik he's half ashamed of. Meantime of course all the fat cats like DeNiro etc. get all the fat contracts & best parts. I tol' M once that if De. had M's politics & M had none (as De. has none), fat cat would get lean & vice versa. Well.

There just isn't the work for someone of M's convictions, it comes to that. He's hung high & nearly dry.

To court tomorrow for ML King action. To Hartford for po'try ash Wed.

D.

[On April 10, the Plowshares Eight received sentences of time served, about which Phil had "mixed feelings" since they "would be forgotten, and so too would G.E.'s war making."]

Friday, 27 April [1990]

Dears,

Last night spent some hours with a home gathering of lawyers, judges & public defenders. In all, a pretty compassionate and inquiring lot. Several of them gave the impression of knowing the Plowshare story quite thoroughly. Most feel trapped in the courts, esp. the p.d.'s. I hope some hope was generated; at least they indicated so.

Sunday, after what the grape vine tells me was quite a rumble, I'm to preach in the local Episcopal church. One can't talk about Easter without bringing up the hideous military occupation of the area, Cheyenne Mt., air force academy etc. I think just the fear of such things being spoken of, wrought the rumble in the first place. So we'll see.

Cesar Chavez is here today; several hundred turned out, and the grape boycott is strong . . .

Guess that does it 4 now—Happy Birthday to Jerry, ever bigger + better!

♥ Daniel

April 3. [1990]

Dears,

This goes to you a day after my return from Jamaica. I'm walking upright, (Whew!), much renewed and more hopeful in spirit—as we face what must be faced.

I'll venture to address this to Jonah rather than to the others of the Plowshares, since I've come to think that certain events in our own past, which is to say, Phil's, Liz's, and my own—are more important than we've allowed. (Than I've allowed.)

I recall that my worst times with y'all (few thank God), are connected with jail time. Let me start way back, far back as Danbury and Phil's verbal assault on me there, for, as I remember, something to do with my excesses in the visitors' room.

As I came through a fog of anguish to understood things, his fury had less to do with my peccadillos at the time, than with his trying to tell me something very difficult; his love for Liz; that in fact you had already married in spirit. I had of course in no way been prepared for this. How could I be?

And yet I stood with you both, and the vow you made. From that moment.

Then there was the scene in Berlin. Phil went into anger and silence, all of it beyond my understanding. He continued a critique of me after our return. It was Planet Mars to me. I did my best to respond.

I'm sick of this. Phil explained it afterwards by talking about his 'demons.' He had been through a particularly hellish jail time that spring and summer. I know that. But it doesn't help me much as to what causes periodic outrage, as far as I can understand it, connected to my life and goings on. To be told, to come to understand, would at least clear the air, which up to this point, is smogged with uncertainty. I dunno what's going on.

Right now I think we're drifting. I don't understand why or in what I seem to keep offending. Or why such events are always connected with jail.

If this is not resolved, I guess we all have to hang out in limbo—a place where I lose you and you me.

To speak of the present, we might succeed in coming to some compromise that would resolve the legal differences of the 'eight.' But our own troubles wd. remain, a source of anguish to you and me. I wonder why, I wonder what my sins are. Why do you on occasion grow so furious at me? What can we do, to come to a better love, a better friendship? Why am I periodically in the way of this?

I have a sense that the issues about the 'eight' which your letter raises, hinge on our facing the above.

The questions are connected inevitably, with jail time; since it is times of jail that have been most hurtful to us; terribly so. Such time accounts for my sole bitter memories of our common life. To raise questions about the effect of our legal moves on the Plowshares community and the peace movement, and to ignore the above, is to me hardly helpful.

There are the deepest reasons I know of, in the lives of Dean and John (and myself) to fight this latest legal lynching. I've nearly died in jail; whether it is a good thing for me to return there, and almost inevitably have to to be plucked from there, is another question that gives pause. Whether jail time is good for Phil, and for Jonah House, is something I question as well, for reasons above. For my part, I'll fight being jailed. To the last ditch.

If the Plowshares prisoners and the peace movement don't understand, so much the worse. But I believe our friends in jail will, if we speak honestly about our situations.

What the future holds as to better or worse times to be locked up, I leave to God. Meantime I have good work to do, in or out. As do all of us. Innumerable ways, as your letter says, of giving life and liberty.

This is the clumsy best I can do, for now. And I'll hope it gets to you before we meet. In any case, I'll bring a copy with me for Phil's perusal.

Love always,
Daniel

[On May 14, Dan received an honorary doctorate of Humane Letters from Loyola University New Orleans, where he had taught summer school for four years.]

17 May [1990]

Dears,

I got back here yestiddy, all tidy & on time. It was a grand ol party in NOhleens, kind of a Good Ol Boy's reunion with everyone in fine fettle & all delicts forgotten but not quite. I referred in my usual intemperate way to this as the second greatest honor etc etc. the first, being convicted in federal court there. . . . That got a laff at least, and a hand. Martin was in good form, he and Janet just in from Paris for the event. Jerry & Carol & I walked a lot in the quarter and out. They had a really first class welcome from the Poor Clare nuns, who gave them an apartment & all the fixins.

Previous day I'd done the baccalaureate at Colorado Col., with some fancy swipes at the air force et al. Good crowd, hard to say what effect. Bishop Buswell tooled in from Pueblo the night before to have dinner with me & the Catholic Worker folk. I left there with fond memories of serious students on their way (at least many of them), and a generally warm reception from the nabobs.

♥ Daniel

July 25th Wed. [1990]

Dear Dan—

I recall you taught Jn. way way back at Lemon [Le Moyne College]. Whadda Gospel! But that could be said of all of them.

Lost my balance—reached for a hard hold and it had disappeared —on a ladder last Mon. Went over backwards, dropped about 12 feet, landed on my back. One side caught a picket fence coming down— that eventuated in a huge bruise. And one knee messed up a bit. Generally speaking however, I was cushioned by angels—no broken bones. I'll try some safe and pedestrian work tomorrow.

Finished up Magee's effort this morning. Mebbe the best we're gonna get. Wrote Sandhaus some corrections and impressions. Some scenes are v. good, others lousy. I suspect that Magee had a tussle with it, and that the tussle ain't over. Liz will read it next. Liz's skeptical, more than you or I. She thinks Hollywood just ain't up to it and ough-ta quit tryin'. But one squeezes thru the cracks betimes, like Romero.

Peace of Christ—
Phil, Liz, everyone at Jonah

[1990]

Dearest bro—

[T]he threads you spin catch everywhere, cables!

And through you and Liz, now and again, I see the impossible epiphany of the worst, transfigured.

Thank you, thank you.

Blessed birthday!
Dan'l

Oct. 16th Tues [1990]

Dear Dan—

Thank you for the excellent, poetic quote on impossibility/possibility—from Barth and from you. That sez it all, huh?—making the possible out of impossibility.

One of the liberation theol. sez the most fundamental division in humankind is that between those who have given up on the world, and those who have not. Yaaas!

Have a trial tomorrow, and another on the 23rd. The second may mean a little contemplation in the dumpster. I can stand bein' with the Poors again.

We're okay and pray yer better still. Hope to see youse comin' thru one of these weekends. Love you.

> Peace + thanks,
> Phil et al. at Jonah

Sun. Oct. 21st [1990]

Dear Dan—

Heard the grand news of 10,000 plus in NYC. Resisters in DC put sand across Pa. Ave—then blood and oil. The cops waited 2 hrs. and then arrested 15–20, incl. Dan Ellsberg.

Just finished a chapter for an Institute for Policy Studies book—Bibl. treatment of the war/pollution connection. Yeah! lotta work. But clarifying to me, if no one else. Now, the Progressive wants some stuff on resp. to Bush's militarism in the Middle East.

Hope you're tip top. Always plenty of folks looking for you. Best love from all—we'll call on Tuesday.

> Phil, Liz, all at Jonah

May 15th [1991]

Dear Dan—

Just talked w/ Jerry. He walked 4 mi. today—God bless him! Sounded like his old self. God is good!

The Queen here to watch a ballgame. She's exposed to all that makes us a great people. Viva House and other Irish plan to greet her with notice of the Irish issue. While our folks are releasing helium filled balloons bearing a banner—Bread not Bombs! Many complications in preparation. But something in a dark time.

So much for now. We send love (much of it) ea. and all. Plus good health and Christ's peace.

Phil

Sun. May 19th Pentecost. [1991]

Dear Dan—

The Fortkamps are busily moving. They laid on us 3 copies of your commentary on Acts, and I'm relishing and absorbing. It's clear to us that you speak and write true theology in an absolutely unique fashion. Beyond the heralded ones from Central and So. America, since you know the empirah and its pomps in a way that they don't. Thank you—it's a superb piece of work. We'll finish John soon, and will begin there, or with the Bk. of Rev. again. Either way—we have your commentary.

Deep gratitude again, much love from everyone, and Christ's Spirit to you on Pentecost.

Phil, Liz, Jim, Greg, George, Patrick, Frida, Katy, Jerry

Friday, 24 May [1991]

Dears,

I finally called Rome yesterday. Bob Keck had relayed that Jack St. George was ill again with the old cancer. It proved alas, true. He's to start cobalt & have surgery this summer on the jaw, where of course he was gouged twice before. This is all so tough to take; he and I had been awaiting his arrival here in Chicago around the first of June; he had arranged an early date so we could have some time together.

Depending on how things go, one of us or maybe both, will go to Rome in late summer, after the worst is over . . .

Did you know Dick McSorley is in intensive care in Gtown. hospital after 5 heart bypasses? Why can't these turkey carvers leave a good man go to God?

The Jesuit powers in Syracuse have sent Tim Lambert packing. He phoned here in an awful state. I told him, shake the dust, you're too good for us.

Jogues wrote a note for my birthday. You'll remember Agatha who used to be at Grady liturgies with us all. . . . Her son was to have graduated Boston College next month, but died. He was a hemophiliac and contracted cancer. I wrote our sympathy through Jogues. Wotta world!

♥ Daniel

July 21st Sun. [1991]

Dear Dan—

A brief scrawl greeting you on return from B.I. Hope it was restful and renewing.

The jail was an eye opener—99% black and mostly run by blacks I was the only white in the cell block—among the prisoners. Dear Christ! What a waste! All those young lives declared expendable.

Adieu for now. Must go to LA on Wed. for the CW.

> Peace of Christ, much love from us all,
> Phil

August 1 (1991)

Dear Rosalie, Jim, Carol, Jerry, Liz, Phil,

Someone sed last night at Ignatius Day liturgy that he felt he was growing younger rather than older. He put the reversal down to the fine community we have here. As Poppa wd. say, I subscribe to that. Or, put me down for 50.

I guess also we had so fine a week's retreat together, that many of the kinks & contrary folds of things got, if not straightened out, at least stroked level. There was a sort of afflicted sense that short of some effort like that, community simply falls to pieces; or at least two dead sos level, a horrid outcome. And one that life in the Apple fosters—& festers as well.

We cooked & shopped for ourselves and had the most sublime mountaintop in creation to ourselves for seven days. There were AM and afternoon and PM sessions each day. As predictable, we had some anger and some reconciling & some close looks at accountability, much of the mentioned highs & lows quite foreign to males not to say Jesuits. Quite a week in sum. Now as they say, the proof of the pudding awaits.

By the bye, I'm praying to Freda (senior) on behalf of brother Tom. It's hard to think that in his last days, there's so little reconciling going on. I feel in my marrow she can intercede.

♥ Daniel

[August 7, 1991]

Hello there dears!

I heard from England Phil's expected there very soon. You'll quickly come I think, to great affection for the FOR folk.

I'm girding for weekend retreat in northern NY. My fourth try and always enjoyable; and the train ride is spectacular.

I missed Hiroshima Day—flu, dammit. 16 arrested.

♥ Daniel

November 15 [1991]

Dears,

It's been quite a week; Chicago then Raw-chester (sigh) once again, the minions of the law in hot pursuit etc etc.

There were many high points to the Chicago gig, being with Liz, then seeing old seldom seen friends again, O'Rourke, he of the mouth adazzle, Callahan shamefully kicked out of this least Society, but unflapped and going on. Carbray looking more & more like his own death mask, but racing to the finish as allus. & so on.

Got out to Evanston and had 4 good hours with Jack St. George, much changed in the phiz, much depleted, but quiet & patrician as allus, and unconquerable of spirit. He kissed me for the first time in my life; I thought of an altogether new tenderness. We walked by the lake, he led me a tour of the house. And of course I must have a hands-on detailed demonstration of his work. It's mostly occult as the 32 degree masonic initiation rite to yrs. truly. He does computer preparation of manuscripts for the Loyola Press. By all accounts he's a genius at this, and work, all self instructed. After he recovers sufficiently, he's to return to Rome for something awful called reconstructive surgery. In effect, it's to rebuild his jaw, and form a complete lower plate.

We talked a great deal about spirited survival, the how & why. He very quietly is determined to live, has great faith, sez his prayers. Good formulas.

In Rawchester I arrived in time for the Wicked Five to put heads together in a coffee bar. We have an old bucko (my age), a retired mailman who listens to nobody & just wants 'to make my point by going to jail.' Admirable, to a degree, but not helpful. Then two women, mothers, the brains & heart of the venture, dear friends. A third woman 35 or so. Wanted to plead guilty, 'can't go to jail'—but they wouldn't budge on a deal, so we're all in the stew together.

The judge is a black woman, member of United Way who, she told us, voted to keep the $$$ flowing toward Planned Parenthood, even tho the latter is close to doing carnage on the unborn on their own propitty. The judge offered to bow out, but we sed, wot the hell, we'll make our point as best we can & you do wot you must.

I've writ the bishop, Clarke [Bishop Matthew Clark], asking if he'll come to the trial & say we're just being Kathlics. We'll see.

Off to Marquette today. Tomorrow, second anniversary of Salvador Jesuit murders. We'll have a memorial at Marquette.

Dec. 2 [1991]

Dears—

I was shook by Phil's account of recent ills in knee + heel. Dammit, we do wax older & given our fizzikul proclivities, not allus gracefully! I sure hope the worst is done & over. My dental woes perdure, in a manner of speaking. He sez much more to come. I bin careful over the years which accounts for the present set of somewhat intact choppers. But it's like an old bldg., we see lots of them on the west side, the mortar gives out. But the brain, mine, is still relatively on its feet so to speak, putting subject to pred. with celerity here & there.

14 of us arrested at RRI last Wed. Martin Sheen along, the scene hilarious as the cops & adversaries jostled about for a smidgin of fame. The poor guy the bldg. uses to lodge the complaint, insisted on sitting in with us for the space of a flashbulb. In the precinct the cops esp. the lady cops, lined up for 'photo opportunities' I buhleev is the phrase, & autographs. The rest of us commoners huddle in outer darkness.

Trial date Rochester Jan 30. I've writ local bishop asking him 2 testify. Also wrote Prexy of Jesuit McQuaid High, after learning that head of the abortion mill is a Jeb graduate + Catholic. The plot thickens.

Well, y'all be well . . .
♥ Daniel

Jan. 9 [1992]

Dears,

Martin Sheen & some of us are vigiling at the UN about sanctions
& children. He and Janet are due to leave the premises around Sunday. He's brought great joy & a sense of conscience to this baliwick,
just like always.

We the SJ's here, go away tomorrow to Kirkridge for the weekend.
I hafta leave there Satiddy night to be bright & bushy tailed for a
7:30 AM liturgy & homily to a hunnert or so—ethicians! who've
come from the four winds to Temple to talk about I guess things
of conscience. This do is arranged by John Raines, brother of our
Bob. It'll be a trek down memory lane in a sense, as it was at John's
church in Germantown I preached while underground 20 or so yrs.
ago.

A week from Satiddy I take off for a week at Wooster College in
Ohio. Then of course on 30th, trial in Rawchester. I writ several bishops asking if they'll appear for us, but no takers so far.

Well, blessed noo year to all!!!!

♥ Daniel

[Dan writes here from Wooster College in Ohio.]

Wed. 22 Jan. (1992)

Dears,

Waal, what we've got ourselves here is a special small town ivy clad
oasis much in the manner of Wesleyan or Vassar or such.

Yesterday at a beat assembly of clergy I was appointed to bring
light to, the chair received a message that turned him to water. He
whispered to me he had to depart in haste, a parishioner'd killed self
+ spouse. Things are not great in academe.

Otherwise, so far so good. I preach (2 Sundays) dispense choleric
opinions in classes, go public tonight with a lecture + Fri. night with
po'try, meet with clergy, dine (last night) at a prof's home + so on.

Love to all. I guess Frida's college decision is near. I'll be home
Tuesday next. So happy Phil's leg is better!!!!

♥ Daniel

Thurs. 12 Mar (1992)

Dears,

There'll be a last hurrah for a week or 10 days. I am off to Jacksonville tomorrow for retreat, then Keck's ordered me to Puerto Rico for a week's r&r. Dentist (sigh), flu & Bush in that order or so, have me in mild thrall. We expect to pass an evening with Bishop Parilla-Bonilla, who's ailing.

We had a healing service for AIDS & caretakers at an Episcopal church in Hackensack Sunday. Very moving for everyone. Under Bishop Spong of Newark, I saw the best Xtian thing yet; afterword a sumptuous meal cooked by parishioners for everyone, some 150. There was a gay male couple in attendance who'd adopted 2 aids children, one of whom had died, the other, black, was cavorting around, free I was told of the virus. How about that for love?

Guess that's it. Many fondest thoughts of Jersey Mc. family + Bill + y'all

♥

9 Apr. (1992)

Dears—

Today after 4 months of travail I purportedly am to get the alleged ultimate choppers. I am assured they're to make me into a satisfactory corpse in due time.

Today I also was roundly pummeled by Dr. Rose who was in rather a distemper & remarked I've put on weight (148) & sed go lighter on the pot stop. This news injures my credibility as a loyal Lenten son of the church, alas.

The good news (?) is that the community wants me to become the new superior here. At the same time they don't wanna interfere with my work including the frequent absences. What with a London semester coming up, and the enclosed proffer for next year, nothing will come of this. Still as Jean Harlow once sed, it's nice to be wanted.

I'm off to Seattle and Santa Barbara on Satiddy. Holy week and Easter with the Immaculate Heart sisters, memory lane all the way. It musta bin '67 when last there. One sister reported me to chancery for doing a general absolution on Good Friday, there was hell to pay on return from the provincial. I suspect things have moved a bit since then. . . .

[The following note from Dan to Phil, appearing in full, is undated. It is written on a card with space for a signature and reads: "I support the position paper of the Association of Concerned Clergy and respectfully urge that servers at the altar continue to be restricted to males."]

This from an asshole brigade somewhere in Jersey. Makes 2 laff?

May 2nd [1992]

Dear Dan—

Wanted to say something inadequate about your birthday, which always brings reminders of your selflessness, faith and pure guts. I reflect that you have both served so many of us thru the years, but more than that, have made us. I for one fall into that category—from the retreat you arranged at St. Andrew's in early '43, to your visit just last week—like Paul breaking in Silas or Barnabas. God knows what a cabbage I am despite your care. But without it, I would be less than a vegetable—wandering, opaque and clinging to idols. In short, you have been grace and gift to thousands, but esp. to your kid brother.

So many prayers this week that God will preserve you and give you good health and long years. You are a vessel of election—may you continue as that for others and for us. We send you much love, much peace and many thanks.

Phil, Liz, Jimbo, Greg, Frida, Katy

[Bill Clinton was elected president on November 3, 1992.]

Wed. Nov. 4th [1992]

Dear Dan,

Waaal, ole Clinton made it. I figger it will take him a year to organize harm in the 3rd world. Whereas, the Bushwhacker had it all organized. So—the Lord has heard our prayers.

Our Bible Study struggles along. As you know, drugees ain't notable for discipline or generosity. But nonetheless, as one of our fundamentalists puts it, "The Word of the Lord is preached."

Will give a call when I get home. Peace of Christ to you, much love, many thanks. Greg sends the same.

Phil

Thanksgiving [1992]

Dears,

A note of sorts to say what a good day this is to say thanks for youse all, for Phil's happy deliverance from the penal pits, for good times always in your company, for the children and what all they give us, for . . . the list is large as the world.

Yesterday some 13 or so of us were detained at the weapons' forge. Everything went spiritedly, we had the fine homeless folk from Emmaus with us, the cops were in almost festive mood. Court dates in late December. So it goeth. Last night I banqueted with Emmaus house, invitation of David and everyone, preceded by moving prayer service in Harlem. Tonight Bob Keck cooks, tomorrow I do the honors.

♥ Daniel

Sunday 7 Feb (1993)

Dears,

My new ears are uncanny. I can now hear Gawd running practically everything. Though there is a certain interference from the principalities. Sometimes a GROWL, sometimes a high keening. Most annoying.

♥ Daniel

2/21/93

Dearest Bruv,

There's a great scrambling around this anniversary year. I see by the media that in May I'm to take part in a daylong thing on L.I. [Long Island] with the likes of General Westmoreland et al. This is for high school students & the general has top spot—as one would expect. There'll be time though for a little truth to hit the fan.

We went to court Thursday, only to have a beetled browed judicial eminence growl, as though he'd bin prodded out of hibernation, that no arresting cops had appeared; so we were again put off for a month. We so seldom see the same judge in this maelstrom here. But this one has bin on our spoor before; he described himself at one tempestuous exchange as a 'field commander in WW 2.' You can conjure up the ursine rage when he hears eg., that people have metaphorically & so to speak, shat-in on the deck of the *SS Intrepid*!

After our group of 4 were disposed of, hizzoner called David Kirk and 2 residents of Emmaus House. David flattened the judge's ears with the wind of truth. RRI wickedly flourishing to wit, and nothing for the homeless. The Bearish One growled something about lawnorder, found the three guilty, and canceled all retributions with a wave of dismissal. So it goes.

Meantime and of course, my noble delinquent friends are busily preparing for another go on Ash Wednesday. Wot fun!

Well I hope all is well under the roof. I hear nuthin' from Tom's or John's direction.

> Love to all there!!! Send us a wing
> & a prayer,
> ♥ D

3/4/'93

Dears—

Now I'm en route down to NYU Law school savants this evening, ('Conscience and the Law'), then off to Loyola Chicago ('Drama and Politics') tomorrow morning.

Wanted in any case to send a report, especially on Jack St. George. He and Bob Keck have happily, soundly decided to stay in P. Rico until next Tuesday. A good sign.

Jack looks for all the world as though he'd staggered out of the World Trade Center bombing. Part of him so to speak are in other parts of him. Miraculous, awesome—that the poor frame can withstand such relentless microsurgical assault, over so long a time, jaw to legs, And still walk the earth. Not well, but on his feet. Very weak, tentative, stricken, a suffering servant if ever one was.

Well we took care of him. Got him eating, somewhat; walking, a bit. Took him on rides round of the island. And in the evenings, he talked, talked, talked. Confessed he'd not had such company in long years.

Anyway it was hard & demanding & altogether wonderful healing time. A species of summing up too. Older friends who were once young friends, kids, movie buffs, students, then mirabile! Jesuits together.

I thought of a play by Pinter on memory; or maybe Bergman's 'Wild Strawberries' film.

Thus it goeth. As I trust all goeth well with everyone—as the wild times allow.

Phil, so great 2 have your letter awaiting on arrival here.

> Much ♥ to all—
> Daniel

[Phil refers here to Jonah House moving to the property with a cemetery.]

Apr. 20th Tues [1993]

Dear Dan—

Nothing much new here. We're trying to get some peacenik to inhabit the cemetery house. That's one of the conditions by which it was turned over to us. And this will wait until we can build ourselves, and then move over there. Meanwhile, we're supposed to work on the cemetery—cut the grass, remove shrubbery etc. In other words, work out the rent.

My reservations about the adventure haven't ceased, or been resolved. But the community wants the move, Liz most of all. And joining the ranks might give therapy to my ego. Which isn't, as I've discovered, the law of the universe.

Best love to you, dear brother. Jerry writes that you're going abroad, to Italy and elsewhere. Right on! After the tour de force in Philly, it will be a worthwhile change and breather.

> Peace of Christ—
> Phil, Liz, et al. at Jonah

Monday, May 3 (1993)

Dears,

Treated meself to "Scent of a Woman" today—have you seen? Ol' Pacino was superb. I remember seeing him with Martin Sheen doing *Julius Caesar* at the Public. But he never came 2 any of Martin's get-togethers—so reclusive he makes DeNiro look like Bush in his cigaret boat.

> Thinking of those on trial—blessings
> on them,
> Dan'l

[It is worth noting that the cardinal-archbishop of Milan at this writing was Cardinal Carlo Maria Martini, S.J. Martini was long considered a potential candidate for pope (and was briefly considered in the 2005 conclave). The term for such an individual is papabile. *Martini resigned from the post in Milan in 2002 at the compulsory retirement age and returned to his biblical studies for the remainder of his life. He died in 2012. Also in this letter, Dan makes another reference to former Provincial Robert Mitchell, S.J., and John Dear, a priest, activist, author, and longtime friend of the Berrigans who edited five books of Dan's writings.]*

Sunday 5 Sept. [1993]

Dears—

Are you all thriving? I'm off to B. Island tomorrow.

As to John Dear & superiors, it's hard for me to grasp the 'problem' [about his participaton in a Plowshares action]. He's already chosen the bottom spot on the totem, among the very poor of DC. One asks, what can they do to him??? Even if he were cardinal of Milan & papable (a Jesuit they tell me is both) what wd. he stand to lose, beside say, the papal piss pot? I jes think, this is a matter after all of faith. They almost kicked me into outer darkness after Catonsville, was saved strangely by so political an animal as Mitchell, who flew to Rome to stop the show. Not mind you, out of anything like esteem for the criminal, but a matter of brute logic; let him go now, the bottom will fall outa the vocation market. . . . Tell John he's called to freedom, not fear. As if he didn't know!

We had intense times at Kirkridge. Some substanial, some shitting green cheese. Ah me.

Many fond thoughts + prayers for brother Bill.

> Write me B.I.!!
> Daniel

11/12/1993

Dears,

Mindful of yall today on the road to Sarycuse, hoping things are smooth & level all the way. At least here, the day is gorgeous.

And so many fond thoughts & blessings as Liz's birthday approaches. Dear, may you always be young in heart & hands as you have always been!!!

John Guiliano called this AM from Chalatenango. A group including the Jesuit John Cortina have occupied the cathedral there since Nov. 1, doing a fast in protest against the death squad killings over the past months. Even the NY *Times* has taken note, and I've sent clippings along to John. He seemed quite up in spirit, sed the thing has taken hold across the country, with many joining the fast. The fasters are to leave for San Salvador on the 16, anniversary of the Jesuit murders, to take the message to the capital. John still hopes to get up here in early December. He asked feelingly for you.

Very sorrowful news on Helen. Kelly called from Chicago, she was at the trial. The judge sed H. owed the state a million dollars. H. responded she was 'short of cash, but would be willing to write a check.'

Jack St. George I jes learned, has decided to come to the NY Jesuit infirmary later this month. Please keep him in prayer.

All for now, y'all crack a jar on the birthday & down one for me!!!

Love,

Daniel

[On December 7, 1993, Phil was a part of the Pax Christi–Spirit of Life Plowshares action in Goldsboro, North Carolina. Their trial began on February 15, 1994, and Phil was sentenced to eight months on July 6.]

1/29/'94

Dearest bro,

I thought of a few things you might just possibly want to take up with the defense folk. Wild, improbably, but wot the h—.

- How about requesting a statement of support & presence at the trial, on the part of all the Pax Christi bishops? Mebbe Sullivan & Gumbleton would get this underway with a letter to the others. . . .
- I think of Coretta King and Nobel prize winners, the Guatemalan woman, the N. American Wald, Tutu—likewise, letters of support, invites to trial.
- How about Geo Anderson inviting the people of John's parish to the trial? And the people John cared for in the shelter? The action an offering of 'relief' from such deprivation? Would they themselves make the connection public, say at a PM gathering during the trial?
- Invite church (black and white) and mosque & synagogue leaders & Native Americans of Lumberton area and elsewhere in NC to testify at the trial on their understanding of Isaiah, swords into plowshares. Or to speak in the evening, or both.
- Is the diocese of Raleigh being approached, layfolk, nuns, priests, for statements, testimony?
- Could there be an official Pax Christi presence at the trial from around the country?
- How about a congress of folks from CW houses?
- How about folks representing the people of Haiti, Salvador, Nicaragua, testifying as to waste & carnage & complicity. Connections.

- Are there invites going out to Plowshares folk in W. Europe, Australia?
- How about the Jesuits? John's DC community—will they support and help out on the DC festival? Could the Maryland Provincial write all American provincials, asking them to announce the trial in their turf, appoint one or two Jesuits from each province to attend, testify, fast, march, vigil, whatever. And report the trial back home . . .

Well, this is probly yelling up a dream, but why not?

Well so long for a while, y'all keep more hearts going steady than you can well imagine. Heart enough and more you are, for so many.

♥ Daniel

2/2/'94

Dearest Bro,

Yestiddy was on Long Island at Stony Brook Medical School for a session on AIDS. They had a classical trio who made music just short of archangelic, between my readings from 'Sorrow' book. I was as always delighted with the quality of medical training, which includes an ethics dep't led by a quite intelligent priest of the diocese.

Ezekiel has me stumped, which I guess is par, as he's been stumping better heads than this cabbage, for many an eon. How to present the burning brand at Kirkridge in April? We'll just hafta enter his whirlwind & see where we land.

Well, LOVE in caps. to all the noblespirited 4!

♥ Daniel

14 June (1994)

Dear Bro,

Liz + fam'ly are not coming to NY shindig. I'll tool down 2 Jonah for a visit next week.

Overflow crowd at CW for Merton reminiscences. Carmen [Trotta] shared + afterword we partied at his friend's walk-up.

Soon's I get an outline on something on the ms. I'll get going here— I pray better health for yez. As to a better spirit—unimaginable!

Love,
Daniel

Sat. 25 (June 1994)

Dear Bro.,

Had a fine 24 hrs. at Jonah. Joe the ex-Jesuit was there for supper and regaled us heartily in ways I hadn't heard for many a year. He is surely a remarkably resilient spirit; as far as can be known, simply going on with work he believes in. I was delighted to be with him again.

We spent most of the next AM at the cemetery house, with Liz offering a guided tour, Peter, Jerry and Frida in attendance. I hadda add what a joy those 2 are—converse, humor, spontaneous helping with chores. You've made a great start! What an amazing place! And so much already done and underway; my first glimpse of it all.

♥ all around,
Daniel

Sunday [Nov. 6, 1994?]

Dears,

The Europe trip hasta be sharply curtailed; Don Moore who was to squire me into Austria and the Jagerstaetters, had to return. They also wanted me in Eyerland & Poland for the start of the 50th anniversary peace walk. But no go. Just 2 weeks in Switzerland & return here in early December.

Bob and I spent last PM with Ned. He's much changed with the poison they are pouring in, zapping & chemo. He looks quite sepulchral, as is usual. I won't go into details; appalling just to listen to the 'protocol' which makes one (him) resemble the slow dying of Hiroshima. The medical nabobs are really in league of spirit with the morticians. But it looks very much as though Ned will go their path to the bitter end. We can't do much but stand by & say our prayers.

Daniel

Dec. 11th (1994)

Dear Brother Mine—

The scene in cou't [court] the other day was a bit astonishing. The lawyers—who wants them around except in a nickel and dime case where the Powers are trying to stick it to usns?—were esp. eloquent. And I tole ole Poretz, gave him a full shot. So inexplicably, he backed off and gave me a ridiculous 2 days, with all other penalties lifted.

Jerry is home and amazes Liz and myself with his maturity and thoughtfulness. No prompting from us, but eventually, I think he's headed for peace work. Purrhaise de Lawd!

We're prayin' daily for Ned Baby. Willa from Viva House told us of a study of cancer patients—sed those prayed for did immeasurably better than those not prayed for. Have you heard of this?

We'll rejoice at sight of you. A blessed Advent, much love from us all, many hugs. And Christ's ineffable peace.

Phil

Jan. 1 ['95?]

Dearest bro—

Just got off the horn + the sun came up. Your voice summoning Dawn! So many thanks, you 4 make the world make sense; just to think of you is to dilate the heart with THANKSGIVING!

All's well here. Because you're there.

Love,
Daniel

May 2nd (1995)

Dear Bruv—

We're draggin' with the cemetery effort—between the City bureaucracy and the contractors. Both are adept at breaking their promises. Nonetheless, we keep hoping to break ground this month.

May is always a reminder of your birthday—a reminder also of what you've meant to us. Taped some stuff for Wilcox today and in the course of thinking about our early years, there is our brotherhood and your inspiration and influence. Which began in High School and continues to the present, even today. The Providence of God definitely enters here—were it not for you and the grace you've been to my life, I would be a purposeless vegetable looking at death and muddling over what I missed.

Am sayin' this poorly as usual, but I sense you get the drift. Thank you for being Dan Berrigan, a true brother to me. May you flourish in good health and grace—and May God grant you many years in the vineyard—to sustain us all.

Much love, many hugs—from us all,
Christ's peace,
Phil

Aug. 20th (1995)

Dear Dan—

You did a sterling job on the editing (best editor I know). Honey Knopp'll have no trouble getting to Abraham's bosom. A great and good woman. Will refer to the St. Andrew's retreat in another chapt. The SJ who gave me the *Exercises* was very tall and bald. You told me he was the Rector or Minister. Sheridan or O'Shaughnessy?—You would know. And the war thing in another chapter. Wilcox is interested in the conversion of a young killer—and I was, God help me, a pretty good young killer. Am trying to get a jail address for Susan and Steve.

> Peace of Christ to you, and love from everyone here,
> Phil

Sept. 16th (1995)

Dear Dan—

Great seein' Carol + Jerry + you. A real transfusion. And your remarks—splendid, indeed. I frequently question my approach—dwelling as I do on the "hard work" of Christ, illustrated by a dose of the Bad News. But then, I reflected that people can stand anything but disinformation and lies. And I don't want to denigrate them by assuming that they're too adolescent to handle a slice of reality.

Anyway, for better or worse, I'll keep screaming, while trying to live what I preach. You can see me going confessional here.

All fine here. I am doing Carol's water cure and finding it extraordinary. I'm pissing away the pounds. Remarkable! Let us know the info on your potion when you get a chance. Seems we're all dipping into the Fountain of Youth.

> Best love, many thanks, Christ's peace,
> Phil

[1996]

Dearest bro—

Your birthday is a holy season indeed. What an honor and joy to be your brother, to have all these years like an unfailing north star to keep me (+ multitudes of others) on a human road! I can never give thanks deep, wide, high enough. Catonsville, which is to say yourself, got me moving.

> All blessings,
> Daniel

[Steve Kelly, S.J., is mentioned in this letter. He is a Jesuit, a close associate of the Berrigans, and sometimes referred to as Primo Nacho. To this day, Kelly maintains an active presence among protesters of war and spends much time in prison.]

13 November. [1996]

Dears

Steve Kelly saw Ramsey yesterday. Can't truly exaggerate the depth & breadth of the blessing Steve's brought us. His deep consistent piety & clarity of thought & speech have won all hearts here.

We had a reading Mon. eve on Isaiah at the local Barnes-Noble emporium on Bway. 8 Jesuits came from here, a record for our moles. There was also a voluble (largely Jewish) standing room crowd. I wuz reproved, but gently, for not working from the Hebrew; I blamed it all on Kelly, who was present peering from behind a pillar in a Harpo Marx nose & wig. He broke into loud pidgeon-hebrew; we won that round.

Love, much of,
Daniel

[Dec. 31, 1996]

Dears,

Last day of '96 (hooray? alas?)

I've been remiss, but thinking of y'all during the Holy Innocents' events, and praying all went as well as the times allow.

For my own there silence, excuses galore. Summed up in a lousy (nearly, now) month of physical depletion et al, due to rare wicked flu swirling from Dante's nether regions, no doubt of it!

Aside from all that, plenty of time to meditate, read, write, keep singing in the rain. And hoping to be somewhat improved as to lungs, reins, blood, muscle and the other human jellies, to start toward Michigan on the 13 Jan.

Trust your Christmas was wunnerfully crowded & noisy & gustatorially beyond words. And may new year (but don't bank yr. roll on it!) improve on the last. This wd. seem a modest hope, in concert with the deity & ourselves. At least here & there, as hope springs.

Blessed '97 to all!
Daniel

Jan. 14th (1997)

Dear Dan,

I figger yer on the mend. Slowly, but on the mend. Purhaise Gawd! We are sooo relieved. How about going to Puerto Rico for some sun? Is that possible? We hope so.

Did you hear that Colman McCarthy has been sacked by the *Babylon Post?* The honchos there sed his columns were no longer of interest to the general public, Haw! Haw! He's been caution itself re the peace movement, and esp. Plowshares.

In any case, I hope you can exercise and eat and regain your strength. Prayers and hugs and love and thanks.

In Christo—
Phil et al. at Jonah

[On February 12, Ash Wednesday, Phil, Tom Lewis-Borbely, Susan Crane, Steve Kelly, S.J., and Steve Baggarly boarded the nuclear-capable USS Sullivans at Bath Iron Works, Maine, hammering and pouring blood on the destroyer. They became known as the Prince of Peace Plowshares. Phil would be convicted of destruction of government property and conspiracy on May 7 and sentenced to 24 months in October.]

Mar. 19th Wed. (1997)

Dear Dan—

We're A-ok—a few ripples here and there. But generally excellent. The Bible Study is a lifeline—5–6 of the guys study with us, and we've evolved a technique (mostly Steve Kelly's) which includes them very neatly.

Did you hear about the abortion flap? In one of my early blurbs, I mentioned "kidling in the womb," and the sh_t began to fly all over the State of Maine, including from some of our supporters. Some of these "progressives" even thought of chasing us from the office turned over to us. Waaaal, the worst is over, and outrage has abated. Right now, like the Administration, we're into damage control.

Got plenty of reading, so that's not a problem. We relish them Jer. notes, I tell you. They make the rounds.

This does it mostly. Prayers and hugs and much love and thanks and Christ's peace.

Phil—for the P of P Plowshares

Apr. 13 (97)

Dear Dan—

The Jer. notes came intact. Thanks so much. They are indeed food for the soul.

Three weeks to trial. I hear word that you'll come and speak at the Fest. of Hope. That'll lend some life to it. Thank you. Tom Gumbleton wrote and I invited him. But it's short notice and he's busy. Gumbleton's a lovely guy.

Doin' excellently here. Study of Jns. Gospel remains a lifeline. The two new C. Workers proving strong and stable—they have good communities at home.

Delighted Liz could see you, Carol + Jerry. Jim tells me Rosalie is recovering well. The hundredfold appears on every side. Please care for yourself. All sorts of Easter peace and hope. And love and thanks from us all.

Phil—for the P of P Plowshares

[This was written on a review by David O'Brien of Disarmed and Dangerous, *Murray Polner and Jim O'Grady's biography of Dan and Phil.]*

April 26 [1997]

Dearest bro—

I guess this is the best shake we can look for. I've written a note of appreciation to Dave O'Brien, a good scout—

I'd hoped to get to B.I. for a breather but we have 2, not 1, bad turns here. Jim Fox had a kidney removed this week. Then another blow; Dave Toolan diagnosed with his second cancer bout—this time colonic. He goes under the knife Monday. We're holding a healing-prayer service here this evening. I know the prayers of the Holy 6 are with us.

Just a week to go until trial! I guess you heard from John a carfull is coming from here. Hope for a chance to visit y'all. Elmer sez the response from Kairos is great + full. We'll see—

Love to all,
Daniel—

[On May 7, Phil was convicted of destruction of government property and conspiracy for the Prince of Peace Plowshares action and held at Cumberland County Jail. This letter seems to refer to a book of scriptural meditation the group once hoped to publish.]

May 15th (1997)

Dear Dan:

As the man sez: "we got a problem!" Our writing has somewhat come to a halt, and we banged heads on what we could do. I suggested that we cull the Bible, and write political commentaries on significant Scriptures, that have over the years, put some fiber in our bones. Assuming we'd do not a scholarly but a purely pol. (radical, truthful etc.) commentary on reading of these Scriptures—beginning w. Gen. + ending with Jns. Gospel. With a view toward n.v. resistance.

So I sifted the whole Bible—not Acts, the Letters, or Bk. of Rev.— and came up w/ over 100 citations. Sorta took the cream from the milk jar. Though I missed perhaps, many magnificent teachings. So—how do we make the 100 passages manageable? Do we deal only w/ the Gospels? As you can see, the 100 or so are too large a bite for us—and too large for a book. Yeah! If I didn't mention it— we'd hope a book would result. A book coming out of community, and out of jail.

Eg. "Your bro's blood cries out to me from the earth!" (Gen.). Killing one another makes certain the wasting of the environment.

Eg. "Choose life that you and your children might live" (Deut.). Life is already in your mouth + in you are heart—you have only to do it, live it.

Your presence here ensured the presence of the other S.J.'s. And it had huge meaning to the other hundreds. Thank you so much. As usual, you are where you should be.

Liz will be up for Frida's grad. on the 17th, with Kate + Jerry also. Then, all 4 will visit here. Jerry graduates in early June, and then, he comes home to face the Powers for that Pentagon testimony.

We're all doing splendidly and hope you're still better. Hope the few days on B.I. were restorative. Best love, many hugs, peace of Christ.

Phil, for the P of P Plowhsares

Aug 7 [1997]

Dearest bro,

Eight of usns took the cuffs at the wicked Intrepid yestiddy. No hostilities from the tourists this time. The CEO, a general somebody was unveiled for the first time, announced hisself as a fervent Episcopal who'd seen the tv program Sunday morning + loved it, but "you + ye brother gave me a hard time when I wuz being shot at in Vietnam defending yr. right 2 stand here today etc. etc." Bill ODonnell called from Berkeley, he + 15 arrested at Livermore. . . . 'Newsday' copied the DC post [*Washington Post*] article in toto on Tuesday, photos and all.

I'm doing pretty well, ol spine groaning a bit like Methuselah's skeleton. . . . I hafta tool up 2 Harlem today 2 retrieve my Soc. Security card, larcenously abducted.

Bob K retrieved from Fred's room 2 folders of letters + Merton exchanges + clippings going back to '64. He came to Danbury Christmas Day '71, no prior phone call, not on visitors' list—and got in!

Love to yez all!
Daniel

August 14, 1997

Dearest Bro,

'Twas 58 years ago today I left streetcar (then bus) Stop 6, old Liverpool Road, on the great odyssey. Good Gawd, thanks be.

And RIP dear Jack St. George. His momma, ever the prima donna, threatened to lie down in the doorway if he tried to go off to the Jesuits. (She didn't mind his becoming a diocesan, the issue of course was control.) Jack came to Freda in some distress. Momma responded laconic; 'Don't worry, Jack, she'll never do it!' Which of course, she didn't.

I wuz sitting on a bench in Broadway yestiddy, reading that wonderful interview in the Catholic paper in Portland; there you are on the front page. I got to the end and was crying like a witless oaf. All that clarity, all that loneliness, I felt it in my bones.

Well, since about 50% of those who wander the street are nuts in one degree or other, I didn't stop any traffic.

Love yez, learn from yez,
Daniel

Sept. 20th (1997)

Dear Dan—

You missed some fun on the 17th. Mebbe Steve told you about it. The judge + prosecution differed strenuously on damage totals, supervised release, fines and restitution. Odd to have ole Carter in one's corner. Anyway, ole Mean Gene, The Time Machine, scheduled another hearing in 10 days/ 2 wks. time. So I guess we'll be here another month or so.

Support was terrific—6 busted at the Shipyard, ending up in the jail here for a day—the award dinner went off famously (Dave Dellinger + Liz spoke), strong presence in the courtroom and outside the courthouse.

Hope them O.P.'s ain't runnin' you ragged. We've met some of their Sisters—really fine types. And we pray the health is holding up. Look for you back in the Big Apple.

> Much love and hugs and thanks and
> the Lord's peace,
> Phil—for the P of P Plowshares

[Oct 1] [1997]

Dearest bro—

Here's a touch of the silly and the sublime to say Blessed Birthday!

Who you are is where you are—a conjunction of conscience and the right place that is truly sublime.

The confounding of the powers goes on, as the dilemma is adroitly tossed into their dark corner. You carried the day in court—as you have done again and again these many years—an evangelical scenario worthy of the original. All honor to you, and good health and spirit— the gifts already given in abundance!

John Dear phoned from N. Ireland where he arrived today, Oct 1. He'd been to France, Italy, + Austria where he visited the Jagerstatter family. On a train in Poland he was robbed of everything en route to Auschwitz—passport, money, clothes. He sends love to y'all.

Monday 6 Oct. we celebrate Bob Keck's 50th in the Jesuits. Wotta guy!

> Love for the day we bless + thank you!
> Daniel

11 November '97

Dearest brother,

Susan died Friday, and today I venture to a neighborhood Jewish chapel to speak as she requested. I'd visited her on Thursday, held her hand and blessed her. She spoke of you, the Plowshares very much on her mind. She had your statement 'what I would have said' printed and sent to her friends—really last hurrah.

There was never in all these months of illness a word of complaint. I was so happy that her last birthday was celebrated here some months ago—when Liz spent much time with her, Susan being in near despair with the world.

So it goeth.

Last night at Fordham was—Fordham. A big evening on rabbi Heschel, including his daughter and widow. The scholarly rabbi who spoke first was fulsome in praise, and I reflected to I'd never heard such words in public from a Jesuit, concerning meself . . .

Love, mucho, and in haste,
Daniel

Nov. 19 [1997]

Dearest,

Just returned from court, where a courteous even compassionate (black of course) judge kept giving out light fines to public drinkers & dismissed charges for peeing in public & likewise for 40 mainly young folk black & white together, who'd sat in at the infamous local housing authority. No one jailed all morning. Finally we 8 were called & with a smile he sent us on our way. How unlike the beetling dinosaur of Portland!

Well the visit of the luminous 3 from B'more was famously restorative to everyone here at liturgy & supper—most of all to the undersigned who was peacock proud to show off such wunerful youngers whether in Central Park or in the house. . . . And of course we prayed for you on your birthday, every year giving new birth of hope to so many! . . . 50 more at very least, please.

Love you, thank you, thank you . . . . .
Daniel

[Phil was sentenced to 24 months for the Prince of Peace Plowshares in October. Dan refers to apparent hardships Phil was having in prison.]

Dec. 12, Sr. Alicia Domon, Martyr, Argentina [1997]

Dearest bro,

I had yr. first letter in weeks yesterday. Took it with me for coffee with Bill McNichols, and we read it together. It was a (nearly) tearful but joyous reading. I'd known something from Liz about the travails, esp. in Lewisburg, but getting it first hand was something other. We were with you in heart all through it.

As to folk here, Toolan is holding his own, Ned is blooming esp. in his weight. . . . I'm off to RIP tomorrow for evening po'try, back here Sunday. Then next week to Syracuse visit. Liz and the 3 wunderkind are due in Jersey before Xmas for McAlister stop overnight, then here for our Xmas liturgy & party Monday 22.

Enclosed some recent brouhaha on Dorothy. Carmen [Trotta] and Jeremy [Scahill] did yeomans' service arranging the exhibit of photos etc. in a little gallery on the lower east side near the Worker.

And hiz eminence here 'improved the occasion' by declaring in St. Patrick's he'd help make her a saint. Many including Colman McCarthy took blistering umbrage at this ol mitred military party scrambling aboard late. . . . Sure as hell, the dead don't own themselves!

Dear bro, I sure hope & pray conditions are more tol'able there, and you have quill & mucho ink & are rarin' to go!

Daniel

Dec. 13th Sat. [1997?]

Dearest Bro. Dan—

Yers always relief, and an infusion + enlightenment. Thanks so much.

The Sch. of the Assassins report very hopeful—beyond expectation. Seems folks gather pizzazz from it more than against the (direct) war-makers. Little shocked by Roy Baby—he's quoted as having no quarrel w/ the military. Hope it's a slip of the tongue. Or perhaps he thinks the kindergarten for assassins is a separate issue from the nucl. + inter-ventionary jocks. Or mebbe Roy Baby has no one to talk sense with.

Hugs and love and thanks—
Phil

Dec 16th Tues [1997]

Dearest Bro. Dan—

Getting adjusted to this dumpster—it takes some doin' because they're top heavy on the rules, and because they enforce them like malevolent little dwarfs. So I gulp the ego, put up w/ their sh_t, and

endeavor to learn the ropes. Gulpin' the ego always good for me—
Mentor used to claim it was our #1 ideal. I believe it.

Bless youse for extending such love to Liz and the kids. They love
you deeply. Can't wish you enuf a blessed and hopeful Christmas. May
it be the best of your life.

> Love, hugs, thanks, peace of Christ,
> Phil

[Dan refers here to what would become his book The Bride: Images
of the Church, *illustrated by Bill McNichols.]*

Dec 18 [1997]

Dearest bro,

Working on a ms. with Bill McNichols on the icons. Such a fine
Advent project, pondering those splendid images of his!

Did I write [that Mairead Corrigan Maguire] the Irish Nobel laureate woman phoned twice from Belfast to announce our nomination
for next year? She wants to have a reception for John Dear, Bill and
myself on new year's day.

All Christmas blessings to yez from the divine cornucopia!!!

> Daniel

Christmas Eve 1997

Dearest bro,

Denise Levertov's death came as quite a shock. She'd written an
essay for my John Dear b'day book, and agreed to read & comment
on the Fordham poems when they appear, purportedly in the spring.
I knew she was ill, but had no idea.

Memories, memories. She and I did what was the very first of my
po'try readings in NY in I think '57, at the YMHA (whence of course
I've bin banished since, due to intemperate notorious Palestine remarks).
She was the only poet of national renown I could count a friend, me not
being terribly impressed or interested in the big names & claims. (The
idiot *Times* neglects to so much as mention that she became a Catholic,
and a fervent one, several years ago.) RIP a dear valiant lady.

Mairead Maguire has been busy about Nobel matters, phoning here
twice. I'm sure the hand of John Dear is in all this.

I'm deep in Bill McNichols' icons, doing a text for an illustrated book Ellsberg wants. Tough work trying to be faithful to those magnificent images!

> Blessed Christmas be yours—as you
> from there, bless us!!!!
> Daniel

Dec. 28 [1997]

Dearest bro,

Christmas day here was quiet & good. I had seven stalwarts for wassail & supper.

Ned I worry about, he's down with pneumonia, & the symptoms distressingly similar to those that first revealed the cancer. Prayers please.

I'll close off with a deep draught of gratitude for you, for where you abide with courage and good spirit, heartening us all. The world a perpetual predawn, certifiably mad in its chief agents, here to Iraq to all but everywhere.

Pray that we bring some measure of light to the Belfast country. There'll be fond inquiries and thoughts of you, all the way.

> Daniel

[On July 17, 1997, TWA flight 800 exploded over the Atlantic Ocean near New York, killing all passengers. The FBI was probing the possibility of terrorism at the time Phil writes here.]

Dec. 30th [1997]

Dearest Brother—

Yours always an infusion of goodness and cheer. Thanks so much.

Got some in depth reporting on TWA 800 today—sent by a friend. 'Twas even as we heard and surmised. And the coverup began immed. The CIA was in on it, threatening those familiar w/ the wreckage—key elements missing—that if they peeped, it'd be prosecution and jail. Waaal, imperialists are liars by definition.

I mourn for Denise L.—a great woman. Imagine what caliber of Cath/Christian she was. I ran into her in DC I think, mebbe 6 yrs.

ago—she and the novelist who used to teach at Sarah Lawrence. Great women, both of them.

Waal, another year. May it be blessed and hopeful. I'm sure God will do her part to make it so. Health and well being and grace, dear brother. And the peace of Christ.

Phil

18 Jan [1998], St. Prisca, martyr under Nero. 'Greet Prisca (and Aquila) my coworkers, who risked their necks for my sake.' (Rom., c.16, v.3)

Dearest bro,

Waal here's a short one just after late nite return from NOhleans. Everything went as such things go, lotsa good folk somewhat lost in the shuffle of Amurika & Church, very good despite all. And Sister Helen [Prejean] unstoppable hopping every fence & ditch. Some 700 showing for the event at Loyola. The rather impervious ambiguous Jesuit Prexy opening the main act & staying on, to what effect even Gawd don't know—or won't say.

I return home with a strong gratitude for life here, no academic malaise, moneygrubbing, bootlicking to the biggies, fencestraddling in the big corral, lollypop tenures, just a passel of tentmakers plying their needles & humming There Ain't no Fleas on the Lamb of Gawd. Ha.

I'm finishing up a text for a book of Bill McNichols' icons. Quite an assignment, trying to measure up to sheer genius. An omadon holding up the train of the saints, or trying to.

Can't think of anything momentous. In fact, can't think. Love & gratitude go with this, enuf.

7 March [1998]

Dearest bro,

Tuesday will see Bob Keck and me winging south to the Virgin Islands for 10 days. Fordham happily is on something euphemistic known as 'spring break'; though with no winter here, spring looks perpetual, if not preemptive.

Life proceeds. Michael Moore called at length last night, full of inquiries about yourself & usns all.

We had some 35 arrests here on Ash Wed. Not bad.

I'll get this off, everything's ok here, the ill are holding their own. Ned much more than that. He's hosting supper for us all at POTS [Part of the Solution] as part of our Lenten observances/bible study.

You being where you are in good spirit & fettle is a blessing beyond measure. We love & honor you.

♥ Daniel

Mar. 14th ['98]

Dearest Bro

Am delighted you're getting away for a breather. May the sun and the Son shine on you and Bob.

Mebbe by now you've heard of the latest nonsense here. In my "Disciplinary Hearing"—the judge—Jesus Lord! They're all so alike—told of his options—back in the "hole," 27 days good time last, suspension of Canteen, mail etc, all privileges or termination of social visits. He had the audacity to tell me that my time in solitary was not "punitive."

But I deeply regret the suspension because it draws the family + community into the punishment.

Prayers and hugs and much love and Christ's good peace.

Love you,
Phil

[mid-March 1998]

"A believer is surely a lover—yea—of all lovers the most in love." —Kierkegaard

Brother Mine—

Two fum yew yestiddy—both of them top shelf. The piece on the universe by Polkinghorne esp. good.

Amy Goodman was here yesterday w/ Jeremy Scahill—did an interview. Amy is exceptional—intelligent + compassionate. And Jeremy seems to be thriving.

Somebody sed the damage to the ecology is so widespread that only internat'l action will suffice. And that's learning on those most responsible in the 1st place.

Got a letter from a good woman on L.I.—interested in giving you, Bill McNulty and myself a peace award in Dec. I begged off, for reasons you know well.

Liz tells me everyone is fine at Jonah. In fact, a couple of them have anniversary aces up their sleeves.

What a great move, getting Bob Keck as Superior. Please give him our love.

And Liz sez you're well and thriving. Thank God!

Will letcha go with hugs and love. See you in June or July—whenever is possible.

> Peace of Christ—
> Phil

21 March JS Bach [1998]

Like an oaf I forgot to bring yr. address with me on departure to St. Thomas. I hope you got Liz's message; Ne Illigitimi . . . I had 2 of yrs. awaiting me here last night, but of course L. had phoned with news of the body snatchers. I'd gotten to John Dear in Belfast & he to Mairead Corrigan Maguire. I presume aftershocks to their minor quakes are impending. Meantime we sits tight on the Lawd.

The week down there was quite restoring of blood & bone. Maureen Toolan left us in charge of dawg & cat & house. The dawg, a noble golden Retriever, proceeded promptly to get sick, as though at sight of the new management. After a day of this, we got him to the vet, the good smoocher lingered on a day or so & then ascended to canine Eden. The verdict was—cancer.

I of course can neither 1) be phoned by Steve, nor 2) visit. Which pretty much settles my hash, except for 1) letters, and 2) prayers. I think latter, from yourself & here, have been salvational of the good mon.

> Love you, lean on you!
> Daniel

Mar. 28th

Dearest Bro—

Welcome home. I hope you gots lots of sun and rest and great hospitality.

Nothing much new here. The appeal (?) is apparently in the works. Liz has done marvelous work in getting public opinion after the honchos here.

The Plough sent on a marvelous little book excerpting Romero's sermons. The guy was a great spirit. Despite his late education, he learned fast and accurately. Gospel n.violence—all the way.

Love you, dearly.

> Peace + love + thanks + all good
> gifts from God's Spirit,
> Phil

30 March [1998]

Dearest bro,

Thursday PM was also F'ham night, converse with Jim Marsh, philosophy prof, exJesuit who gets arrested with us regularly, also attends my class. About 200 showed up for enlightenment of sorts. Remember our old friend from Danbury days, Billy Bones? He comes to class regularly. He's quite frail now, gimp more pronounced, but indomitable. We got him library access & he eeets it up. He sends love.

We're gearing up for Good Friday. My class is involved, looks good.

Hope you're getting something of the sunshine raining down in buckets here. Love & all honor. A coven of clowns rule the imperial roost. Not funny, just despicable.

> You make the days & nights bear-
> able,
> Daniel

Holy Thursday, April 9 [1998]

Bonhoeffer; 'Living unreservedly in life's duties, problems, . . . experiences and perplexities. In so doing, we throw ourselves into the arms of God, taking seriously not our own sufferings, but those of God in the world—watching with Christ in Gethsemane. That, I think is faith; that is metanoia.'

Dearest bro,

Today we have liturgy & guests for supper; tomorrow Jerry departs—& how proud we are. So good talking with him, so fine a one to pass the vocation of hope & compassion to!

Friend S, it appears, is in semi solitude for one month. Appears he objected to a 'breath-alcoholic' test. Two from here were to visit him, alas no no go. This gent has put all here through our paces. But I think he also shakes our seams out; one has a nightmare of clerics clotting together, older and fatter & routine ho-hum. . . . I think strangely enough, whatever Jesuit fire here & there has pretty much passed over to folk like the Bruderhof. I've invited them for the Stations.

Tonight I meet with 25 or so Jesuit Volunteers from around the coast, who wanna talk cd tomorrow at end of Stations. This is a great advance, the original only a year ago engineered by John Dear. Holy Saturday I tool over to Brooklyn where they're lodging, to review the Friday events.

Of course, long pondering talk of you, and much love to be sent. I never liked him more.

I'll pass this on, thanking you for our Easter Man.

Daniel

April 14 [1998], St. Justin Martyr; 'You can kill us but you cannot do us any real harm.'

Dearest bro,

News yesterday of Sr. Jogues Egan's death, a long long shock. I will try to make either the wake or the funeral Thursday, and today we'll have a eucharist invoking her rest.

What a history! In the volatile '60s I came to understand that she sought from me something I was unable in principle or temperament, to give. She pressed me at every turn; it became clear (and is clearer in hindsight), that what I saw as a friendship was becoming an unworkable torment on both sides. So I walked away, for sake of whatever good sense or sense of direction I could muster.

After her stroke, I had hoped things could resume on a better basis. But she dropped strong hints that the past, as she saw and desired it, had far from evaporated. So I kept away, except from a cool word now and then—all I could manage. And then she died.

Sorrow and gratitude and regret. She supported me in dark times, when I was shipped out in '65. She wrote my tawdry secretive provincial a strong protest, and she and many others forced a moratorium on the savagery. I came home. But the conflict of expectations, and the maneuvering, never stopped.

The episode is one of the most mysterious and painful of my life. May she rest in peace, a great and good woman.

Well we have a small Easter gift. Liz gave the news that the nabobs have limited your punishment to late June. A small victory for you, and all of us, Deo gratias.

25 of us arrested Good Friday at *SS Intrepid*.

Thass about it, I hope Easter brought you joy & sense of some solid achievement, so richly deserved!

♥ Daniel

[1998] 23 April, Cesar Chavez ('27–'93) 'It is my deepest belief that only by giving our lives do we find life. I am convinced that the truest act of courage is to sacrifice ourselves for others in nonviolent struggle for justice. To be human is to suffer for others. . . . '

Dearest bro,

Was visited the other day by a young woman from the farm workers here; the current contest is with the strawberry owners, including scandalously enough, the biggest biggy of all, the Driscolls, who are incalculably rich & Catholic Californians. So there's much to help with . . .

We're amid annual visit by the provincial, who announced that the new superior is to be Bob Keck, a lagniappe for us all, though some of his multifarious dooties on behalf of us all will hafta be divided up now. But we're blessedly to be free another 6 years from outside reformers who could wreck the place & us . . .

♥ Daniel

Apr. 28th Tues. [1998?]

Dearest Brother—

We're lookin' at your birthday again in a few days, and I've been hunting for some good poetry to share. Michael Espada—a Latino (teaches lit. at the U of Mar.) sent me a book of his poems, and I read them carefully. But Michael baby came outa the lumpenproletariat, and his poems are mostly about that struggle. And hence, not eggsakly suitable.

So, as a substitute, here's a statistic from Wink that I found encouraging. He wrote about the slow, yet perhaps inexorable (given God and the Gospel) spread of n. violence in the world. In 1989 alone, 32% of humanity sponsored n. violent resolution—some 1,695,100,000 people. Add to that those people touched by major n. violent actions since '86—the Philippines, S. Korea, S. Africa, Israel, Burma, N. Zealand—plus the struggles of the century—India, Ghana, the overthrow of the Shah in Iran, Argentina + Mexico, the anti-Vietnam and anti-nucl. movements in the US, and one has 64% of humanity—3,337,400,000 people.

This is of course, a radical contradiction of the assumption that n.v. doesn't "work" in the real world.

You have had as much or more to do with this heartening situation than anyone I know. It sums up your life, springing from your allegiance to Our Lord and His Kin-dom. So, as your birthday beckons—I can merely say, this is just the beginning. "Greater deeds" await you. Many years, good health, dear brother.

Peace, hugs, my love, and always,
always thanks to you,
Phil

[This was attached to letter from America *to Dan informing him that "the editorial board of the Catholic Book Club, a subsidiary of America Press, has unanimously voted you to receive the 1998 Campion Medal, given yearly to a distinguished Christian person of letters."]*

[1998] 29 April, St. Catherine of Siena, Doctor of the Church.

Dearest bro,

This funny (form) letter arrived a while ago. Well, the gents at *America* mag just about beat the undertaker.

And imagine sending a letter to a Jesuit explaining who St. Edmund Campion is, what *America* mag is? It made for mannny a lafffff hereabouts . . .

The Kelly saga continues. Seems they shipped him to another part of the grab bag through no fault of his. So he's under a different chaplain, & we start all over again, the prospective visit of 3 from here tomorrow, canceled. A more serious item is K's. uncared for eye troubles. He was to see an ophthalmologist last week, now no go. It's becoming an issue where in my judgment, we need a lawyer's help. Keep yuh posted.

I've finished at Fordham Monday. Nice class reaction & gift of a book of po'try. Fine young folk.

Love, gratitude!
Daniel

[Bishop Juan José Gerardi Conedera, auxiliary bishop of the Archdiocese of Guatemala, was bludgeoned to death April 26, 1998, in

response to his work for justice. His assassination was linked to the highest Guatemalan governmental officials.]

[1998] May 6,

HD Thoreau, 1817–1862; 'How does it become a man to behave toward this American government today? I answer that he cannot without disgrace be associated with it.'

Dearest bro,
We had the 65th anniversary Mass of the C. Worker on May day. Large crowd in attendance, prisoners of conscience fervently remembered. Some 200 for dinner afterward at Mary House; candles, flowers, table cloths, they'd worked like young beavers to put on a beautiful setting & meal.
I enclose words on the appalling murder of Bishop Gerardi; Dennis Leder phoned from Guatemala City; the whole country was shaken. By all reports, the bishop was a man of singular courage & modest. It's beyond reasonable doubt he was x'd for his expose of the crimes of the military over the years of war. Now, continuance of same by 'other means.' And we are granted another advocate, a second Romero.
Ramsey by the way, flew yestiddy to Iraq together with Gumbleton & Arnold & others mainly from the B'hof, 100 strong. The pilgrimage & 2 chartered jets is underwritten by—you guessed it—the Bruderhof.
Every day you, Steve, all prisoners—our glory—are in my heart and prayers. Such as you stay the hand of God against this 'crooked generation' (Acts).

♥ Daniel

[1998] May 13, Julian of Norwich: 'As truly as God is our Father, so truly is God our Mother. Or Father wills, our Mother works, our good Lord the Holy Spirit confirms'.

Best of Bro's,
Tom's birthday. RIP good man!
As to the friend from L[ong] Island & the award, of course I couldn't go ahead except you agreed; she knows that. I'm not big on such things, as I know you're not.
Which brings up the point of Nobel prizes. I feel strong too, about turning the thing down, and maybe we shd. start thinking of a press release or something as to why??

Did I send along notice of the Jesuit Campion award in October? I'm accepting as 1) this is strictly a literary kudo, and 2) it was the 'America' editors who in '65 helped with the Spellman coverup when I was shipped south. So they owe me (not the same eminences of course) a touch of belated compensation.

Love yeh, thank yeh!
♥ Daniel

[On May 17, two nuns, two priests, and Catholic Worker Kathy Boylan entered the Andrews Airforce Base during the Department of Defense Open House and poured blood and hammered on the bomb bay missile hatches and plane doors. They became known as the Gods of Metal Plowshares.]

May 19th Tues. [1998]

Dearest Bruv—

Be sumpthin' if Bish. Gerardi's murderers were grads of the School of the Assassins.

Called Sun. night about the new Is. mtn. climbing, and Liz gave me a few particulars. The $2 billion dollar boondoggle B-2 heavy bomber was the target—the one for whom the arms slaves must provide an air-conditioned hangar because of its sensitive skin. Anyway, rejoicing is in order—2 nuns, 2 priests and a magnificent CW woman. The ole Church still spawns the martyrs, and the splendid witnesses.

As for the L.I. award, please go ahead if that strikes you right. It's another chance to speak some truth. Liz just accepted a Pax Christi award—that's her decision. As for the Nobel, I agreed to accept it only on the faint hope that I'd still be in prison. There are some very worthy types nominated and our chances in '98 are faint. Mebbe in '99 or 2000, and then you and I can figger on accepting it or no.

Peace and love and thanks,
Phil

[The following one-sentence letter was sent on a copy of Dan's old test for his students.]

Now you know why I wasn't asked back to good ol' Berkeley!

1980 Spring Semester
Jesuit School of Theology at Berkeley

You may answer all, any, or none of the following questions . . .

1. Is there such a thing as a theologically indefensible position? Explain.

2. How many different ways can you spell Schillibex?

3. Has the church always taught anything? Be specific.

4. Reflect on the Seven Deadly Sins. Describe how you have integrated these in your life.

5. Who wrote the Summa Theologica, and why?

6. Why is Simon Stylites important in the history of Eccentric Spirituality?

7. Compare the discernment process of Ignatius with that of Sherlock Holmes.

8. Does Karl Rahner believe in verbs?

9. In light of recent papal directives, discuss the hundred button cassock. Should the garment properly be unbottoned at the top, bottom, or middle? Discuss the pros and cons in light of the above, of a six foot zipper. Given the sacred male priesthood, are not 2 zippers too much? Discuss by way of contrast, the possibilities of a hundred button fly.

10. Construct, on a single legal size sheet, a mockup of the Trinity.

11. Chart the progress of a mystic climbing Dante's Mount of purgation from the inside.

12. Make an ethical critique of a hypothetical proposal to establish a papal sperm bank.

13. If the headquarters of the western church are at Geneva and Rome where are its hind quarters? Illustrate.

14. In light of post-Fruedian theory and the return of the Roman cassock, discuss the following proposition of canon law; 'Father must now dress like mother.'

15. Taking in account the view of Norman Vincent Peale that Christ had everything going for him, and blew it, refute the Servant Songs of Isaiah.

16. If transcendental meditation grew immanent, would its devotees disappear into a black hole in space? Interview at least 5 t. mers. on this question.

17. Reflect on the status of a male priest who undergoes sex change surgery. What has occurred regarding his/her 'necessary likeness to Christ'? Locate this likeness and illustrate.

18. Which of the following do not belong in a given group?—
   a—Rahner, Kung, Howdy Doody, Dulles, Schillebeeckx
   b—Ecclesiology, Christology, Mariology, Phrenology, Eschatology
   c—Esther, Dolly Parton, Ruth, Judith, Sarah
   d—bishop, cardinal, priest, deacon, cowboy
   e—John XXIII, Malcolm XXX, Paul VI, John Paul I, John Paul II

19. In light of protestant theology of the '60s, discuss the neo-Gothic towers of NY's Riverside Church. If God is indeed dead, has the church buried him standing?

June 30th

Dearest Bro. Dan—

Tom Gumbleton sent on an article he did on Iraq. Devastating! esp. for a Bishop. What's more, he breaks w/ the club, castigating the moss backs who have said nothing, done nothing. First time I've seen that. I figger w/ a little cultivating, he'll do a Plowshares yet.

Your test for the Berkeley crowd a howl! No wonder you ain't invited back.

Finished yer pomes. Better'n a meditation.

> Peace to you, much love, many
> thanks,
> Phil

Sept. 3rd

Dearest Bro.—

As Freda would say—"Hearing from you is a treat!" Thank you.

Reading in Chronicles how Yahweh came down hard on David for Census taking. The obj. of which of course, was to find out how many men could "draw the sword." we thought the same thing when the Poors (temp. job) came around the last time. And refused any info.

Bin watchin' Clinton + Yeltsin on CNN. What a sorry pair of sobs! Clinton looking like Atlas w. the world on his shoulders, and Yeltsin barely able to speak a coherent sentence. And the "yellow" press— how they deserve that description! Quest. galore about Monica Baby, nothing about Iraq, virtually nothing on disarmament.

No ripples here, save a few with my cellmate—a Venezuelan edu- cated here, picking up the worst of the kulchah. He's a squeeky clean guy who objected to my "stink." To point, he was right, so I took some measures to reduce the stink, and he still raised hell. So I told him he smelled himself because he had his head up his _ss. Since then, there's been a blessed silence.

Glad yer takin' on Job—another book for the times. No worries toward us—I'm muckin' thru, w/ God's help. Liz comin' on Sept. 10th. Sendin' you hugs and much love and constant thanks.

> Peace of Christ—
> Phil

24 Sept. [1998]

Dear bro,

Had a scrawl from Steve; a guard informed him Sunday PM; don't eat anything tonight, surgery in the morning. So we're hoping & praying the gents with the keys came through at last.

Liz reports the 5 Plowshares acquitted (!) themselves nobly, eloquently, honorably, informing hizzoner (or herroner?) (s)he had been given a chance to issue a verdict helpful to the world—& of course failed to do so. So no further cooperation on their part. So they're in lockup until sentencing in Jan., which as Liz avers, is prob'ly more time than the da. would ask for!

I'm recovered from the transcontinental jumbo jetting in 34 hrs. The San Diego scene is sunlit & nightmarish, with nukes in the harbor alongside sailboats & religion for the most part mum. But the Episcopal cathedral where I held forth is an eden amid hell, with a fine outspoken pastor & thoughtful congregants. I preached sort of, on Isaiah 2 & in the PM we had a public forum, mainly on the Plowshares.

♥ Daniel

Oct. 2nd

Dearest Bro Dan—

Have given restitution and supervised release some thought. No $ for them—that's clear. I can't, but if I could, I wouldn't. The superv. rel. is another matter. These P.O.s are amoral hounds—I never told you of their harassment after action in NC. And then, finally, violation. Ramsey helped to bail me out. (I recall you experienced similar when you left Danbury. So you know the drill.)

I'm torn between total non-cooperation and stringing them along. I know how to string them along—lots of experience. If you've got ideas, please tell me.

Little thievery going on here—my cellmate stripped a radio, and myself a book of stamps. So I'll send this thru a friend in Me.

Weather gorgeous here—cool nights and warm days. I'm fine and pray you're tip top.

Peace of Christ to you, much love,
continual thanks,
Phil

Dearest bro,

My heart is not big enough to hold the gratitude your birthday brings—and brims.

Your offering on behalf of a demented, demoralized world, is boundless before God—and immeasurable to us. We know only, if we know anything, that we live from the spiritual riches amassed by our beloved prisoners.

They (you) make sense for our sake. We may, if lucky and attentive, draw on that grace of compassion and fearlessness—and make small sense too, where we live.

But always, I think, our grace is from you; from that cell we can take soundings + direction in the world, as to the cost of human behavior exacted by inhuman times.

Well this is by way of admiration and gratitude + a fervent prayer like a big embrazzo. Blessed birthday, many years, for all our sake!

♥ Daniel

"That's exactly why there will be change, because all they have is guns." —Aung San Suu Kyi (Burmese Nobel Peace Laureate)

Oct. 17th

Dearest Bro—

Normal Sat. routine here—answering mail. Hope the week in Pa. is not too exacting. But they always are, aren't they?

Am listening to the hacks down at their firing range. They really shoot up a helluva lot of ammo. The morning was absurd and ludicrous. A moderate fog appeared at 6am—the turnkeys went into hysteria—count + recount—guns appeared outside the razor wire. We finally got a bite to eat at 9:30. These poor bahstids exactly reflect the warden and his spirit—which is a combination of neurosis and militarism. (I recall what the Bk. of Rev. had to say about the militarized spirit.) It pretty much sums up everything wicked about us.

Am doin' a piece on Amer. arms sales—now nearly 60% of the world's total. Another facet of the Beast's outreach. We subsidize poor countries to buy, and then, when they can't pay, the poor taxpayer picks up the tab. Then the $ goes directly to Lockheed Martin or Boeing. It's another argument for the Prin. + Powers.

Guess Jerry will make it to the SOA. Our brother sees Caesar nothing if not clearly. Hugs to you, much love, constant thanks, peace of Christ.

Phil

15 November [1998], St. Roque Gonzalez, martyr of Paraguay

Dearest bro,

Seems fitting to send a wing & a prayer on this day, recalling too the making of the Mission film. And my last note to you before the great Friday Freedom Day!

As far as our fate with the wicked landlord, everything in the courts is in abeyance for a month, while the judge peruses the paper storm launched by both sides and fallen to her podium. After that, either a 'summary judgment' for Gawd knows which side, or a decree to proceed to trial. So we shall see.

The utterly demoralised Clinton is rattling the war drum night & day. God help the poor folk of Iraq.

Soon. Days, hours, then HOME!

Congrats, immense gratitude,
♥ Daniel

Jan 12 Sun. [1999]

Dearest Brother—

Nothin' like recycling govmint paper. The old Beast is good for sumpin!

Liz, Kate, Carol, Jerry here yestiddy. We had great palaver. I plumb choked up in sayin' goodbye to Kate—won't see her for a year or more. Got a deeper understanding of Jesus isolating the bloodline (w/ ego and possessions) as an obstacle to the Cross.

The kids went to the ocean and on the way back, had supper w/ Jim and Rosalie. Kate sed both looked "frail." Hey! we're all closer to the Beatific Vision, I'm learning how beguiling good health is. Gives you visions of immortality.

Jerry tells me he'll try one more semester of teaching. Then something else—which shure as H won't be retirement.

Everything hunky dory, though the dustbin tempers that. Hope you get a decent break on B.I. Love you, thanks and peace and well being,

Phil

29 Jan. [1999]

Dears,
    Helen Prejean got to the pope who spoke up. At last.
    John Dear is assembling Nobel winners for the trip to Iraq in March. I ast him if he'd approached Kissinger. He had, no response so far. Now if the dying children could only redeem that lost gargoyle!
                                        ♥ Daniel

6 Feb., '99

Dears,
    Kairos is planning an Ash Wednesday vigil at a 'detention center' of 'illegals' near Kennedy airport. We're trying to enlist churches and a campus of Empire State U. to help. 200 inmates languish within, from Africa, Asia, L. America; their crime, seeking asylum. The place is a 'run for profit' pit, squeezed by a nefarious private outfit with purported CIA connections. Stench.
    Then for Good Friday, the usual Stations across Manhattan, ending up with vigil (and undoubted arrests) at the SS Insipid [*USS Intrepid*] War Museum anchored in the lordly Hudson.
    Class at Fordham blooming amid winter. Young folks are smart & alive & curious.
    Meantime a big flap on Kathlik Universities in the *Times*. Seems the Pope's treading on their tail, they're 'losing K. Identity.' With of course a big stake in what's politely called 'gov't $$$,' a euphemism of note. For which read ROTC megabucks.
    My notion, strictly minority, is that they're burying themselves (hardly) alive. Like old nag Maj, they now and again kick up a fart & a post mortem hind leg.
                                        Luv & gratitude,
                                        Daniel

Feb. 13th

Brother Mine:
    Yours memorable as always. Just back from an FOR mtg. at St. Al's in DC. J[ohn] Dear presided, though he was pale and half sick. He points to 2000 rather than trying anything this year. John sez yer gonna get evicted. Is that so?

Frida got her job. Meanwhile, she's quite stricken about no service of the Poor, and no resistance. So, she moves toward the CW and Kairos. Praise be!

You're in heart, mind, prayer, love. Good health + well being.

> Peace of Christ—
> Phil, Liz, et al. at Jonah

19 Feb [1999]

Dearest bro & all

Ash Wednesday we joined, Kairos and Catholic Worker (wonderfully, Frida was there), to vigil at a detention center for 'illegals' (detestable word) out near Kennedy airport. They snatch these folk, coming in from Asia, Africa and Latin America, when the plane lands, whisk them away to this hideous warehouse, which is in the hands of a ravenous corporation, 'pro profit.' We found they increased their loot by some 35% last year.

We had in attendance law students, lawyers, 2 fine priests of the area, relatives and friends of the prisoners. Lotsa medium interest. We read scripture and vigiled in silence for an hour. At the end, the chaplain came out to say he'd told the prisoners of our vigil. He distributed among the vigilers cards with the names of prisoners, and people pledged to write them. We left flowers at the scene and came home. Good Lenten start.

> And love to all,
> Daniel

March 3 [1999]

Dears,

Well Bob K. and I had a retreat for the homeless last weekend at Esopus NY; the Redemptorists gave us their magnificent seminary & a warm intelligent welcome. Bob gave massages to all comers; I venture it wuz the first time such suffering folk ever felt on their frame the hands of Mother God. I did some Isaiah; never seen in Israel such faith.

We had final arguments in court last Friday on our (un)real estate. One sensed her honner was sympathetic, but detected too a note of fear in her voice; doing the right thing, then being reversed on appeal. So the career might just freeze in place.

> Love, gratitude abounding,
> Daniel

Sattidy, March 6 [1999]

Dears,

This is to register a midwinter gripe; concerning what momma used to call 'the pip.'

A touch of background. The architecture of Fordham at Lincoln Center is roughly based on low intensity incarceration. Mebbe I wrote of this. Windows are sealed shut, air (of sorts) circulates, so to speak. (My desk is bolted to the floor—but that's another threnody.) Youngers, themselves sealed 'for the duration' in a high rise dorm next door, cough & snuffle in semi hibernation through the winter. So inevitably do their profs. cough & snuffle. Among whom to wit, me.

So, a week of flu.

Send a prayer our way. Toil & trouble. Brother Ned Murphy is shaking us up with his didoes, chiefly involving his 'sons,' the aberrant title he gives two wayward manipulators. The first walked out of a drug program midway last week. Ned is once again easing him into the building, despite all orders. The second as I may have written, muzzy with booze, tore the lock off Ned's door one midnight, frightening the neighbors.

> Love & warm days under the roof-
> tree!!!
> Daniel

Monday, 22 March [1999]

Dears,

Florida was restoring to soul & frame & we returned here braced for another round in the fanatica, fantastical town.

Which round was not long in sounding. Friday 25 or so including several NY State assemblymen were arrested at the cop hdqtrs. downtown. Rev. Al Sharpton has been holding daily events there for almost 2 weeks now since the police murder of Amadou Diallo. It was brown, black & white together in a way I hadn't seen in years.

A lieutenant on Friday's detention scene quipped to me; 'Aren't you a week early this year?' They were on best behavior—for a change. Enough tar (or blood) has stuck to them long since.

> Love,
> Daniel

March 28th

Dearest Bruv—

The Internet gave extensive *NYT* coverage of the bombing in Kosovo and wider Yugoslavia. Predictably, the Serbs won't give in. They'll merely step up the heat on the Albanians. It appears that (NATO/usns) will have to forsake the bombing or send in troops. Our violence + stupidity is putting us between a rock and a hard place.

I figger that one by one, we'll follow T. Lewis back into the dustbin.

I heard you were dusted over the police murder of that young Haitian. Called several times on Sun. but you were out.

The choir is on a rocky trail—some deviousness, lotta mouth and blustering. With several, I'm the main problem. Heh! heh! heh! But we'll muck thru.

Adieu—God w/ you. "He is risen, he is not here!" That sez it all. Love you.

> Peace of Christ,
> Phil

May 30th 1999

Dearest Bruv—

We go to [Secretary of State Madeleine] Albright's house in Georgetown for "Memorial Day." Three or four will risk arrest. It strikes me that our peacenik comrades are a bit demoralized as Clinton's madness rages on in Iraq and Yugoslavia. Milosevic seemed ready for real compromises in his palaver w/ the Russian. But we'll have no part in it, save unconditional surrender.

Behind Clinton's "humanitarianism" of course, are the real reasons—we won't tolerate a socialist regime in Europe. And lust—Kosovo has the largest and richest mines in Europe. Then too, both Iraq + Yugoslavia flank the largest nat. gas and oil reserves in the world, and provide access to them. The puzzle of our politics there is really not a puzzle.

Thinking of you and sending best love, thanks, the peace of Christ.

> Phil, Liz, et al. at Jonah

Memorial Day [1999]

Dears,

Anniversary time. This PM I take wing for Camden and play whooping crane at Sacred Heart for McDoyle's 40th. Home same night, off Wed. for Italy; Parma rendezvous with Carol and Jerry. Three days there, three off to seaside Venice, and home.

Hopes & prayers that the situation concerning the wicked powers vs. those we love, is under yr. control. What dark times—& what a hell for the innocents under the bombs, and shunted about the globe! Be there a God, someone(s) will pay dear.

Kairos et al. are planning cd here June 3. The group also goes to court that day for the Good Friday action at Intrepid. Joe Cosgrove is coming to town to represent my (absent) butt.

Many blessings befall thees! (That's both a prayer and a fact.)

Daniel

[On May 11, Eqbal Ahmad, a Pakistani political scientist and antiwar activist who was a defendant in the Harrisburg Trial with Phil and Liz, died in Islamabad of heart failure.]

Monday, May 17 [1999]

Dears,

Such sorrowful news as just reached here this AM with a call from Bob Keck, the death of Eqbal. So the circle of friends narrows here and widens elsewhere. . . .

My sense of loss is compounded by his silent withdrawal over the years. I'd been unable to take part in the retirement ceremony at Hampshire. Then one day within a year, his daughter stopped me on Broadway to say her father was in town, and 'surely would want to get together.' To be sure, she took my phone no. Nothing came of it. I had a sense that he was bowing out of old friendships, even of marriage, in favor of a new start in Pakistan.

A flood tide of memories; I officiated at the wedding, then Harrisburg with the tiny new daughter. He felt his third-world scholarship was unacceptable here (it certainly was, along with [Noam] Chomsky and [Edward] Said). I'm so happy Frida was exposed to a consummate teacher and scholar, rare bird indeed.

Love yez,
Daniel

June 4th [1999]

Dearest Brother—

Yours happily rec'd. 26 good folks busted at the Blight House yesterday, incl. T Gumbleton, who spoke eloquently and then, joined the naysayers. A sizeable clutch gone in that direction today—incl. a baker's dozen from Wi. and Mn. happily escorted by son Jerry. So good to see the old scampe.

You're off for Italy—hope you don't find Carol too exhausted. And that Kate is brimming w/ pizzaz. We miss that young 'un also.

> Sending you much love, prayers,
> thanks, the Good Lord's peace,
> Phil, Liz, et al. at Jonah

June 29 [1999]

Dears,

SLC [Salt Lake City] was quite a scene. Very articulate pros of every stripe & profession. Women ordained, gays included. Yet, yet—they don't start Jonah Houses or Kathlik Workers or go to jail.

The ethos seems to be; talk, argify, probe the courts for liberal loopholes.

Quite a bag of contradictions; Xtians, atheists, Jews, ex-everything. Much like Rowe retreat writ large.

Had to pass by my 60th class celebration. That was hard, as we're a remnant of boisterous beginnings.

Day by day here we're living in a furnace stoked with damp firewood. Suspect it's likewise there. Wuz thinking of taking off for B. Island, but don't as yet have much soul breath. We shall see.

Year One always gives to ponder.

> Thank you,
> Daniel

July 1st 1999

Dearest Brother—

Liz sent away this one. Hope you're feeling better. Carl Kabat's mother died. No rest for Carl. Helen Woodson called up—she's gonna sue the govmint—involving her in its lying.

Went to a reception for Bishop Frank Murphy, afflicted w/ cancer. Lovely guy—one of the peace Bishops. He seems hopeful about recovery. Cancer is an epidemic, mostly environmental in cause. We love you—

Peace + thanks,
Phil, Liz, et al. at Jonah

MEMORY (60 years a Jesuit, 1999)

> A huge percussion
> brought back and back;
> memory. As though
> the heart of things
> beat on, despite.
>   I wish I knew
> where that sound wends its way.
> I don't. The drummer boy
> mum, muffled, won't tell.
> He goes, all said,
> spellbound.
>   (Or can't).
> Like the next beat,
> walks in and out of.
> Hear it;
>   Yet, yet to be.

Scoops of love,
Daniel

Sept. 15th

Dear Brother Mine—

They tell me Clinton gave a speech on Global Warming. Hah! First he's sed in nearly 5 yrs. The sucker has a talent for fogging over his own crimes, and broadscaling his responsibilities.

But it looks like Dame Nature will have her say about the abuse she takes from us. And if we don't listen . . . ? I envision her shaking us off as a dog shakes off water after a good dip.

Much love, thanks to you, peace of
Christ,
Phil

[around Sept. 20, 1999]

Dear Dan—

[Sister] Chris Mulready [Plowshares activist] died of cancer this morning. She went into a coma and died without becoming conscious. Our nuns, who loved her deeply, were there.

And Art Laffin's brother Paul was stabbed to death on Mon. at a shelter he helped to found in H'ford. With the elder Laffin dying from that auto accident—all this comes hard and fast for all the Laffins.

Lottsa rain here. A new UN report on global warming and the weather made public. It judged much of the harm irreparable, but hoped it wouldn't be added to. It appears that we're too deeply into our "Way of Life" to retreat from it.

We're all okay and send you love and thanks and Christ's peace. Year One on its way.

Phil, Liz, et al. at Jonah

[late Sept., 1999]

Dear Dan—

Liz just got the *H'ford Courant* on Paul Laffin's funeral. Remarkable account! The family totally forgave the poor man who murdered Paul, and asked his family to meet at their parish church to pray with them. Priests and Bishops flocked to the altar. The liturgy, and the words spoken will help them, I think.

Good health + well being, much love, many thanks, Christ's good peace.

Phil, Liz, et al. at Jonah

Oct. 1 [1999]

Dearest bro,

I took note this AM of the turn of the year and your birthday. A day that does what few days can do—makes the larger picture bearable. Even cause for celebration. What an exemplary life; and how yours reverberates at large-and-at-small—in my own. ¾ of a century and more, granted you, surely for sake of us all! How grateful we are, even as we hold out breath and send fervent prayer on view of another bold foray for God + creation.

Happy birthday, as your friends rejoice in you—and you so richly merit!

> Happy Birthday Big Guy!
> Daniel

Oct. 20th

Dearest Brother—

New development here—a food strike, total participation. So total in fact, that a handful of laggards were shamed into joining up. This is the second day—the turnkeys are apesh_t, they have us locked down now—nobody's working. And the threats abound—we'll ship you, cut off phone + canteen. But the spirit remains good and resolute. Praise the Lord!

I find the food rough but adequate. But those who work in food service report that the kitchen is filthy, with ample vermin. And most complain steadily about food quality. It is certainly, the worst I've seen in any fed joint.

What's the next step w/ the landlord—take him to court? Some direct action? This guy has the spirit of a slum lord.

Have no concerns about me. A little fasting will do me good. I did 5 days on water at Lewisburg in transit here, and never felt better.

That's it from this cabbage. The Lord is good, and caring for us in unimaginable ways. I can see the digitum Dei in bringing ole Clinton down.

> Peace of Christ, all sorts of love,
> thanks, well-being,
> Phil

Oct. 31st Sun.

Dearest Bro—

And the Bruderhof—Greg and I were there in W. Pa. for talks Sat. + Sun. When in doubt—sing! Dear Lord!! They sing at the slightest provocation. And sing like angels. A little overdone at times—one stretch—45 minutes. But kind + welcoming, and w/ many young Turks.

Saw Dorothee Soelle in Philly on Mond. last—Liz and I. She asked after you at length. Gave us a thou. clams, her honorarium for a prestigious lecture.

Hope the back has cleared up. All over, requests: "How's Dan?" I tellum, "Never better!" Love youse.

> Prayers and thanks and Christ's peace,
>
> Phil, Liz, et al. at Jonah

Nov. 23

Dearest Brother—

Ramsey spoke in DC last Sat. and we went to see him to inquire about the possibility of an internat'l law defense. He spoke soberly, "not a helluva lot better than a pro se defense" to expose the military and its conduct in Iraq + Yugoslavia. I dunno where that leaves us, but it'll straighten itself out.

When folks here get an acc't of weekend happenings, they'll send on a packet of info when the crunch comes. We'll hope to get it around.

Love you much. Forgive the brevity of this. Constant thanks, peace of Christ.

> Phil, Liz, et all at Jonah

Dec. 14th Tues.

Dearest Bruv—

Did I write you that we lost another citizen from the choir this past week? He had been staunchly w/ us for a year. But a combination of dreads and incapacity afflicted him. So tomorrow nite, we begin the last short haul in a long haul. Prayers, please. I figger it's only the prayers of friends that got us this far.

And we will be with you in strong spirit and prayer on the 16th. Please God, this scan will promise you some relief.

Thanks to you and the SJ's for the lovely hospitality and warmth when Liz and I visited. I was somewhat blotto, but nonetheless, it was a stellar time.

Much love to you. Gratitude galore and Christ's peace. Will write Jerry for his 80th.

> Phil, Liz, et al. at Jonah

[On December 19, Phil, Susan Crane, Steve Kelly, and Elizabeth Walz damaged two A-10 Thunderbolt aircrafts at the Air National Guard

base in Middle River, Maryland. The group became known as Plow-shares vs. Depleted Uranium. In March 2000 Phil was sentenced to 30 months in jail.]

Apr. 25th 2000

Dearest Bruv—

Your card spoke of healing, for which we thank God. Better still, Steve tells me you and other SJ's will be here on May 1st. If you hadn't progressed, I don't think you'd attempt the trip.

Sorry about making noise over a house keeping item—but was moved to a cell yestiddy. Steve follows sometime in May when another guy leaves. Then we'll juggle to get the same cell. Lord be praised! Some days the boob tube had us on the ropes. And we thought of plucking it from its cage and dropping it on the floor.

Liz visited yesterday and told me of 1,300 arrests at the World Bank/IMF, most of those jailed refusing to give their names, and the cops releasing them despite. Also of our Faith and Resistance retreat (3 arrests at the Pentagon for gore) and a splendid Easter Vigil at our A-10 base. It seems that a growing NO! against the money changers and warmakers, is arising around our polluted paradise. Please God!

We'll look for you w/ rejoicing on May 1st.

> Love galore, constant thanks, peace of Christ—
> Phil

Apr. 28th

Dearest Brother—

Your approaching birthday always an occasion for stock-taking. It's a time when I regain some grasp of the truthful and the real.

That has to do with the realization of your inspiration in my life. I doubt very much that even the priesthood would be possible were you not here—always there to me. Unquestionably, you've been the greatest example and prop to me. Even your criticism was totally beneficial—in fact, I rarely listened to any other.

So "thank you" sounds empty and superficial—since the debt is more than I can ever pay. It is like the one I owe God, and Christ and God's Spirit. One consolation is that you don't expect even gratitude—your humanity and Christianity is repaid in the doing.

But I can pray for you, your wellbeing and healing. And pray also that God give you more years of service to us as you enter your 79th. Pray also that I grow to love you as you deserve.

So—blessings and love on your birthday, dear brother. Please read between the lines—words fall short of the occasion.

> Peace of Christ—
> Phil

May 18th

Dearest Bruv—

Sed a Te Deum after reading your letter. You did that whole retreat w/out considerable pain. Lord be praised!

Fascinated by the quote you sent. The barbarians are our own people. It seems to me that in different ways, you and the Jonahs have been saying similar things for years.

Kelly's up the hall a coupla doors, celling w/ a spic 'n span, veteran prisoner. He's good—getting adequate sleep which makes all the difference. We go into a rec area for Mark every morning and shout at one another over the boob tube. He tells me that the only reason he stays out of the "hole" is myself. So I lay out a big case for staying in population and working w/ guys. But he sees it differently. I have no doubt that he'll do every day of 27 months.

The Cath. chaplain is a Josephite nun—who has 3 dustbins of this size to minister to. She's a nice person, but subject to the Christian heresy—me'n Jesus.

Just finished EPICA's new book on Romero. Anecdotal from those who knew him, and helped him grow up. Splendid!

God bless those women who give you therapy. Please do them exercises. One of these days we'll see you.

> Hugs and prayers and love, thanks,
> Jesus' peace,
> Phil

June 1st

Dearest Bro—

Ched Myers recently at the house. Gotta touch of heart trouble, trouble breathing while asleep. I'm reading his little *Say to This Mtn.* [*Mountain*] on Mark's Gospel, which he wrote w/ others from DC.

His part is fine, though he attributes the 2 feedings in the desert to sharing. Ain't that a howl? These Prots. . . .

Sendin' youse much love, hugs,
thanks, the peace of Christ—
Phil

July 13th

Dearest Bro. Dan—

There are a coupla turnkeys here who have done many favors for Primo + myself. One just got me a do-nothing job in the barbershop—flushing me out to the library where I can do some writing and praying. But he's an odd mixture, a weekend warrior (Nat'l Guard), a collector of guns and a breeder of fighting cocks. He reveres Catonsville. Ain't that sumpin?

This comes w/ daily prayer.

Much love, wellbeing, mighty
thanks, pax Christi,
Phil

July 26th

Dearest Brother—

I'm reading Job and finding it superb. Your comparisons w/ Is. and Paul classic. We could stand some questioning of God today, as Job did. We get mighty blessings from the Almighty, but we don't get much relief from the Empirah, do we?

Somebody wrote today about praying for enemies. I'm gonna answer and suggest she pray for the cruds in power—who lie to us, betray us, threaten us w/ their Death Rows, abortion mills + weapons, and convict us in their kangaroo courts + lock us up. They're the only true enemies we have. The barbarians are at the gate again—this time they're our own people.

Much love to you, love to all the SJ's. Big hugs. And thanks to God for what you are.

Peace of Christ—
Phil

Aug. 17th

Dearest Bruv—

Thanks for yours. Hope you're feeling tip top. Has anyone sent you our book *Disciples + Dissidents*? I wince at the title, I didn't pick it. Anyway, bin thru these essays 4–5 times and they still blow mah mind. Guess I'm being subjective. Anyway, the editing's good, good Introd.—the whole thing hangs together nicely. Let us know what you think.

Do me a favor. I snapped at John Dear because he ends his letters w/ "hang in there!" Anyway, it got damned irritating. It shouldn't have, but it did. John's a sensitive guy and I'm sure he was hurt by my blustering. Please tell him I'm sorry. I'll apologize when I write.

> Sending you hugs, love, thanks,
> peace of Christ—
> Phil

Sept. 6th Wed.

Dearest Brother—

The eye is beyond expectation. I'm celling now w/ Primo (watching my steps re cleanliness) and working on a variety of writings. The latest is a quote from Mt.: "Blessed is the one who finds no stumbling block in Me." Tried to work the apocalyptic into that one, discovering to amazement that the apoc. is a distinct element of faith.

Prayers that the back is okay and the flu crud has fled. Do we hope for you and Bob Keck on the 8th? And how about K'ridge—did you feel up for that?

Primo is fine. Before our nuns left for the West, they voiced their view of his relationship to the SJ's. Namely, that he should make concessions, get out and get cleared away with the criminal injustice folk, return to Ca. and do Tertianship. Primo has it under advisement. In different ways, you and I have told him the same.

Adieu—God with you.

> Much love, constant thanks, the
> peace of Christ—
> Phil

Sept. 20th Wed.

Dearest Bruv—

One from you always cause for rejoicing. Thanks so much. I'll drop Dar Williams a note. As you probably know, she did a benefit for the CW in Duluth, and is close to the heart of our three young'uns.

I liked the review of Job in the *Phila. Inquirer*—understatement but still good, given the mass media. I think it unlikely that any of the current crop of theologians would have the faith to put in God's mouth: "Because I said so!"

I'm slogging along, trying to do a little writing—horrified and appalled by Rosalie Bertell's contention that the nucl. club—led by the US—has killed, maimed, or sickened 1.7 billion people since the Doomsday Race began. Nor is the end in sight, for with the use of DU [depleted uranium] in Iraq and Yugoslavia, DU promises to be more lethal than the Hiroshima and Nagasaki bombs. Hence, the cancer epidemic and a great deal else that ails us, spiritual and physical.

Care for yourself—you're the best hope against the barbarians at the gate.

> Constant thanks, pax Christi,
> Phil

Oct. 11th

Dearest Brother—

We're going thru some changes w/ Primo, selected for a random urine test which he refused. Which means he's headed straight for the "hole." I recall the tribulation at 98th St. when he was in a Pa. fed jail. Waal, it's a replay. I've argued myself blue in the face w/ him—poor issue, everyone here subject to it, breaks up Bible Study, breaks up the remarkable influence he has on the compound etc. etc. It doesn't look as though we've dented him. This morning, w/ his permission, I aired it before the Bible Study group, and in the main, they told him to piss in the bottle. It's the Mitch Snyder syndrome—the sacralized individual conscience, w/ little awareness of a community conscience. He hasn't had my advantages—I've been 27 yrs. in community, and I've been overruled in decisions frequently. It was good for me! I've learned that the consciences of most in a community of good people are a helluva lot superior to my own.

It looks as though I have to look for a new cellmate. Waal, a jail is a jail is a jail.

Whaddya think of them nuns? Ain't they crackerjacks?

Lastly, there's the plight of Carl Kabat—the Oblates are on the pt. of kicking him out. And Carl Baby isn't lifting a finger. Typical. I've written a statement denouncing the whole sorry railroad, and have sent it on to CO, where an ex Oblate is supporting him. But it looks bad. Card. George of Chicago, an Oblate, is silence galore. And he's a contemporary of Carl's. 'Twas ever thus.

> Love you much, many thanks, peace
> of Christ,
> Phil

Oct. 18th

Dearest Bruv—

Yours always a deeelight. Thanks so much.

77 has come and gone. No change—except I'm meaner + closer to senility.

Read a slashing review of the opera "Dead Man Walking" in the *Wash. Post.* It sed the opera sugar coated the issue, concentrating on injection (painless), fumbled with morality etc. etc.—missed the point of Prejean's book. In contrast, the *Times* review seemed vapid.

Much love to you, thanks + peace of Christ. Hope the Ca. trip went famously.

> Phil

Nov. 20th

Dearest Bruv—

Word from you always a blessing. Thanks very much. Prayers that you're well, and that the SJ housing gets resolved.

At your suggestion, I've written John for the 2nd time apologizing for our rhubarb, and for my spleen. I hope he accepts my apology.

This is strictly inter nos—but I don't know at the juncture if I'm going to be paroled to the feds in Dec. I'm told it's up for "review." My only explanation is this—the Powers wanted to see if I'd do something in solidarity w/ Primo. As for me, I'm indifferent—whatever comes down is okay, ie more time here or more after Dec. Voluntas Dei.

I'm having great sessions w/ my cellmate on John's Gospel. He's a black guy from Balto. The other group folded w/ Primo gone and myself having to work.

> Loving you greatly—constant
> thanks, pax Christi—
> Phil

[mid-Dec., 2000]

Dearest Brother—

Waal—yestiddy was a rough one—sudden snow, and the walk to chowaglaze. I fell twice, twice, hitting my hip and messing up my bad shoulder further. Thank God—no bones broken. The guys now walk me as the snow continues. Today, they put salt down—a big improvement. So I'm okay—just some bruises and stiffness. Praise the Lord!

Guess you heard that the "election" in FL was "stolen." The Bush Boys staged a coup. Seems that ole AL [Al Gore] won both popular and electoral votes. Not that it makes that much diff. in this benighted society. I'm convinced that the job rules the man.

Hope yer thriving.

> Much love, thanks, peace of
> Christ—
> Phil

[Dec. 29, 2000] St. Thomas Becket

Dearest bro & Steve too!

Enclosed a few matters I hope get past the bars & bolts. The account from Scotland particularly hopeful, along with mention of the German judge & old friend, evidently still at the ramparts.

I was awaiting some work from the dedico-medicos before winging this your way. Yesterday my second opinion arrived ahead of the first; Dr. Ligouri who's a good friend & capable, reported that his radiologist 'whom I trust implicitly,' sed there was no evidence from the cat-scan that laser beam surgery would be of help. I'm still awaiting a report from our man at laser hdqrtrs., surgeon Dr. Choi. . . .

So there we pretty much are, back to Dr. Rose & make the best of it! I'm leery about proceeding with the surgery in face of Ligouri's conclusion, even if Choi urges it. Bob Keck agrees. We'll try to get a copy of the radiologist's report to bring Dr. Rose.

I venture forth to the desert on Friday, returning PM Satiddy.

Jerry Jr. brought me a momentous table of fir wood now gracing the premises. He & Frida attended Xmas liturgy & dinner here & were the usual stars of the show.

Thass about it for now. Heartfelt thanks for creating an island of sanity in a demented time.

♥ Daniel

PRISON, 2,001 (for Philip)

> This is dignum et justum, the exact
> address of the just.
> This fits like a skin a frame
> the tegument of noble souls, your soul.
> Over hill and dale of nightmare,
> for the crowning of saviors—
>   barbed wire,
> miles of it, indicting, arresting the sun,
> betraying pure light for a Judas shekel—
>
> woven on hell's loom, bristling with ironies
> hell knows nothing of,
>   it keeps the unjust out (judges,
> sheriffs, beware) who throw the just in,
> into this thorny nest
> where the future broods precious eggs unborn.
> O my brother, ten like your soul, only ten,
> and the times are redeemed.
> You, Susan, Greg, Steven—God keeps count,
> wills the total—
>
> like a priest's cup passed, full, unfailing
> breathing sacrament.

[Phil was released from prison on January 12 but sentenced to one year in jail on February 2 for failure to pay restitution.]

Dearest Bro,

Just a word 2 say your 'proposal' 4 a strike went out yesterday, together with a covering letter signed by John D + me; to *Cath Worker*,

Other Side, Nat. Cath. Reporter, Richard Deats at FOR [Fellowship of Reconciliation] + *Sojourners.* So we'll see.

I bin collecting enclosed material on D.P. You see you're on 2 something!

Off to a weekend retreat in Stamford, CT,

Love + hurry Daniel

Apr. 12th Holy Thurs.

Dearest Brother—

The chaplain seems a good sort—just recovering from serious stomach surgery. He's asked me to conduct a Cath. Bible Study. I hope to have it more than once a week.

Am prayin' for all the Holy Week efforts at justice/peace—yours, the Jonah's, CW's etc. God help us! The darkness seems to gather, but so do awakenings and NO's. Prayin' too for your celebrations—I know it'll be a humdinger. What an unmatchable life you've had! In the next week, I'll write a little statement and send it to you. Understatement all the way!

Got the Kissinger article—devastating. You know Hitchens writes for the Nation—I've followed his stuff for years. He's an up and downer—brilliant and very bad, went Apeshit on Mother Teresa etc. But helluva job on ole Henry K.

Without crying "wolf!"—good and bad days w/ the hip. Sometimes I over exercise and undersleep. So gotta carve out an acceptable regimen. But I remain functional—at worst, it's slightly painful and annoying. That's all. No need for concern.

Wishing you a blessed Easter. He has risen! That sez it all.

Much love, many thanks, Christ's peace—
Phil

July 30th

Dearest Bruv—

You might have heard—a jailbreak here, throwing the turnkeys into a frenzy. One of the principals was a cellmate, placing me immed. under suspicion. They tossed me in the SHU [Special Housing Unit] for 4 days, meanwhile, shaking down the entire dustbin. I lost addresses, papers, clothes. Part of an effort to punish us—we're still on lockdown after a week—and to cover their buttocks w/ the cretins in DC. As they say, if you're in pharaoh's court, you lie and cover your ass.

I'm uncertain about visits for Aug. 3rd—they're suspended now. But will be in contact w/ Liz, and hopefully, you. Sending you much love + gratitude, plus the peace that surpasses the understanding—
Christ's peace—
Phil

Aug. 27th

Dearest Brother—

Toilin' thru the week's mail, but thinkin' of youse.

Martin Sheen will visit sometime this week—Mon. or Tues. I'm astonished how he manages these dustbins. Since the jailbreak, I've been under a cloud—no press, no visits from those outside the family. But Martin manages, guess his integrity and charm rules the turnkeys.

In a word dear brother, I'm making it and making it fine.

Liz writes that Primo Nacho arrived in Balto and is probably in P'land now, before Mean Gene Carter. He expects 18 mos., and of course, he'll non-cooperate all the way.

Hope you're thriving.

Sending you best love, constant thanks, the peace of Christ—
Phil

Sept. 1st Sat.

Dearest Bruv—

Found my credibility w/ staff and prisoners immeasurably advanced by Martin's visit. Heh! heh! heh! Ain't that a huge joke? To me, it speaks volumes of the devilish capability of the System to tailor + manipulate the Amer. spirit. Of course, Martin does his best to combat this—w/ his integrity and love.

The hip seems to slightly improve. No great difficulty, no great pain. I hope by release in Dec. I will have backed it into a corner.

Reading *Bonfire of the Vanities* again—Tom Wolfe. It lays bare the scam of Wall St. about as well as anything I've seen. Very talented little guy—this Tom Wolfe.

Frida + Liz due this Fri. My friends and family indulge me. Fer shure!

> Prayers and well being and thanks
> and much love and Christ's good
> peace,
> Phil

[The "enormous tragedy" referred to here is the attacks on September 11, after which Phil was placed in solitary confinement and held for two days without outside contact. His letter indicates that he is unaware of the reasons for his treatment. Subsequent letters detail his hopes of avoiding a violent response to the attacks and the effect they had on prison life, capturing their effort to make sense of the event.]

Sept. 13th Thurs.

Dearest Brother—

Am pencil writing from solitary (3rd day), following that enormous tragedy on Sept. 11th. I'm "under investigation" again.

I bleed for the thousands of victims.

Please call here and ask "what investigation?" And when? For all I know, the pharaohs are going into knee jerk and rounding up the naysayers. Remember the Japanese during WWII?

Don't worry—I'm okay. Came here w/out my glasses and have been agitating to get them. Like punching a wall of marshmallows. Prayin' for the victims. And victimizers.

Love you much. Many thanks.

> Christ's peace,
> Phil

Sept. 22nd

Dearest Brother—

I hope Liz has got to you with news of release from solitary. Had a meeting w/ the Warden yesterday and was able to assure him that I'm not into jail house reform.

But God help us—the psychos in powah don't promise anything but more death + destruction. The Jonahs are pushing the theme—no retaliation—as strongly as they can. Because if we wipe up Afghanistan, escalation toward the nuke will happen. And there's no stopping counter-terrorism. That's what Sept. 11th was—counter-terrorism.

More than enuf to keep the prayer mat warm. You're in heart and mind and prayer.

> Love + thanks + Christ's peace,
> Phil

Oct. 6th

Dearest Bro.—

Thanks for the b'day greetings, and the undeserved accolades. It's part of your sterling character to be overgenerous w/ this cabbage.

Hideous scene here last night, 3AM. Screams woke me up. One guy had poured boiling water on the head of another (asleep) and then beat him about the head w/ a lock wrapped in a sock. The cops came in, the lights went on and everyone nearby checked out for implication or no. I pray for the poor prisoner + hope his eyes are okay. Jesus Lord! the things we do to one another—an aftermath of Sept. 11th, no?

Went for the 2nd p_ss test in 10 days this morning. When I questioned the cop who took it, he said, "I dunno!" And they're snooping thru my mail, and withholding some of it. And I can't get Carol + Jerry's no. corrected. So they're screwin' w/ me. What else is new? At Bible Study we went thru portions of Jn 15—on persecution. We're all persecuted, we all have to live under the BOMB, and at the whim of these savages in power. And most don't even know it.

I get reports from all over of more + more people catchin' on, working w/ one another, taking to the streets, issuing a public NO! Thank God! Apart from the official knee jerk after Sept. 11th, mebbe this is a corner of sorts turned. Thank you for the Big Apple reports. The Jonahs tell me of the Beltway + events in Babylon, and I get consistent reports from Albuquerque, of all places. A young teacher, friend of Jim Reale.

Great talkin' wid youse the other evening. I'll try to make it more frequent.

> Love + blessings and thanks and
> Christ's good peace,
> Phil

Nov. 6th Tues.

Dearest Dan—Brother!

Bin neglectin' youse recently re letters. But talkin' on the phone was balm to my spirit.

Wanna jot down in orderly fashion the gist of material sent me—from reliable sources. This may be the most colossal swindle in history. The war was 4 yrs. in preparation (1997); around 9/11, the Brits, NATO and ourselves had 60,000 troops on maneuvers in the mid-East and So. Asia; the BBC reported before 9/11 that reliable sources (basically Amer.) predicted that hostilities in Afghanistan would commence by mid-Oct. In reality, the war is about So. Asian oil from the 4 republics clustered around Afghanistan + Pakistan. We already have a military base in one, and one can be sure, the 7 Sisters are there. We need a base in Afghanistan to protect pipelines, once production begins.

As for Bush, some claim he had foreknowledge of the mayhem and destruction of 9/11. But even if he didn't, he did nothing, not even leaving that FL elementary school to call a meeting. His strategists translated the counter-terrorism of 9/11 (completely ignoring our global terrorism) into a "war on terrorism." I watched the Bushwhack-ers on CNN this morning, addressing the Coalition on Terrorism, and then that craven network brought out Dr. Kissinger to respond. So the major media have gone belly-up completely.

At Bible Study, we've been discussing Jn 5 where Jesus links lying and murder to Satanism. That's probably as close as we're gonna get to demonism.

I'm okay—within the context. Hope you're twice as good. The press shut out—Mike Gallagher has been tryin' to get in for months. Liz due this Fri.

> Love you much, thanks galore,
> peace of Christ—
> Phil

[The letter here was attached to a copy of "After 11 September, is there hope for peace?" by Cardinal Carlo Maria Martini, S.J., archbishop of Milan, with the following passage highlighted:]

"The evil in which we are immersed is being revealed, the absur-dity of a society wherein money is the god, whose law is success, and whose time is marked by the opening bell of the world's stock exchanges; a society making a fool of itself in its breathless search for virtual investments, its frenzied ratings-driven media, and its messianic drive to export this way of seeing throughout the world."

[December 2001]

The good Cardinal might be describing ourselves! The Berrigan quotes are partial alas.

Received a copy of the report of Liz on Holy Innocents retreat. Wonderfully heartening! We keep plugging along on the apartments, like sea creatures with no land in sight. A tough discipline but good for us.

Don Moore leaves for Jerusalem Jan. 3. God bless him.

> Love to all,
> Daniel

[Dan's letter implies more of the heightened security Phil experienced in the wake of 9/11.]

Jan 25 [2002]

Dears,

Well, quite a roller the poleece put us through, no?

I have a brainstorm that next time, we've got to put an end to this (mutually) degrading charade; no chains, we're not convicted murderers, a sit-down if required, let them deal with that. They're turning a simple cd. into a tormenting survival run. . . .

I had a session with Dr. Rose on Thursday. He inquired solicitously after Phil. Told of the hip situation, he strongly urged surgery. 'It's the most successful of the replacement protocols, certain to end pain and lead to eased activity.' So there. I was delighted and surprised, as he's quite conservative regarding surgery, except as final resort.

Back in class at Fordham last Wednesday—though hardly in top form!

> Love yez, hope all is pacific as
> wicked times allow!
> ♥ Daniel

Jan. 29th

Dearest Bruv—

Got the hip prospect in motion yesterday—Liz and I going to Social Security. One way or t'other, I'll pry casts from this govmint. Things complicated because the last $ I paid into the System was '52 while a Seminarian. Haw! haw! haw!

Prayers for Dave Toolan and all the cancer victims. I can't help but think, whenever I hear of another victim, of the 650 million killed, maimed or diseased by our nucl. blackmail. Those responsible (damned near everyone) had no eye to consequences. The leeeders in fact, had the consciences of alley rats.

> Sending much love, thanks, peace of Christ,
> Phil, Liz, et al. at Jonah

Feb. 2nd Sat.

Dearest Brother—

Profuse thanks for the book. Sooo considerate of you.

Might take as long as 60 days to get approved for Medicare/Medicaid. They won't even give approval for x-rays. So am taking one last fling w/ the homeopathic stuff—a combination of allegedly Australian herbs that are supposed to build cartilage, clean the joint and relieve pain.

Strange weather—another sunny day. We've got a tiger by the tail w/ this global warming thing. And our military's war exacerbating it further. Another mark of the pharaoh's love for us.

> Blessings + Christ's peace. Plus constant thanks + much love,
> Phil, Liz, et al. at Jonah

Friday, 22 Feb. [2002]

Dears,

We've had ourselves quite a week here. Last Friday Dave Toolan was on his feet, came to supper as usual, helped wash up afterward though stone deaf & greatly scrambled in articulation. Next morning we found him on the floor of his digs; he'd evidently never made it to bed. Ambulance in a hurry, to nearest hospital. He was in & out of this world all week. Yesterday we conveyed him to the infirmary at Fordham where he'll have 24 hr. skilled care. Send us a prayer.

My Fordham class puts up with me nobly. Everyone is against the war, but nudging the young into Union Square on Satiddy goes slowly.

I was emerging from St. Paul's church, just south of Lincoln Center, en route to class. A woman spotted me on the steps, peered closely and inquired wuz I 'one of the Berrigans?' I fessed up. She introduced herself, Susan Rosenburg, just finished 18 yrs., 10 of them in solitary in the women's supermax in Lexington, Ky. She knows everyone in & out, asked for Phil feelingly. I invited her to visit my class. She asked for a hug & we went our way.

Love yez. I hope Phil's proposal is taking hold. It's light in a sullen time.

Sure hope the surgery nears!

Daniel

3 April [2002]

Dears,

Sunday last, Easter, Lyn came to the cottage with a hurried message; Dave had taken a large turn. We summoned Bob Keck down at the parish center. The parish priest phoned and was able to get us on the 11AM boat to the mainland. So we arrived in the Bronx by 4PM. To find out beloved brother indeed in deep coma and breathing shallow & slow.

So it's bin daily pilgrimages from here. Dave comes & goes in this world and the next landing. At times we think he knows we're hovering, others not. But as of today, he's still (remotely) with us.

Driven out of its collective skull, our proxies & pyromaniacs continue throwing gas on the world's blaze. And the church, demoralised, its britches down to its knees, sees no evil. Pretense, control, secrecy; 3 indelible marks. Thank God for one another.

And thanks for wonderful Holy Week booklet! And hope and hope—day of relief for Phil nears.

Love
Daniel

May 1st

Dearest Brother—

Get Jim's Birthday and your own confused, so send this off, recalling that both were in early May.

If I were in better shape, I could tell it better. But words have their limitations, and at best, mine do in regard to you. Thru the years of hurly-burly, you have been exactly where you belonged—brother, friend, counselor, bulwark of decency and integrity, shining example. And I love you for all this, but will never love you enough. You deserve better. So you have my gratitude as you face another one in the empirah. And pray God to keep you with us as long as needed.

> A brother's love, and Christ's peace,
> Phil

[This was attached to a newsletter, in which Phil writes, "At home, at 2am on April 24th, I fell, answering a nature call and broke my left arm near the shoulder. That accident delayed hip replacement. Now, I hope for removal of the cast from my arm in 3 weeks time, and hip replacement early in July."]

May 10th

Dearest Brother:

Liz and I tried calling you on your birthday.

I'm on the mend, thank God. Today is the first one when I've been relatively free from pain.

I'm doin' the 24th chapt. of Jeremiah—the 2 baskets of figs. A good reminder that we're all in exile.

Blessings and love. Hope yer thriving.

> Thanks + Christ's peace,
> Phil, Liz, et al. at Jonah

May 17th

Dearest Bruv—

Your lovely card arrived—and the books. Gifts and gifts galore. the best one of course, was yourself. You burst on our dour scene like a June day. Thank you so much for coming.

Our folks at Andrews AFB yesterday—another of their air extravaganzas. We're praying that this Congressional Investigation of Sept. 11th goes somewhere.

All here send love and thanks and Christ's Peace.

> Phil, Liz, et al. at Jonah

May 25th Sat.

Dearest Brother—

On Thurs., Gd. Samaritan took off the cast—a deliverance. I assure yew because that sob cast was digging into my old hide. And the lesions got infected. Don't know which was worse—the stink or the pain.

I'm doin' simple exercises for the arm, and healing proceeds apace. The doc sez it's got a good start toward knitting—by the time I see you in MI. it should be in good shape. Praise the Lord!

Thanks for the encl. The essay on pedophilia very helpful—all about powah.

> Love you. So many thanks, peace of
> Christ—
> Phil, Liz, et al. at Jonah

Dears—

Word from Kate + Frida that the operation is on for July 5. Much rejoicing here, esp. from the undersigned. It will be a task of paradise on-the-ground, when this venture brings relief and renewed energies. Soon!

Dave Toolan dreams on. Last visit Bob K did a careful massage of arms + hands, wh. tend 2 swelling + clenching. We think the sweet skills evoke a spark, momentary—but hearing, seeing, speaking are gone. What a sleep—of God?

Vigiling continues. Wot we need is some restorative c.d.—which I hope will come soon through the 'Voices' 40 days here.

> Love yez,
> Daniel

July 5th

Dearest Brother—

As Freda would say, a "rare treat" talkin' wid youse the other day.

Had a good demo—about 30 of us—at the NSA yesterday. Of course, it was tepid enuf—we need, even as you say, constant, robust civil resistance. And currently, folks ain't up to it. The nuns, God bless them, are studying Mi 4, but that's down the road a piece.

Yesterday was not only savagely hot, 104 degrees here, but indicative of the hysteria and paranoia of both leeeders and public. It's a demonic exhibition, how the propaganda grinder has whipped the public into such a state. But a couple of friends got atop a B-52 at a Langley AFB air show and showed their colors God bless them! Just what we needed.

Love you, blessings, thanks, peace. We all give thanks to God for you.

Phil, Liz, et al. at Jonah

July 8 [2002]

Dears,

We're whirling the prayer wheels for Phil's big day, at long last, Friday. Freedom now! Everyone sends loving support and firm hope that full restoration is on the way—and soon.

Folks have retrieved on e-mail the Hiroshima–Nagasaki days of retreat. Admirable as always. We're gearing up here for arrival of "Voices" folk from Chicago and elsewhere. 40 days of fasting, frequent cd—and this in the August dog days!

Up to Bronx yesterday for a coupla hours' vigil with Dave—Bob Keck, Bob Carter + I. Evidence of good care, no change. We pray, hold him. Bob does massage. But it's indefinite bedridden, no wheelchair, no recognition.

Love yez—this Friday. What a blessing!
Daniel

Aug. 9th

Dearest Brother—

A word of thanks for making the long trek to Balto. You refreshed and renewed us all.

Ardeth told me this morning about one of the Mi 4's decision. I too was pretty appalled, since I know the response to people dropping out after 12–18 mos. study. It's happened several times, incl. Pl. DU at Warfield.

With due respect for conscience, I surmise too that the politics of her [Anne Montgomery's] decision leave something to be desired. We are among the few people in the world w/ a priority of disarmament.

Lastly, pulling out at the last moment from a community of these nuns is bad nonviolence. She has done exceptional work for justice/ peace in the US and West Bank. No one has done more. Yet to my mind, it is an unfortunate decision + bad n. violence.

I hope you can talk w/ her. God speed to Ireland and back. Love you much. This comes w/ love.

> Thanks, peace of Christ from all of us,
> Phil, Liz, et al. at Jonah

Sept. 5th [2002]

Dearest Brother—

The *Newsweek* acc't sed 1,000 dead of thirst or suffocation. This one 4,000. While our troops stood by. What a terrible way to die. Ah, the glories of war!

I'm doin' great. This morning, I walked a block using just a cane. Without noticeable pain. And the l. arm gets a little better daily.

I wrote our friend, gently suggesting her priorities were off the mark by resolving to go to Hebron/Iraq. And that it was bad n.violence to pull out of a Mi 4 choir at the last moment. She answered graciously that both might be true but her heart carries her to the Middle East.

Thass it, dear brother. Be fabulous to see you at K'ridge.

> Blessings + love + thanks + Christ's peace,
> Phil, Liz, et al. at Jonah

9/16 [2002]

Dears—

Just got to 'Year One,' as usual (+ so unusual) riveting + nourishing, both.

Good hours at Kirkridge. Your insights were pure gold. Phil's spirit radiated all over the place. We pray the good restoration of suppleness + energy goes apace.

Sr. Prejean phoned to invite me to Opening Night of *Dead Man Walking* opera 28 Sept.

Next Friday to Detroit for po'try + I hope a bit of time with the Kellermans.

Blessings, gratitude,
Daniel

[*This letter reveals that Dan was named after the Irish radical Daniel O'Connell, known as "The Liberator," who agitated for Catholic political representation and freedom from British dominance.*]

24 Sept [2002]

Dears,

Shaken also to read from Phil that the recovery has slowed down. And praying the therapist will shed light and suggest something helpful!

Was in Detroit overnight for poetry and anti war discussion. Bill Kellerman drove me to airport. Jeanne is only so-so and life continues hard for the family. But Bill's holding on—the guy's pure gold. I've agreed to help with the Philadelphia meeting of Word + World.

To Bard College this Thursday. I'm intrigued with the place though this will be a first visit. They have a reputation much like Frida's Hampshire; liberal + secular + students quite active. We'll see.

At long last I'm reading a life of Daniel O'Connell. (Dado told me I was named for D.O.C., the 'Great Emancipator.') Was moved to learn he was resolutely nonviolent vis a vis the bigoted British, and won important concessions without bloodshed.

Bush leaves me agape, wordless. If only he + his thugs could be given mental therapy on some remote island, with a view toward rehabilitation. God help us!

Isaiah sez, "Hope on."

Love yez,
Daniel

Sept. 26th Thurs.

Dearest Bruv—

I sense we've been thoughtless in not calling after the fiasco at Mt. Sinai—where an MP and old friend, has an office. I went to her yesterday to get an opinion on month-old general lassitude and weakness, and no progress w/ the hip. She started testing me and the bottom dropped out. A possible bloodclot near my lungs etc. etc. etc. She held me overnight—no sleep, always another test, and meanwhile her fear was proven illusory. So Liz brought me home— no sleep, no food for nearly 24 hrs. and both arms looking like pin cushions.

It's terrible to fall into the hands of doctors with technology at their call! Now it's my liver. I informed her that my liver has been the best—no pain. And I've never been an excessive drinker. No matter, I must return for a "scan" test. Whereas, the only thing clarified is that I'm losing weight—mebbe 20 lbs.

Oh vell! Hope to be in shape for Oct. 10th when Liz and I go to LA for a CW retreat, LACW. If not I won't go, just load my stuff on Liz and hers to read it. Liz is fantastic, a pillar of iron.

So a long winded way to explain why we were negligent. I came home and went to bed for the day. A priest is now with us—tomorrow in comes Elmer w/ a new chair.

Love you much.

> Blessings, thanks + peace,
> Phil, Liz, et al. at Jonah

Oct. 7th

Dearest Brother—

Am awaiting a report of the liver biopsy. Soon . . .

Liz and I will tool out to LA on Fri. for the CW retreat. I'll see if I can weather it.

Everyone else at the Death Penalty vigil.

> Blessings + love + thanks + Christ's peace,
> Phil, Liz, et al. at Jonah

14 Oct [2002]

Dears—

I go to Toledo OHIO tomorrow, back in the PM.

Saturday I face John Richard Neuhaus [Richard John Neuhaus], former compatriot along with Rabbi Heschel, in Clergy Concerned. Now he's a fervent acolyte of Bush's onslaught. This at Riverside Church—God help us.

> Awaiting word on Phil's condition,
> in prayer + love,
> Daniel

2 full page ads in *NY Times* today against the war.

19 Oct [2002]

Dears—

Primo Nacho was here for 2 days. In top form + mood. Addressed my class with eclat + point. We had meals together and a eucharist to invoke light on all involved in coming events. I was so moved, he spent 2 nights, to + fro, on the dilapidated grey Beast bus. Jesuits don't do such things for one another—but that one did. Alleluia. May his tribe increase.

> Love,
> Daniel

PS—As things fall apart, don't the STAMPS get more sterile and chauvinistic? Ugh!! Flags, skyscrapers . . .

[Phil speaks here about his diagnosis with cancer. He also makes reference to John Grady, trusted friend of both brothers and fellow activist, who died on October 23.]

Oct. 24th Thurs.

Dearest Brother—

Another momentous week. The oncologists want more blood work before deciding on the chemo for remedy. They promise to start next week (the chemo).

We'll come to Maywood on the 1st of Nov. and leave Sun. Nov. 3rd. On Wed. we had a tearful, painful meeting w/ Frida and Jerry to gauge their reaction to the cancer. They were admirable, shaken but lurid. Jerry's been here all week and has been immense help. So has Frida.

I'm taking the homeopathic stuff faithfully and feeling blah! blah! but tol'ble. Liz is a rock—my dearest comrade. J.P. Grady has passed— Liz and some will go to the funeral on Mon. He was one of the great, early ones against Vietnam.

I pray for healing daily, but if not that, may God's Will be done!
> Blessings, love, peace of Christ, and
> thanks, thanks thanks,
> Phil, Liz, et al. at Jonah

Nov. 10th

Dearest Bro—

We'll have Veterans Day off. The ole warriors will be struttin' like roosters in parades. Many of them have had their soul seized by the military. They're one main reason why the Pentagon can stay in the driver's seat.

I hear you're comin' to Jonah for that weekend of release. Huzzah! We'll drop a tankard or two. Though my tolerance won't be great.

All downhill now, mostly coasting. I'm leavin' behind some good people, and that's cause for regret. 'Twas ever thus! Until I see you— much love, constant thanks, good health, peace of Christ.
> Phil

[With the recognition that Phil's time is short, he and Dan plan what to do with their collection of papers, books, and documents, hoping to avoid storing them at Cornell, with whom they had long fought over their contract.]

12 Nov—[2002]

Dears—

All this was initiated 1) to get us out of Cornell's clutches and 2) to get some bucks in favor of the BI Cottage, since the Stringfellow estate was greatly diminished. The de Paul tag is hardly maxibucks, but still

. . . I propose ? your correspondence, ? mine + ? the books collected
from BI and 98 St. If Loome sends me check here, I could forward
yr. share—IF this is presentable? 4 thou? The future correspondence
from us + Jerry + Carol is still in question, I'll take it up with Loome.
Love + ongoing prayer—
Daniel

*[On December 6, 2002, Phil passed away at Jonah House, surrounded
by family and friends. Dan wrote the following ten months later, in
October 2003.]*

On what would have been my brother Philip's 80th birthday, October 4, friends held a public event at Judson Memorial Church in
Manhattan. Heartfelt thanks to friends at the Catholic Worker in NY.
They worked night & day, in the midst of a searing and witless war,
to mount a celebration of zest & spirit.

Saturday's event opened with a video of Phil's last public talk, at
a vast antiwar assembly in DC. He was terminally ill. One will not
soon forget his wan but passionate departure from his text, reminding the gathering, 'You are the answer!' and 'Don't get tired!' Indeed,
he himself, to the end offered a pristine answer to the war lords. And
tireless and on his feet, proclaimed the gospel command of love and
no enemies.

Then Ramsey Clark, Howard Zinn and other friends and cowork-
ers, had their say, bracing and heartfelt. Of the family, Liz McAlister,
Frida and I spoke. There was talk of Phil's legacy, song and poetry.
The crowd was deeply moved, attentive.

Sunday morning marked a return to the source, we celebrated
Eucharist at the Catholic Worker. There in the 'forties, I first heard
the liberating word of nonviolence and peacemaking from Dorothy
Day. For almost sixty years, she was a prime influence on our family.

Toward Sunday noon, we assembled in Bryant Park and began a
solemn procession across Manhattan, bearing placards with Phil's
photo and quotes from his writings. Our goal was the *SS Intrepid*,
a hideous, overbearing war museum anchored in the Hudson River.
There 29 of us crossed a police line and were arrested. All honor to
a noble spirit. Philip lives!

Index